POLITICS, STRATEGY, AND
AMERICAN DIPLOMACY

POLITICS, STRATEGY, AND AMERICAN DIPLOMACY

Studies in Foreign Policy, 1873-1917

by John A. S. Grenville and George Berkeley Young

NEW HAVEN AND LONDON, YALE UNIVERSITY PRESS

FOR BETTY ANNE AND MARY

Preface

THESE STUDIES WERE WRITTEN in the belief that a contribution to the better understanding of the history of
American diplomacy might be made by examining foreign
policy in its political as well as strategic context. Both authors
were members of Samuel Flagg Bemis' postgraduate seminar on American foreign policy held at Yale University. Although two decades separated their respective attendance,
they share a common approach to the subject. The collaboration which led to this book was undertaken at the suggestion
of Mr. Bemis, who has taken a lively interest in the progress
of the work. We have benefited greatly from his deep understanding of the period and his instinctive grasp of the issues
involved. Any merit this book may possess is but a small return for his interest and devotion. Of course the authors alone
are responsible for the views expressed.

It is pleasant to record our debt to the many friends who
have helped us: to E. K. Wickman, Lansing V. Hammond,
and Martha English of the Commonwealth Fund of New York,
and to Yale University. Admiral E. M. Eller of the Division of
Naval History, Department of the Navy, permitted the examination of the records in his care, and Dean Allard ensured
that this research proved fruitful and pleasant. We are also
grateful to George Cabot Lodge for permitting us to quote
from the correspondence of Senator Henry Cabot Lodge
and to the Massachusetts Historical Society for their hospi-
tality. Walter M. Robinson of Nashville, Tennessee, allowed
us to look at the papers of William L. Scruggs at considerable

trouble to himself. James E. Hewes, of the division of Army Historical Research, discussed the whole subject with the authors. His criticisms, especially of the last two chapters, have led to significant improvements. W. D. McIntyre and H. C. Allen read parts of the manuscript and gave us the benefit of their learning. Richard Webb, J. P., Reader in the Department of Law at the University of Nottingham, read the whole of the manuscript in its first draft and drew the attention of the authors to mistakes in fact and style with exemplary zeal and unfailing courtesy.

In common with many authors we owe a tremendous debt to the staffs of the National Archives and the Library of Congress who spent many hours on our behalf searching for the documents we required.

The Yale University Press lavished valuable and specialized care on the manuscript, and we are particularly grateful to Marian Neal Ash and Jane Isay for ensuring that what had remained obscure in the manuscript would be clear in the book.

To our friends and colleagues too numerous to mention who have aided us in many ways, we can only express the general hope that they will consider the results worthwhile. We have taken the opportunity of this reprinting to make some minor alterations. The discovery of two further war plans against Spain (p. 276) has also enabled us to show with more detail how naval planning influenced the outcome of the war with Spain. In other respects the new printing is identical with the first edition.

J. A. S. G.

G. B. Y.

August 1969

Contents

[ix]

Contents

[x]

Introduction

THE ERA BEGINNING AT the close of the Civil War and ending with American participation in World War I witnessed startling and revolutionary changes, among them the transformation of the United States from a predominantly rural society to an industrial one. During the early decades of this period, the problems of international relations troubled few Americans; absorption with domestic problems was almost complete. By 1917, America was drawn into the mainstream of world politics. The interrelated studies here presented are concerned with the men who perceived this change and influenced the American response to it.

The structure of this book is biographical rather than purely narrative. Such a presentation imposes certain limitations, but at the same time it may serve as a useful reminder that the conduct of diplomacy is not determined in the abstract, but influenced by personal prejudices and idiosyncrasies. Historians, in their endeavor to trace the principles and doctrines that govern diplomacy, are perhaps inclined to impose order on what is frequently an irrational pattern of events. Often the interplay of personal assessments and the resolution of rival pressures are determining factors. Politicians are not always conscious of the personal motivations for their conduct; they may even persuade themselves that they are acting according to some hallowed tradition. They certainly neglect few opportunities to invoke principle and tradition to lend dignity to the policies they decide on. For many years after the Civil War George Washington's advice to steer clear of permanent alliances was cited more frequently than the Monroe Doctrine. A reference to the Founding Fathers could serve as an excuse for inaction. On the other hand, the Monroe Doctrine imposed a responsibility for action whenever a European power endangered its principles.

The purely diplomatic approach cannot offer a complete analysis of American foreign policy; on occasion, party politics played a predominant role in its formation, as did the considerations of strategy. The influence of strategy on the course of American policy during the years under consideration cannot be equated simply with the influence of Alfred Thayer Mahan. Fortunately, the discovery of new archival sources and the rediscovery of old material now enable the historian to reveal aspects of American foreign policy too long neglected.

The first chapter of this book is devoted to a naval officer who, with his supporters, challenged the traditional views of the majority in the 1870s and 1880s. These men recognized that the conditions of American safety that Jefferson had described more than half a century earlier were passing away: "We especially ought to pray that the powers of Europe may be so poised and counterpoised among themselves, that their own safety may require the presence of all their forces at home, leaving the other quarters of the globe in undisturbed tranquility." [1] But the European balance of power during the last quarter of the nineteenth century led to consequences Jefferson had not foreseen. Bismarck's masterful diplomacy in Europe had created a temporary stalemate. The great European powers fought out their rivalries in Africa and Asia. It seemed possible, even probable to some, that an attempt to partition parts of South and Central America would follow the partition of Africa. The United States herself might fall

1. Saul K. Padover, ed., *Thomas Jefferson on Democracy* (New York, New American Library, 1946), p. 145.

prey to European aggression. The expansion of American commercial and strategic interests in the East were also endangered by the growth of European power in Asia and the Pacific. These changing conditions led a small group of Americans to ignore the pressures of domestic politics and to reexamine the traditional tenets of military and foreign policy. Among these farsighted men was Rear Admiral Stephen Bleecker Luce.

Only a few years after the close of the Civil War, the United States Navy practically ceased to exist as a fighting fleet. In these, the darkest years in the history of the Navy, the service produced an officer of rare talent, a leader of men, and a great reformer. Unknown today, his stature and success entitle him to occupy at least an equal place with Mahan, his most brilliant pupil, whose fame obscured the contribution of his teacher. Unlike Mahan, Luce worked behind the scenes, manipulating with dexterity the political forces that alone might ensure the success of his mission. Although he left no self-adulatory account of his work, his published articles, private papers, and the papers of others clearly evidence the towering influence, generous personality, and remarkable political skill of this great naval officer. Luce did not seek to further the cause of any particular party. He was as ready to work with the Democrats as with the Republicans to bring about the regeneration of the American Navy. Grover Cleveland's attitude to party politics was very different.

The influence of party politics on the course of American foreign policy has been the subject of much comment. The study of Cleveland's first Administration (1885–89) shows a President utilizing diplomacy as a weapon of domestic politics. The diplomatic maneuvers to which Cleveland was willing to resort in order to assure his reelection, secure domestic reform, and keep himself and his party in power are examined in the second chapter. His main concern was to stabilize the currency; he attempted unsuccessfully to use diplomacy to restore the gold standard. Scarcely less important to him than sound money was the tariff; he used the Chinese immigration question as a diplomatic diversion to facilitate the passage of a new tariff law. The good faith of the United States was sacrificed to political expediency, and the Chinese received something less than justice. Partisan politics in the Senate meanwhile fatally mutilated and delayed an immigration treaty with China and defeated the wise convention negotiated by Secretary Bayard to settle a potentially dangerous dispute with Great Britain over North Atlantic fishing rights. During the critical preelection summer months of 1888, Cleveland denounced the Canadians, the Chinese, and the British in an attempt to recoup his declining prestige and garner votes among the electorate. Other nations were not slow to regard this as evidence of the true inwardness of American foreign policy, and this attitude handicapped the conduct of American diplomacy.

The Harrison Administration bequeathed Cleveland a substantial hemispheric foreign policy. The background and formation of this policy are discussed in the third chapter. But Cleveland and Gresham, his Secretary of State, were unable and unwilling to pursue this foreign policy when, in 1893, Cleveland was returned to office.

They rejected the policy of annexing Hawaii, after nearly a year of hesitation, and initiated a vituperative and strictly partisan debate on America's role in world affairs which identified the Democratic party with the cause of anti-imperialism. Thus at a time when economic and social conflicts were increasingly obliterating any substantial differences between Cleveland's domestic policies and those of the Republican party, the President chose to destroy any chance of evolving a bipartisan foreign policy.

After the death of Gresham in May 1895, it fell to his successor, Richard Olney, to determine American policy over the Anglo–Venezuelan boundary dispute. Olney sought to settle the problem by diplomacy but instead plunged the United States into a serious international crisis. Cleveland and Olney have been acclaimed for their successful settlement of the Venezuelan crisis. But their policy was far less consistent than has generally been supposed.

Cleveland's claim that his foreign policy was determined by ethical principle does not withstand scrutiny. His gullibility (and that of the American people) in the mid-1890s is well illustrated by the success of William Lindsay Scruggs.

That Scruggs played some part in influencing American public opinion in favor of Venezuela has long been recognized. The magnitude of his role in shaping national policy is revealed by his manuscript journals. Their story would appear almost incredible were it not verified by other sources. Dismissed for corruption by Harrison from his post as Minister at Caracas, Scruggs entered the service of Venezuela, and changed the course of American policy. The skill, determination, and success of a lobbyist in the pay of a foreign power reveals how dangerously ill informed Congress and the Executive were, how ill equipped they were to deal with complex diplomatic questions.

It is a curious paradox that Cleveland has been credited with a firm grasp of diplomatic principles and McKinley is portrayed as a weak politician who allowed himself to be forced into war by political pressures. Senator Henry Cabot Lodge, Theodore Roosevelt, and Mahan have been singled out as being among the most influential of the "jingoes." The ideas of Lodge and his circle are explored in the study entitled "The education of Henry Cabot Lodge." The policies of McKinley are discussed in the two following chapters.

Lodge's voluminous and, for the most part still unpublished correspondence leads us to believe that the Senator has been misjudged and misunderstood, serving as a useful symbol of the "arch-imperialist" in the 1890s and as the "arch-isolationist" in the 1920s. To say the least, this credits Lodge with an extraordinary degree of inconsistency. Lodge has been blamed for concocting a plot with Roosevelt to seize the Philippines several months before the outbreak of the war with Spain. This notion belongs with the legends of history. Lodge emerges from the manuscripts as a high-minded and responsible politician. He did not share many of Roosevelt's wild notions during the years before 1898. His influence on national politics during the decade of the 1890s was, moreover, far greater than that of his celebrated friend. Lodge too came to recognize McKinley's strength as President, writing during the campaign for the President's reelection: "I think he has shown great ability and that he will stand very high in history, much higher than he does in contemporary opinion." [2] The prophecy remains to be fulfilled.

McKinley understood better than his predecessors how to manage the politics of American foreign policy. He was determined to reach a tolerable solution of the Cuban crisis, peacefully if it could be done, but by force if necessary. Although the President displayed judgment and skill in his handling of Congress and in his assessment of the changing public mood, it must be admitted that he did not grasp the strategic implications of his decisions. The influence of one particular war plan on the course of American foreign policy provides

2. Lodge to James Ford Rhodes, Aug. 6, 1900. Lodge MSS.

evidence that a few unknown men in relatively humble military positions can affect the course of national history.

The subject of the final chapter is, in contrast, devoted to the work of an American naval officer whose name is a household word. Admiral George Dewey is remembered as the victor of the battle of Manila. He last appeared publicly in 1899 as a short-lived contender for the presidency. He then was ridiculed for his political ineptitude. Dewey's contribution to the shaping of national policy during the last fifteen years of his life has remained unknown for more than half a century. As the chairman of the General Board of the Navy from 1900 to 1915 and of the Joint Army and Navy Board, Dewey was the principal adviser on military and naval strategy to three successive administrations. His labors are revealed in the records of the General Board. The relationship between the strategists and President Wilson in particular, emerging from the military and naval records of his administration, are of extraordinary interest. This new documentary material suggests conclusively that the views of the "revisionist" school of historians can no longer be sustained; it reinforces the other evidence to the effect that to the very last moment Wilson did not contemplate war—the decision was forced upon him by Germany.

The management of foreign policy in a democratic society poses a number of fundamental problems. Diplomacy can rarely be conducted successfully in the glare of public debate. At the same time, any responsible government has to win a broad measure of popular support for its policies. To reconcile national interests and public feeling is frequently difficult. The task becomes complicated beyond measure—if not indeed impossible—if either party seeks to derive partisan political advantage from the handling of foreign policy. Unhappily, the division of powers and responsibilities embodied in the United States Constitution provides ample opportunity for members of Congress to undermine politically the diplomatic measures of an administration. By the same token (and it is sometimes overlooked), the constitution also tempts the Executive to enhance its position by adopting a partisan posture in its dealings with the Legislature. The baneful influence of politics on American foreign policy during the period here discussed is a significant thread that runs through all these studies. Another is the role of strategy in the shaping of foreign policy.

An examination of the years from the close of the Civil War to 1917 prompts the conclusion that the harmonization of strategy and foreign policy was more often a matter of chance than of design. In short, these studies illustrate how an excessive regard for political advantage and a lack of attention to strategic considerations has in the past handicapped the conduct of American diplomacy. They do not, and cannot, provide a complete record of all important aspects of American foreign policy from 1873 to 1917. These reappraisals may, however, encourage others to study American policy in depth: in its political, commercial, and strategic contexts.

Chapter One
The Admiral in Politics:
Stephen B. Luce
and the Foundation
of the Modern American Navy

REAR ADMIRAL STEPHEN B. LUCE is almost forgotten today. His portrait in the Naval War College, Newport, Rhode Island, depicts a rather fusty, elderly, conspicuously "Victorian" gentleman, dressed in Rear Admiral's uniform with an enormous sword at his side; his face is adorned by luxurious side-whiskers, and the painter has carefully allowed the light to illuminate a domed head going bald on top. But for the arresting eyes which seem to peer out directly from the canvas, no feature distinguishes the portrait of the Admiral; not even a single naval engagement is associated with his name. Yet this is the man who has the best claim, not even excepting that of Alfred Thayer Mahan, to be regarded as the father of the modern American Navy. He advocated proper training for the crews and officers who manned the warships; he founded the Naval War College and guided Mahan's first steps as a naval historian; he stressed the need to prepare for war in times of peace; he placed himself in the forefront of the fight for a battleship fleet and the acceptance of strategic principles designed to win wars. After bitter political struggles he got most—if not quite all—of what he wanted.

On any reckoning Luce must rank high among the few Americans who shaped national policy during the twenty-five years after the Civil War.[1]

How is his comparative obscurity to be explained? His career appears to be overlooked mainly because more attention has been devoted to the glamorous 1890s, the years of fulfillment, than to the two decades of preparation, the 1870s and the 1880s. During those twenty years, the relations of the United States with the rest of the world caused only an occasional ripple in the national consciousness. Few people took any serious interest in America's foreign policy or armed services. The annual debates on naval affairs were more emotional than effective. The United States Navy consisted almost entirely of wooden ships unfit for contemporary warfare. They rotted in government navy yards, where their (ostensible) maintenance in serviceable condition provided fortunate seaboard senators with political patronage that ensured substantial votes at election times. The large sums voted annually by a Republican Congress for the Navy to squander received Administration approval. Most of the funds were in fact a subsidy to secure the Republican votes of the many workmen and merchants who profited from spurious contracts. The 1870s and 1880s were the decades of the party machine, of the railroad monopolists, of financial tycoons, and corruption which

1. Luce has not received the attention he merits. Rear Admiral Caspar F. Goodrich in 1919 wrote a brief appreciation of his life: *In Memoriam, Stephen Bleecker Luce* (New York, The Naval History Society, 1919). Rear Admiral Albert Gleaves prepared a fuller study six years later, in *The Life and Letters of Rear Admiral Stephen B. Luce* (New York, Putnam's, The Knickerbocker Press, 1925). Although it is a useful work which reproduces important letters from the Luce papers, its documentation and scope are limited and incomplete. The Luce Papers in the Library of Congress are the single most important source for Luce's work, but of almost equal value are the articles by Luce during the 1870s and 1880s. See also Elting M. Morison, *Admiral Sims and the Modern American Navy* (Boston, Houghton, Mifflin, 1942) for an important appreciation of Luce's work and the early years of naval reform.

permeated both political parties.[2] The complacent attitude that all was well with the Navy was first shattered when in 1873 the United States faced the possibility of war with Spain. The revolt of the Cuban people in 1868 had increasingly drawn the interest and sympathy of the American public. As a responsible viewer of the situation, Senator John Potter Stockton of New Jersey warned his fellow senators in the spring of 1872, during the course of a debate on the Naval Appropriation Bill: "I deem it my duty as a member of the Committee on Naval Affairs to say to the Senate now, that if a difficulty should occur to-day on the coast of Cuba, you are simply sacrificing gallant men, brave and experienced officers. . . . [From] having one of the finest navies of its size in the world, we are now the most helpless of all great nations on the water, more helpless than this country ever has been before." [3]

In the same debate a Republican senator from Illinois, Lyman Trumbull, demanded to know what had happened to all the money spent on the Navy: "Millions and tens of millions of dollars have been appropriated and used by the Navy Department since the close of the war . . . and what have we got to show for it?" These speeches did not represent the prevailing mood, however, as the Republican chairman of the Committee on Appropriations, Senator Cornelius Cole from California, countered, "we have now . . . a very good Navy. It is not very large; but we have a considerable number of excellent vessels, first-class vessels, well manned, well equipped, and well provided." [4] In the House two years later, a

2. For the best general accounts of naval development, see Harold and Margaret Sprout, *The Rise of American Naval Power, 1776–1918* (Princeton, Princeton University Press, 1939), and George T. Davis, *A Navy Second to None* (New York, Harcourt, Brace, 1940). For an appraisal of the less savory aspects of American politics, see Matthew Josephson, *The Politicos, 1865–1896* (New York, Harcourt, Brace, 1938).

3. Senator Stockton [Democrat], *Congressional Globe*, 42d Cong., 2d sess. (May 1, 1872), 4, 2963.

4. Speeches by Senators Trumbull, Stockton, and Cole, ibid., 2963–64.

Democratic representative from Maryland, Stevenson Archer, warned of the dangers of pursuing a forceful diplomacy without a Navy to back it up. He contrasted the "high ground" reached in proclaiming the Monroe Doctrine and in claiming exemption from the rights of search (which had led to the War of 1812) with Hamilton Fish's policy which, if the Secretary of State persisted with it, could lead to war with Spain. This time, however, the United States possessed no adequate Navy;[5] and neither President Grant nor Secretary of the Navy Robeson could have harbored illusions to the contrary. When faced with the *Virginius* crisis in 1873, the Administration could no longer overlook the fact that the United States did not possess a Navy that could dare quarrel with anyone.

The *Virginius* had been chartered by the Cuban exiles to engage in filibustering expeditions. She had an American captain, and the majority of the crew were American and British citizens. The vessel's right to fly the American flag was doubtful; her mission was unlawful according to the accepted canons of international law. But when the Spanish authorities arrested the crew and brutally executed the captain and thirty-six of the sailors as well as other persons on board, their conduct smacked of the Dark Ages and aroused the American people to extreme indignation. This Spanish action helped transform American feelings of dislike for Spanish colonial rule in Cuba into demands for active intervention.[6] In Feb-

5. Representative Archer, *Congressional Record,* 43d Cong., 2d sess. (Dec. 7, 1874), 3, 215–17.

6. For a thorough and scholarly analysis of the Cuban crisis and the *Virginius* incident, see Allan Nevins, *Hamilton Fish, The Inner History of the Grant Administration* (New York, Dodd, Mead, 1936), pp. 615–37, 667–94, 871–87. See also Joseph V. Fuller, "Hamilton Fish," in Samuel Flagg Bemis, ed., *American Secretaries of State and Their Diplomacy* (New York, Knopf, 1928), pp. 177–203. The facts are well established, although the authors do not share all Nevins' reflections on Fish's diplomacy.

ruary 1874, at the height of the *Virginius* crisis, "the fleet" had been assembled in the waters of Florida. Unhappily the maximum speed reached in maneuvers was 4½ knots; Chief Engineer Baker explained that, although the vessels had originally been capable of 12 knots, the boilers were now worn out. One naval officer informed the chairman of the House Naval Affairs Committee that the assembled fleet was composed of "antiquated and rotting ships," which a single modern war vessel could have dispatched to the bottom of the ocean without suffering serious damage.[7] Hamilton Fish engaged in some inglorious diplomacy which sought above all to avoid conflict, while securing from Spain the payment of compensation to satisfy American honor. His policies did not aid the Cubans; the only positive good that came from the incident was that the helplessness of the American Navy aroused the concern of Congress. Washington Curran Whitthorne of Tennessee, a Democratic representative who was to become one of the chief spokesmen for naval preparedness, exclaimed in 1877, "the United States Navy has sunk so low as not to have a standing among the navies of the world."[8]

During the 1870s the exponents of naval reform in Congress repeatedly pressed two arguments: without an adequate Navy, a foreign policy faithful to the principles enunciated by Washington and Monroe simply could not be executed; the United States would be exposed to grave danger unless she prepared for war in time of peace. These were to remain the classic arguments for the expansion of the Navy.

The 1880s witnessed the evolution of a third argument, the historical thesis. Representative Whitthorne expounded an

7. Commodore Foxhall A. Parker, "Our Fleet Manoeuvres in the Bay of Florida, and the Navy of the Future," *Record* [later known as *Proceedings*] *of the United States Naval Institute,* 1 (1874), 163–76.

8. Representative Whitthorne, *Congressional Record,* 44th Cong., 2d sess. (Feb. 14, 1877), 5, 1567–68.

embryonic concept of the influence of sea power upon history, declaring that only those nations possessing a powerful navy and a large merchant marine had, in the past, flourished.[9] During this time, international developments increasingly alarmed a group of senators and representatives. These men belonged to both parties and represented all sections of the country. They created a favorable climate of political opinion in Congress that made the building of new warships possible. The United States, they argued, could no longer remain defenseless when other nations were increasing their armaments daily. The growing power of Chile and her hostility to United States policy in South America, the probable effects on American interests of a transisthmian canal, the energetic commercial policies of European countries in Latin America, American-Canadian differences over the fisheries question, the Samoan imbroglio, and the possible repercussions of restricting Chinese immigration—all these were among the major foreign situations causing concern to Congress and the Administration during the decade of the 1880s. The congressional debates on the state of the Navy provide a good barometer of this concern. The senator who complained in 1884 that "the navy yards of this country are used more for political than for naval warfare" was stating an obvious fact.[10] Needless to say, he had no navy yard at his disposal; he belonged to the party out of office.

9. For an interesting analysis of congressional debates on naval matters in the 1880s, see especially, Robert Seager, II, "Ten Years before Mahan: The Unofficial Case for the New Navy, 1880–1890," *Mississippi Valley Historical Review*, 40 (1953–54), 491–512.

10. Senator John Roderick McPherson, of New Jersey, especially, *Congressional Record*, 48th Cong., 1st sess. (Feb. 26, 1884), 15, 1387. On the administration of the Navy Department, see Charles Oscar Paullin, "A Half Century of Naval Administration in America, 1861–1911," *Proceedings of the United States Naval Institute*, 39–40 (1913–14), 165–95, 111–25. For a good summary, see Leonard D. White, *The Republican Era: 1869–1901* (New York, Macmillan, 1958), pp. 162–74.

Further arguments for naval expansion were also repeatedly advanced: the need to protect America's neutral rights, her trade, and eventually her shipping; the necessity for physical force as essential backing for an effective foreign policy; the proposition that a navy is an attribute not only of power but of civilization; the contention that the time to prepare for war is in time of peace.[11]

More effective than these rather abstract ideas, however, was the stress laid on America's vanishing security. Several speakers pointed out that isolation from complications with Europe was disappearing; the defenseless state of America's seaboard cities might prove a great temptation to an aggressive nation. Chile was frequently referred to in this connection, for its *Esmeralda* was a ship more powerful than any in the service in the United States. This fact, it was argued, rendered the Pacific coastline practically defenseless. The danger to many other cities from a variety of possible aggressors was also frequently evoked. But for sheer imaginative horror, the following peroration of Senator Joseph Norton Dolph from Oregon has probably never been excelled. (He did not invent the imaginary catastrophe he was describing; a San Francisco correspondent had envisaged the consequences of a possible British ultimatum delivered by the commander of five British warships and demanding the surrender of San Francisco.)

11. Seager, "Ten Years before Mahan," *Mississippi Valley Historical Review, 40* (1953–54). For Luce's views on war as a means of shaping national character, see his "The Benefits of War," *North American Review, 153* (1891), 672–83. The relationship between commerce and naval supremacy was brought out well by Charles Belknap, ten years before Mahan's work, in the prize essay of the United States Naval Institute for 1880: "That commercial and naval supremacy are coexistent is undeniable. The great commercial power of the world has always, for the time being, been also the great naval power, and history teaches us that when the naval supremacy of a nation has been overthrown the decay of its commerce has followed as an inevitable result." *Proceedings of the United States Naval Institute, 7* (1880), 375–91.

The demand is refused. Twenty-four hours are allowed for the departure of the women and the children; then the two ships take up a position inside the bar, south of Point Lobos, within seven miles of the city hall. Suddenly a roar is heard, followed by another and another; soon the screech of the shells is followed by the crash of falling buildings; fire breaks out in a hundred different places; the fire department is helpless; the socialist and anarchist revel in the wholesale destruction, and strip and burn the buildings which the shells have spared; the whole city is on fire; men are looking out to save themselves, leaving their property to the mercy of Providence. San Francisco, the pride of the Golden State, is destroyed, and the enemy has a foothold on American soil which it will cost many lives to recover. A city with 233,000 inhabitants, $245,000,000 of property, 800 steamers or sailing vessels in its harbor, and vast interests of various kinds is dead, or so stricken that it will take years and years to nurse it back to its present prosperity.[12]

Fantasies, of which this is a good example, carried weight not only with congressmen representing seaboard cities but also with those from the interior who contemplated the disastrous destruction of trade.

Even more arresting are the speeches revealing an early awareness that America could no longer count on her geographical isolation as an assurance of safety. Possibly the clearest exposition of the many delivered in Congress on this theme during the 1880s was that of a Republican senator from Maine, Eugene Hale:

We have gone on for years safely with a dwindling navy. Papers will be put in before this debate closes which will

12. Senator Dolph, *Congressional Record,* 49th Cong., 2d sess. (Feb. 16, 1887), *18,* 1810–11.

show how that navy has dwindled, how feeble it is to-day, and the man is blind I believe who does not realize that at any time the United States may be called upon to maintain propositions with regard to the American continent, with reference to its influence, with reference to its control, with reference to its transit, upon which the American people are substantially of one mind. I do not believe that it will be possible for the United States for the next twenty-five years to be kept from contact and complication with foreign powers, as it has been fortunately for the last twenty years. The Old World and the New are being brought nearer together every day. Commerce and traffic increase daily; the ocean passage grows shorter; submarine cables bring the two worlds together so far as the doing of business goes; the commerce of the Pacific, to be, very soon it may be, of a magnitude that no man has dreamed of, may be the great prize of the world; and the United States can not afford to lie supinely and let that commerce be monopolized by any European power. To-day a foreign enterprise, with foreign capital, purely under foreign management, has undertaken the task of piercing the isthmus that joins North and South America and letting the two oceans flow together. I, for one, am not prepared to take my position with any party or with any sentiment that will leave this Government powerless and with no means of asserting power whenever the United States shall feel that the day has come for it to announce firmly to other nations that the control of the transit of the American continent can not be left in the hands of any power outside of the American continent.[13]

The congressmen who denied that the United States needed a Navy, despite these weighty arguments, also became more

13. Senator Hale, *Congressional Record*, 48th Cong., 1st sess. (Feb. 26, 1884), 15, 1382–84.

vocal. They argued that the threat of war was generally remote; a large Army and Navy were both un-American and a danger to the liberties of the people; in any case, naval expenditure was a wicked waste at a time when the farmer was struggling against a growing mountain of debt.[14] A year later, the Secretary of the Navy conceded, "we have nothing which deserves to be called a Navy." [15]

The strategic concepts of the Navy Department, moreover, were as outdated as the warships. Statistical comparisons of the American Navy and the navies of European powers, of Chile, Brazil, China, and Japan, were annually presented to Congress. They made depressing reading; the United States Navy was outclassed by navies of minor powers, and Representative Long, a future Secretary of the Navy, did not mince words when in 1885 he described the American fleet as "an alphabet of floating wash-tubs." Successive annual reports of the Secretaries of the Navy drew attention to the derelict state of the so-called warships comprising the fleet; Democratic and Republican administrations endorsed a policy of naval expansion. But the real debate in Congress was not between those who wished to expand the Navy and those who did not. It concerned the type of ship best suited to defend the country: should it be large, or small; would considerations of speed outweigh weight of armor and armament; was sail preferable to steam, or could the two be used in combination? Although debate was also marred by mudslinging—the Democrats accused Chandler, the Republican Secretary of the Navy, of financial corruption—the 1880s nevertheless witnessed the construction of the first modern American warships, the steel cruisers later to become known as the White Squadron.

14. For typical examples of such arguments, see speeches by Representative William Steele Holman of Indiana during the appropriation debates of the 1880s and William Calvin Oates [Democrat, Alabama], *Congressional Record*, 51st Cong., 1st sess. (April 10, 1890), *21*, 3258–60.
15. Secretary of the Navy, *Annual Report, 1885*.

It is, however, perhaps understandable that historians should have tended to write off the naval officers of the 1880s as men set in their conservative ways who were not shaken out of their stupor until Captain Mahan preached his doctrine of sea power. Even as late as the year 1889, a senior naval officer could still be found to advocate the construction of vessels with steel spikes, designed to ram holes in any enemy battleship that ventured to blockade the United States. The defense of a few seaports, meanwhile, was entrusted to clumsy monitors left over from the Civil War.[16]

The year 1890 in fact appeared to be the *annus mirabilis* of the new Navy. In that year Mahan published his celebrated book, *The Influence of Sea Power upon History, 1660–1783*, the Policy Board issued its famous report advocating a large battleship fleet, and Congress voted the necessary funds for two battleships. How very tempting, then, to link Mahan's book with these changes—even though the chronology of events does not fit.[17] The chief credit for America's naval renaissance does not belong to Mahan. It belongs to Benjamin Tracy and to Stephen B. Luce. Mahan appeared relatively late on the scene, and his doctrine of sea power was not original. The concept, as has been noted, had been discussed for two decades by a number of congressmen and naval officers. Mahan had attempted to demonstrate its validity in history; he had followed in the footsteps of Luce. For Luce, the creation of a battleship

16. Captain W. T. Sampson, "Outline of a Scheme for the Naval Defense of the Coast," *Proceedings of the United States Naval Institute, 15* (1889), 169–232. For the best treatments of administration naval policies in the 1880s, see George Frederick Howe, *Chester A. Arthur, A Century of Machine Politics* (New York, Dodd, Mead, 1935), pp. 232–39; Leon Burr Richardson, *William E. Chandler* (New York, Dodd, Mead, 1940), pp. 293, passim; and Mark D. Hirsch, *William C. Whitney, Modern Warwick* (New York, Dodd, Mead, 1948), pp. 253, passim.

17. For instance, Sprout, *Rise of American Naval Power*, p. 207, surmised: "Whether Mahan drafted certain passages, whether Tracy had access to Mahan's manuscript, or whether he merely consulted him, it is difficult to say, but the ideas were indubitably Mahan's."

fleet marked a fitting climax to a career devoted to laying the firm foundations for the new Navy.

Luce was born on March 25, 1827, in Albany, New York. His family claimed descent from the early settlers. They were sufficiently well connected to enable his father, Vinal Luce, to present his son to President Van Buren in the White House. With the President's recommendation, Luce, at the tender age of fourteen, entered the Navy as a midshipman.

Luce was a self-educated man and began early to display a literary bent and a passion for learning. He diligently wrote in his journal, read widely and, it must be conceded, rather indiscriminately. It was an unusual young officer who spent his leisure time at sea devouring the *Spectator,* the works of Dickens—which must have greatly impressed him, for he wrote of his reaction to them that "my vibrations are frequent and rapid"—*Antony and Cleopatra, Paradise Lost,* and Charles Macklin's *Love à la Mode.* Later he became passionately absorbed in the study of history, which profoundly affected his outlook. History, Luce was convinced, provided examples and lessons pointing out the correct paths that future national policy should follow. General strategic principles could be distilled from historical experience: "It is by the knowledge derived from the history of naval battles that we will be enabled to establish a number of facts on which to generalize and formulate those principles which are to constitute the ground-work of our new science." What he had in mind, he explained in 1886, was not a mere recital of events but the philosophical study of military and naval history.[18]

Although nineteenth-century America offered little opportunity to naval officers, Luce's early career had already marked

18. For his early life and career see Gleaves, *Life and Letters,* pp. 35, passim. Luce, "On the Study of Naval History. (Grand Tactics)," a lecture delivered to the Naval War College, Sept. 1886, *Proceedings of the United States Naval Institute, 13* (1887), 175–201.

him as a man of exceptional abilities. At the age of thirty-six he compiled the standard work on the handling of sailing vessels. It took ten more years, however, until he was promoted to the relatively senior rank of captain. Luce's gifts as an educator were first revealed when he was appointed head of the Department of Seamanship at the Naval Academy in 1862. The Civil War was raging, and the Department of Seamanship had been evacuated to Newport, Rhode Island. That autumn Mahan was detailed to join him in training the increasing number of midshipmen required by the Union Navy. In the following year Mahan, as Executive Officer, accompanied Luce on the practice cruise which took the training ship *Macedonian* to Europe. So began a momentous association. At the end of the Civil War, Luce returned to the Naval Academy (now back in Annapolis) as Commandant of Midshipmen. There he soon formed a close friendship with the Superintendent, Admiral David Dixon Porter.[19]

His career as a practical reformer and politician began in these postwar years. His attention turned first to the need for skilled American seamen. Even the modest demands of the Navy in the years immediately following the Civil War could not be met. For example, in 1872 five ships of the Mediterranean squadron were manned by rough and polyglot crews. Indeed the crews were drawn from no less than thirty-five nations, and only a third were American citizens. Desertions were frequent. "The majority are ignorant of the Navy and its tradition, indifferent to honor and reputation," Luce wrote to the Secretary of the Navy, "impatient under discipline, and . . . go through with their military duties under protest as it were." Such crews, Luce recognized, would stand no chance if they were ever called upon to fight a well-disciplined navy. Luce

19. Gleaves, *Life and Letters*, pp. 103–06. See also Richard S. West, *The Second Admiral, A Life of David Dixon Porter, 1813–1891* (New York, Coward-McCann, 1937).

pointed out that the lack of trained American seamen not only made any question of the expansion of the Navy unthinkable but also rendered the few warships of the 1870s ineffectual. He put it forcefully to the Secretary of the Navy in 1872 when he wrote, "the seamen who man our ships, fight our guns and follow our officers into battle are as a clan inferior to those of almost every navy having the slightest pretensions to respectability." He suggested a remedy—the establishment of nautical schools to train boys for the Navy. As the Department in Washington was not responsive to new ideas, Luce did not hesitate to argue his case outside the official channels.[20]

Luce publicized his views by delivering a lecture in 1874 to the United States Naval Institute entitled "The Manning of Our Navy and Mercantile Marine." The Institute had been founded in October 1873 for "the advancement of professional and scientific knowledge in the Navy." In his lecture Luce explained the basic objective of this and all his subsequent reforms—national preparedness for war. Geographical isolation and pacific intentions, he was convinced, could no longer ensure freedom from all conflict: "Shall we wait for the declaration of war to drive us to exertion, or shall we unite at once to discharge the duty which so long has stared us in the face?" He drew freely on historical analogies to underline his point. The Crimean War had found England unprepared, the Franco-Prussian War had caught France unready; as for the United States, he discerned "the cloud of war already hanging darkly on the horizon . . . [Cuba] with her thorn ever pressing in our side . . . lies bleeding at our doors, a prey to contention, and rent by fierce civil strife." All this was stirring stuff compared to his calm and businesslike proposal for a bill to be placed before Congress to "promote the efficiency of masters and mates in the merchant service, and to encourage the estab-

20. Gleaves, *Life and Letters*, pp. 137–38.

lishment of public marine schools." [21] Luce realized of course that the officers who listened to him at the Naval Academy could do little to promote such a bill; the pressure would have to be brought to bear on Congress by more influential groups.

With this in mind, he sent letters to the Chambers of Commerce, Boards of Trade, and Boards of Education in Boston, New York, Philadelphia, and Baltimore. He laid less stress on the need to prepare for war—an argument not likely to appeal to traders and peaceable citizens—but rather emphasized the moral and material benefit that would follow from the establishment of nautical schools. The life and condition of seamen would be better; he claimed that a well-ordered merchant ship was the best missionary to spread through distant seas the manifold blessings of Christianity and civilization. Commerce would be increased; ships would be safer; insurance rates would therefore be lower. In short, Luce nicely balanced spiritual and material benefits.

He succeeded brilliantly. Congress passed the Marine Schools Act in June 1874, authorizing the use of a naval vessel as a nautical school. Other nautical schools were established shortly thereafter in New York, Philadelphia, and Boston and, in 1875, Congress authorized the enlistment of 750 boys as naval apprentices. This was the beginning of a permanent naval training system with which Luce remained closely associated for several years.

Luce's next venture into naval politics was a campaign for the foundation of a school to train officers in the science of war. There was no likelihood that the United States would embark on a building program matching the American fleet in size to the warships of the European powers; but Luce saw no reason why the United States fleet should not be superior

21. Luce, "The Manning of Our Navy and Mercantile Marine," *Record of the United States Naval Institute*, 1 (1874), 17–37.

in quality, and especially in the quality of its officers and crew.

Luce first advocated a postgraduate course for naval officers in August 1877. "Extraordinary as it may appear," he wrote to Secretary of the Navy Thompson, "the naval officer whose principal business it is to fight is not taught the higher branches of his profession." [22] A year later the Navy Department sent an officer abroad to study the systems of naval education in other countries. One of the bureau Chiefs presumably pigeonholed his report, for nothing further was heard of the scheme for years.

His proposal aroused the derision and annoyance of many conservative officers. The majority of the bureau chiefs in the Navy Department resisted all change. Commodore Ramsay, the Commandant of Annapolis, saw no place for any rival institution. Senior officers scoffed at Luce's idea of providing postgraduate education and at his notion that the Navy was an army afloat, whose disposition was governed by strategic principles similar to the ones that determined the handling of armies on land. The unlikely alliance between dogged, seagoing officers and bureaucrats tied to their Washington desks frustrated Luce for years. To combat them, Luce looked for support in the Navy and in Congress. He forged ties of interest between the new naval strategy and politicians who clamored for a new approach to foreign policy. This community of interest is personified by the association of Roosevelt, Lodge, and Mahan. It was Luce in his efforts to establish the Naval War College who brought them together.

22. Gleaves, *Life and Letters*, p. 168. More than thirty years later, Winston Churchill followed in Luce's footsteps. After he became First Lord of the Admiralty in 1911, Churchill was responsible for the appointment of a committee to report on the organization and creation of a Royal Naval War College. See John Terraine, "The Training of Naval Officers, Lord Haig's Notes on the Report of the Committee on the Royal Naval War College, 1913," *Royal United Services Institution Journal*, 109 (1964), 357–62.

Luce followed up his August 1877 letter to Secretary Thompson by encouraging discussion of the subject among active members of the Navy. It was surely more than a coincidence that the United States Naval Institute—with which Luce was closely associated—announced in the same year that an annual prize would be awarded for the best essay submitted on a subject chosen by the Institute: naval education. It was won the following year by Lieutenant Commander C. F. Goodrich, who recommended the establishment of a postgraduate course for officers and the foundation of a Naval College for this purpose.[23] The seed fell on stony ground. Four years later, in 1882, Luce delivered a lecture to the United States Naval Institute drawing attention to the need for a War College.[24] In Washington, meanwhile, he had interested his old friend Admiral Porter in his plans.

Porter's house at 1710 H Street had become a meeting place for officers and politicians.[25] But Admiral Porter was not in a position of favor at the Navy Department. He lamented that the Secretary did not consult him and that the bureau chiefs, who kept all business in their hands, always combined against an outsider.[26] Luce nevertheless continued to pull strings and enlist anyone who could possibly be of help. His doggedness was rewarded in the end. He received an invitation to Washington to explain his views to Secretary of the Navy William E. Chandler and the assembled bureau chiefs. Fortunately the senior bureau, the Bureau of Navigation, was headed by a progressive naval officer, Commodore James G. Walker. With his and Chandler's support the objections of the other bureau

23. C. F. Goodrich, "Naval Education," *Proceedings of the United States Naval Institute,* 5 (1878), 322–44.
24. Luce, "War Schools," *Proceedings of the United States Naval Institute,* 9 (1882), 633–57.
25. West, *The Second Admiral,* p. 336.
26. Porter to Luce, Feb. 21, 1883. Luce Papers, Library of Congress.

chiefs were overruled, and Luce was appointed to head a board of inquiry to investigate the feasibility of the scheme. A few weeks later, this board submitted a cogently argued report in favor of the establishment of the War College. In October 1884, Chandler added his approval. The Naval War College was assigned to Coasters' Harbor Island, Newport, and placed under the protective control of the Bureau of Navigation; Luce was appointed its first President.

This did not prove to be the happy end of Luce's persistent efforts, but rather the beginning of a fierce struggle between Luce (aided by the friends of the College) and his opponents.

The Navy Department merely proposes; Congress disposes. Without adequate funds, the War College would have been stillborn, and Luce's tenacity alone kept the College alive during the first years of its existence. The House of Representatives was controlled by the Democrats. The opponents of the College, headed by Commodore Ramsay, worked hard—and with success—on the House Committee on Naval Affairs to deny the College support. The College possessed no more than the shell of a building, a former almshouse. Scrounging some chairs, desks, one lamp, and a quantity of coal, Luce and his indefatigable aide, Lieutenant William McCarthy Little, managed to get the class of eight officers started in September 1885.

Luce had at this time only one firm friend in the Navy Department, Commodore Walker. Admiral Porter, too, did what he could to aid Luce. These two officers were responsible for the favorable accounts of the work of the College included in the Secretary of the Navy's annual reports of 1885 and 1886. But with the change of Administration in March 1885, the Democrats had come to power and the new Secretary, Whitney, mistrusted everything the former Secretary of the Navy had done and did his best to discredit him. The War College was one of Chandler's innovations, and so Whitney and the

[18]

Democratic majority in the House did nothing to further its prosperity. Party political considerations thus help to account for Whitney's cold indifference to the War College.

In June 1886, just before the second session of the College was due to begin, Luce, now Rear Admiral, was appointed to command the North Atlantic Station. Mahan, who had been preparing his lectures since the previous summer, was appointed to succeed Luce. Unhappily, Mahan and Whitney had started off on the wrong foot. Having accepted Luce's invitation to lecture at the College, Mahan was impatient to get away from his seagoing assignment, command of the *Wachusett,* cruising off the coast of South America. In May 1885, he sent a tactless letter to Whitney requesting to be relieved of the command of his ship, a request which the Secretary refused. Mahan had to wait another year for his release and appointment to the War College post. Tedious service on the South American station in a third-rate wooden screw steamer soured Mahan. He had already spent thirty years in the Navy, and his career had proved rewarding neither professionally nor financially.[27]

Mahan joined the War College in August 1886. That summer the College survived by a narrow margin. Luce's attempts to secure an appropriation during the previous spring had failed, despite the support of Senator Nelson Aldrich of Rhode Island.[28] At the Navy Department, Commodore Walker nonetheless was doing his best to tide the College over "until it has more friends. I have had pretty hard work to carry it as the Secretary is not at all in its favor." [29]

The College session in the autumn of 1886 was a tremendous success. Luce arrived in Narragansett Bay with the North

27. Hirsch, *William C. Whitney,* p. 267.
28. Senator Aldrich to Luce, May 27, 1886. Luce Papers.
29. Walker to Luce, Aug. 21, 1886. Luce Papers.

Atlantic Squadron and delivered the opening address and four lectures. Mahan lectured on naval history. Another lecturer was Tasker Bliss, then an Army lieutenant. A class of about twenty men attended the courses. They were joined by the officers of the squadron. Luce had chosen Coasters' Harbor Island as the site of the War College in order that the North Atlantic Squadron could participate and cooperate practically in the work of the College. Ever since the disastrous experience of 1874, the American "fleet" had for all practical purposes ceased to exist. Ships had been sent singly to possible trouble spots. Luce now devised tactical exercises to enable the ships to act together.

The enthusiasm of the officers who attended the courses and the protection of Commodore Walker kept the War College alive during 1886. Rather optimistically as it turned out, Walker wrote to Luce in November of that year: "I think the War College is now on pretty safe ground. I think the boon given it last summer has modified the Secretary's views very considerable . . . It came very near being broken up last summer." [30] During the winter the building was empty; Mahan and Little practically camped out. The Newport winters are bitter, and it was only by a happy chance that Mahan got hold of some coal which someone had left at the College by mistake. But the work of preparation for the summer of 1887 went on.

Walker had managed to insert $12,000 in the naval appropriation of 1887 to equip the War College. But the opposition to the College was also gathering force. The battle was fought on the floor of the House on February 25, 1887. Luce's farsighted project was not denied on its merits. Political partisanship marred the debate. Commodore Ramsay persuaded the Democratic members of the Committee on Naval Affairs, who

30. Walker to Luce, Nov. 28, 1886. Luce Papers.

suspected the Republicans of seeking party advantage, that if postgraduate naval instruction were desired it should be given at Annapolis. The Republican Representatives from Connecticut and Rhode Island, John Ransom Buck and Henry Joshua Spooner, both spoke in favor of the College, but Democratic Representatives William McAdoo of New Jersey and Hilary Abner Herbert of Alabama set the tone of the debate, as McAdoo declared:

> In a country like ours, where the people are rightfully fearful and wisely jealous of military pageantry and display, it is a great misfortune that our military schools should be established in connection with watering places, and characterized in certain seasons of the year as scenes of social display and dissipation. . . . There was no opposition in the Naval Committee to this postgraduate course for naval officers nor to the war college proper, but there was a well-founded suspicion that this so-called munificent gift [of the college building] on the part of the State of Rhode Island to the United States Government was given for the purpose of enhancing the charms of her well-known watering place, the city of Newport.

No doubt, he added, the wealthy hotel owners might favor the appropriation but, while the naval officers could add to their knowledge of military science by attending the College, "they [will] find some time to devote to the festive dance; and the giddy maidens, who disport themselves on the rocks in sun-bonnets in the latter part of the summer season, find quite a romantic charm in sometimes strolling on the shining beach with the epauleted, embryonic admirals of our decaying and dilapidated Navy." He recommended that appropriations for the "alleged war college but really a dancing school" be refused. In closing the debate, Herbert characterized the appropriation as an extravagant demand on the American people and voiced the hope that Congress "will here and now nip this thing in the bud." Congress acted on this advice, and the appropriation was defeated by a vote of 81 to 70.[31]

Commodore Walker sent Mahan another class of twenty in the autumn of 1887, but the days of the College seemed numbered. Whitney was planning to rid himself of what he considered an encumbrance. Anchored off Coasters' Harbor Island lay the *New Hampshire,* the training school. Not unnaturally, the officers of the training school hankered after the War College building, a haven of comfort and sanitation compared with their quarters aboard the ship. It was especially galling to the training school's officers to see the College building in use during only part of the year. Whitney hoped to solve the problem neatly by removing the War College from its buildings and consolidating it with the Torpedo Station on neighboring Goat Island.

During the critical winter of 1887 Luce endeavored to rally support for the College. He organized a petition against the removal of the College from Coasters' Harbor Island; he appealed to senators, to congressmen, and to members of the congressional naval committees. He also wrote to Theodore Roosevelt.[32] Luce's letter to him is a good example of the way in which he attempted to win friends for the College. It also reveals how Roosevelt's momentous association with Mahan and the War College was brought about.

I beg you will excuse my addressing you on the subject of your admirable work entitled "The Naval War of 1812." But on reading it recently I have been so struck with its impar-

31. *Congressional Record,* 49th Cong., 2d sess. (Feb. 25, 1887), *18,* 2287–90.

32. Luce to Roosevelt, Feb. 13, 1888. Roosevelt Papers, Library of Congress.

tiality and the care with which you have sought information from original sources that there is no question in my mind the work must be accepted as the very highest authority we have on the subject.

It teaches the Naval student the great value of Naval history when written in a spirit of fairness.

We are now giving some attention to the subject of Naval history, or what may be called a philosophical study of Naval history; and on the part relating to the war of 1812 your work must be our text book.

The Navy Department in recognizing the necessity for an advanced course of study for our officers, in which they will be lead [sic] to draw from the lessons of the past, the true policy of the future; has recently opened a Naval College on an island in Narragansett Bay. Some idea of the work carried on there may be gathered from the short article herewith enclosed.

May we not hope that the study you have given to the early history of the Navy will lead you to take some interest in a naval institution now struggling through the ills of infancy?

The next college term does not begin till September, but Captain A. T. Mahan, U. S. N., the President would be glad to see you at any time, and explain the objects and ends he has in view.

Roosevelt responded with zest and enthusiasm. He not only came to the War College to make Mahan's acquaintance, but also, unable to resist Luce's friendly and appreciative reference to his book, stayed to lecture on the "True Conditions of the War of 1812."

Despite Luce's efforts and the zeal of his allies, the class of 1888 was the last one assembled in the original Naval War

College building. Although the classes were small and their duration was short, Luce had ensured wide recognition of the College which he once called a "poor little Poor House."

During the early years, Luce drew attention to the work of the College by inviting the leading citizens of Newport to attend ceremonies at the beginning of the term. Although Newport's status in those days as a fashionable resort was used as a weapon to denigrate the War College, once a year the summer residents paid a call on the College to hear the opening address of the term. Luce also invited anyone of influence, the friends of the naval officers who were attending the current course, and, above all, congressmen and senators. By such expedients he filled the lectureroom to capacity. A reception and luncheon which followed marked the one day in the year when the War College basked in the reflected wealth and distinction of a glittering array of guests.[33]

Lobbying in Congress by the friends of the College finally produced tangible results in 1888. The College secured an appropriation of $10,000. Unfortunately, this infuriated Secretary Whitney, who wanted the College out of its building. During the previous summer he had already reduced the duration of the courses from four months to three. Now he decided to abolish the College altogether. "I spent yesterday up at the Senate," he wrote to his wife in July 1888. "I got mad about a small thing and concluded I would make a fight in the Senate . . . It was about the infernal war college at Newport. These officers have been working behind my back all winter and I recommended, but I didn't seem to get it as I recommended, and I finally awoke to the fact that the whole

33. Luce, "The notes of an address to the War College, June 1906," "Talk on the history of the War College, August 20, 1906," "Notes on the War College, December 19, 1910," Luce Papers. Gleaves, *Life and Letters,* pp. 168, passim. Alfred T. Mahan, *From Sail to Steam, Recollections of Naval Life* (New York, Harper, 1907), pp. 296–301.

thing was being set up and worked in Congress behind me. I will wipe the whole thing out shortly." [34] Whitney was as good as his word. First he removed Mahan from the presidency and sent him three thousand miles away to investigate the suitability of Puget Sound for a navy yard. Luce at once appealed to Walker to allow Mahan to remain at the War College, prophesying that when Mahan's work was complete, the United States would rank first in knowledge of the science of war. Walker explained that he could do nothing, since Mahan had been detailed by the Secretary himself. Having removed Mahan, Whitney abolished the office of president of the College and ordered consolidation with the Torpedo School on Goat Island. He also removed the College from Walker's supervision. All this was done during the dying weeks of the Democratic Administration. Luce was determined to badger the incoming Republican Administration as soon as possible to reestablish the War College as a separate entity.

President Harrison appointed Benjamin F. Tracy as Secretary of the Navy in March 1889, and so began a notable period in the history of the Navy. Tracy, despite his lack of previous experience in naval affairs, proved himself to be the most outstanding Secretary of the Navy during the half century between the Civil War and World War I. Tracy had hardly taken up the reins when he received a long letter from Luce, outlining the history and value of the College and requesting that the College be allowed to return to Coasters' Harbor Island. Tracy promptly sent a sympathetic reply, assuring Luce that he appreciated the importance of the War College.[35] Moreover, he chose not to act on the previous con-

34. Whitney to his wife, July 25, 1888. Hirsch, *William C. Whitney,* p. 339.
35. Tracy to Luce, March 30, 1889. Luce Papers.

gressional appropriation which provided $100,000 for the construction of the Torpedo School and War College on Goat Island.

Luce also sent a stream of letters to Admiral Porter asking him to see Tracy and to intercede personally on behalf of the College.[36] Porter was not very hopeful. He had been cold-shouldered by the Department for years. The only ray of hope he could hold out was that his personal friendship with President Harrison might secure him greater influence in Washington. The trouble lay with the bureau chiefs. For one thing, the archenemy of the College, Ramsay, had replaced Walker as the head of the Bureau of Navigation. The bureau chiefs, Porter ruefully commented, are "a hard party to deal with . . . They have pocketed every Secretary who has ever gone in there—even Whitney who thought he had grappled with and conquered all the evils, was completely hoodwinked by the Bureaus." Porter had no better opinion of Tracy, whom he described as an old gentleman of sixty-two, who would do nothing in a hurry, "having passed many years in the study of the law." [37] A week later, after he had seen Tracy, Porter enthusiastically reported: "I have had but one special interview with the Secretary and came away much impressed with the profound knowledge he possesses of naval affairs which I think must have been born in him!" [38]

Tracy spent the next six months working on his famous first report in which he advocated a battleship fleet. He found the time to appoint Mahan, on his return from the Pacific Northwest, to the staff of the Torpedo School and War College. In October 1889 another class—the last for two years—assembled at the College and heard Mahan lecture. Mahan

36. See esp. Luce to Porter, March 9, 1889. Gleaves, *Life and Letters*, pp. 185–86.
37. Porter to Luce, March 14, 1889. Luce Papers.
38. Porter to Luce, March 21, 1889. Luce Papers.

was assigned for the next two years to special duty in the Navy Department (more about this later), but he continued his historical work. There were no classes in 1890 and 1891.

Despite the lack of Mahan's guiding hand, these two years were not barren for the War College. With the benevolent approval of Tracy and Republican control in both houses of Congress, Luce successfully appealed to Senator Chandler to obtain proper appropriations for the War College and to insist on its return to the old building. Chandler and Senator Aldrich did in fact secure a handsome appropriation of $100,000 in June 1890 for a new War College building to be erected near its original site at Coasters' Harbor. The new building was completed in 1892; Mahan was again appointed President. But the sands of the Republican Administration had nearly run out, and, with the swing of the political pendulum, the War College was once more plunged into danger of immediate dissolution in 1893.

The War College could hope for little from the new Secretary of the Navy under Cleveland, Hilary A. Herbert. Like Tracy, Herbert was a staunch supporter of the Navy, but the pernicious tradition of decrying the work of the previous administration—if it were of the opposing party—was firmly rooted in almost every aspect of American government. The War College had been established by one Republican Secretary of the Navy, was supported by another, Tracy, and was a matter of some importance to the Republican Senator from Rhode Island. All this made the Democratic Secretary look upon the institution with disfavor and suspicion. As a congressman, Secretary Herbert had ridiculed the War College and had opposed appropriations for it. Next to him, the second most important person in the Navy Department was the Chief of the Bureau of Navigation, and Ramsay was confirmed in this position in 1893. To add to the War College's troubles, the Democrats gained Senate and House majorities.

The worst fears of the supporters of the College were soon confirmed: Mahan was once again removed from the presidency and ordered to sea. Luce could do little, but in his fight to save the College he had gained the support of two young Republican politicians, Lodge and Roosevelt.[39] Paradoxically, in being repeatedly threatened with extinction, the War College served one of its most important functions. The threat that he might lose his audience at any time stimulated Mahan to publish his lectures; his books and articles in turn provided the basis for a new concept of foreign policy that won the support of an ardent group of representatives, senators, and newspaper editors.

The imminent removal of Mahan from the War College now spurred the tireless Luce into action once more. Roosevelt wrote to Mahan (May 1, 1893):

Last evening Lodge, Harry Davis, Admiral Luce and I held a solemn council of war . . . and as a result, taking advantage of Herbert's absence, I went up to see MacAdoo [the Assistant Secretary], who is much more civilized, to-day. He is on our side; but he can do very little. I fear all hope for the War College (which is nothing without you) has gone; our prize idiots here have thrown away the chance to give us an absolutely unique position in Naval affairs . . . Oh, what idiots we have had to deal with! [40]

In appointing Captain Henry Clay Taylor, one of Luce's disciples, to succeed Mahan, the Navy Department had chosen one of the ablest officers of his generation and a determined fighter for the College. It cannot be established clearly

39. See p. 210.
40. Roosevelt to Mahan, May 1, 1893. Elting E. Morison, John M. Blum, and John J. Buckley, eds., *The Letters of Theodore Roosevelt,* 1 (Cambridge, Mass., Harvard University Press, 1951), 315–16.

whether the friends of the College had contrived to get the right man into the right position, or whether the appointment happened by chance. During the summer of 1893, Herbert paid a visit to the War College, and a story is told describing how, en route from Washington on the *Dolphin,* he underwent a tremendous conversion. The Captain of the *Dolphin* arranged that Herbert's enforced idleness on board should be occupied reading Mahan's *The Influence of Sea Power upon the French Revolution and Empire.* He read the book with interest and admiration. When returning to Washington he admitted to the Captain of the *Dolphin* that he had set out to break up the College but that Mahan's book alone had been worth all the money spent; he now intended to help it. If all this really did happen, then Herbert's good intention evaporated rapidly. It is more likely that some portions of this tale are apocryphal;[41] certainly the contemporary correspondence does not bear it out.

Luce, on the retired list since 1889, was nevertheless still the War College's guardian-in-chief. The old rivalry between the Training School and the War College, both on Coasters' Harbor Island, continued to blight the future prospects of the College; Captain Bunce, Commandant of the Training School, attempted to oust the War College from the new building it occupied. While traveling in Europe that winter, Luce received an urgent appeal from Taylor: "College affairs are at their lowest ebb." He feared that the opponents were attempting to get the College appropriations omitted. "Every effort that I can make is being made, but some methods of working with Congressmen I do not wish to dabble in, even though the cause be lost for the lack of it." He dared not take strong

41. Luce provides the most detailed account of Herbert's visit in 1893 in his "Talk on the history of the War College," which he delivered Aug. 20, 1906. Luce Papers.

official action, for this would appear to the Secretary as insubordination; he therefore asked the Admiral to write to his friends "both Republican and Democrat." [42] Luce wrote to Senator Lodge and others in Washington, but Lodge was not very sanguine: "I have just received your letter from Geneva. My interest in Captain Mahan and my appreciation of his books are of long standing and I have always been a friend of the college. I exerted every influence of which I was capable to prevent Captain Mahan being sent to sea, but was unsuccessfull [sic]. Roosevelt and myself and others have been at work in behalf of the college and I had correspondence with Captain Taylor about it." Lodge pointed out that Commodore Ramsay and the Commandant of the Training School were trying to destroy the College, that the Secretary was very lukewarm and, while not recommending the withdrawal of the appropriations, would take no active steps to help the College. Lodge gloomily concluded that the "most we can hope is to keep the appropriation up and the college alive and wait for a change in the Bureau of Navigation and for better times." [43]

Taylor soon overcame his reluctance to dabble with congressmen. In his letters to Luce during the spring of 1894, he graphically depicted the declining fortunes of the War College. He thanked Luce for his efforts and explained that he, too, had been busy.

I am trying to sow the seed all over the country and thus create an atmosphere which shall presently arouse Secretary Herbert and change his nominal approval to active interest, so that he will stop the persecution of his chief adviser, which, if continued, must soon destroy all vestiges of the College . . . The more you can stir up your friends the

42. Taylor to Luce, Dec. 28, 1893. Luce Papers.
43. Lodge to Luce, Jan. 22, 1894. Luce Papers.

better it will be. I am beginning to work up Boards of Trade, Chambers of Commerce, and other commercial bodies all along our coast and lake frontiers, and I propose, if the College is to be buried, that it shall require a large grave to be dug for the corpse.

Taylor's declared purpose was to force Herbert to coerce Ramsay through the pressure from his other bureau chiefs, senators, representatives, "and a lump of correspondence from myself which—if it does not kill, must permanently enfeeble him—but all of no avail." [44]

The blow fell in March 1894. The Commandant of the Training College had reported Taylor for improper advocacy of the College. Herbert thereupon warned Taylor that any further attack on the Training College by the Naval War College or its friends would lead to the immediate abolition of the College. On March 14, by general order of the Navy Department, the Naval Training Station, the Naval War College, Torpedo School of Coasters' Harbor Island, and the Naval Torpedo Station of Goat Island were consolidated into one command and placed under Captain Bunce. The President of the War College was specifically subordinated to Bunce—and Bunce was the most determined opponent of the College. [45]

But despite the somber outlook, the Naval War College was not abolished. Mahan's growing fame soon overshadowed the petty, internecine rivalry that had impeded the development of the College during its early years. The year 1894 marked the turning point in its fortunes; thereafter it was not again in serious danger. Passages from Mahan's books were frequently cited by the advocates of naval expansion. In his annual report of 1894, Herbert himself justified the need for a

44. Taylor to Luce, Feb. 9, 1894. Luce Papers.
45. Taylor to Luce, March 10, 1894. Luce Papers. Navy Department General Order, March 14, 1894. Luce Papers.

battleship fleet by a thinly veiled reference to Mahan's second book. The War College, or rather Mahan, had thus provided Secretary Herbert with a reasoned case for naval development. In fact, Cleveland's Secretary of the Navy was—despite his earlier opposition to a Naval War College—a conspicuous adherent of that large policy which now began to transcend party politics and take its place as a major point of foreign policy.

In this favorable climate of opinion, the War College experienced a new boom. Its stature grew with Mahan's fame. At Luce's suggestion the College began in 1895 to study the problems of a possible war with Spain over Cuba. "What you say about Cuba and Spain interests me very much and will I fancy produce greater results than you fancied," Taylor wrote to Luce, "for it decides me to do what I have been thinking over for a long time, to use this winter, to prepare with a permanent staff, full plans for the Gulf of Mexico and vicinity . . . I hope some day you will find that your suggestion about Cuba has borne good fruit." [46] A war plan to meet the eventuality of a conflict with Spain was drawn up during collaboration with the Naval Intelligence Division the following year.[47]

The College played a crucial role in the development of America's foreign relations during the decade of the 1890s. Not only did it train naval officers in the science of war, strategy, and tactics, but also—and most important perhaps—it raised a generation of young naval officers on the doctrines of Mahan.

It was Luce who founded the War College, who launched Mahan, and enlisted the support of Lodge and Roosevelt for

46. Taylor to Luce, Aug. 5, 1895. Luce Papers. See also p. 272.
47. See pp. 273–76.

the work of the College in general and for Mahan in particular. It was Luce also who recognized the need for practical exercises to enable the fleet to act as a fighting unit; these exercises he had conducted in conjunction with the War College when he was Commander-in-Chief of the North Atlantic Station. It was Luce who had taken practical steps to ensure a supply of trained and loyal seamen for the Merchant Marine and for the Navy. This impressive list of achievements does not encompass the range of the Admiral's interest in and influence on the development of the United States Navy. He also demonstrated with devastating clarity the mistaken strategic concepts that lay behind the construction of the new Navy in the 1880s and successfully campaigned for the creation of a battleship fleet.

The United States Navy before 1890 was composed of cruisers supposedly designed to act as deterrents to an enemy contemplating war. These cruisers, it was thought, would roam singly over the Atlantic Ocean and cripple the merchant shipping of the enemy. Luce called for the construction of powerful fleets of battleships capable of defeating the battleship fleet of any potential aggressor. He pointed out that the United States could only defend herself by attaining command of the ocean approaches to the Western Hemisphere. His arguments were accepted by Tracy, who in 1889 issued his revolutionary annual report publicly endorsing Luce's proposals. Thus a few months before the publication of Mahan's *Influence of Sea Power upon History, 1660–1783*, the Navy Department asserted the need for a massive program of battleship construction.

Three years earlier, in 1886, the Cleveland Administration had already taken an important step forward when Secretary Whitney proposed the construction of two large armored vessels, later listed as battleships. His recommendation was fiercely contested in Congress and signaled the start of a debate not to be resolved for several years. It was concerned not merely with technical arguments but also with the purpose of the Navy, and, beyond that, America's role in world affairs. The concept of a combination of commerce-destroying cruisers, to deter would-be aggressors, and monitors and static fortifications, to defend the coast from attack, was essentially defensive and isolationist. The construction of a battleship fleet with a large coal-carrying capacity, on the other hand, would make possible the assertion of American power beyond the continental confines. The opponents feared that once America possessed such a battleship fleet the United States would soon abandon her traditional policy of aloofness from world affairs. Such a view was expressed, for example, by Representative McAdoo, a member of the House Committee on Naval Affairs, during the naval appropriations debate of 1890. He opposed in committee the construction of three battleships and advocated: "Low free board monitor-type vessels for coast defense only." If a large battleship fleet were created, he now declared, "then I would not be responsible for the peace of the United States for twelve months." [48]

It was Luce who had led the demand for a Navy capable of meeting the battleship fleet of an enemy on equal terms. This meant constructing American battleships of equal, if not superior, capacity to those of any foe. Mahan in 1889 was engaged in his historical researches and philosophical speculations on the elements of sea power, and he was singularly pessimistic about the time needed to create an American battleship fleet. He wrote that the United States would only possess a real fleet when the revival of the Merchant Navy had created sufficient demand for its protection. He was mistaken:

48. Representative McAdoo, *Congressional Record*, 51st Cong., 1st sess. (April 8, 1890), *21*, 3167–68.

he overemphasized the economic motivation of sea power. Fears for national security played a greater part than Mahan expected in the creation of a Navy. Before Mahan published his views, Secretary Tracy's annual report of 1889 had proved that his misgivings were unreal.

A few months before Tracy sent the report to Congress, Luce had published a remarkable article in the *North American Review*, entitled "Our Future Navy." He advocated the construction of twenty battleships—precisely the same number as Tracy proposed later that year. Luce detected much woolly thinking about the role of a fleet within both the Navy and Congress—thinking that sought to distinguish defensive capacity from offensive power. In his view, no Secretary of the Navy had yet proposed the creation of a fighting fleet. What Luce now set out to do in his article was to tear away the strategic misconceptions that still prevailed late in the 1880s.[49]

Luce reminded his readers that half a century earlier, in 1836, the Navy had assessed its needs more realistically when it endorsed a program calling for the building of fifteen battleships; "to-day we need twenty at least. When we shall have put one half that number afloat we may begin to talk about rehabilitating our navy without provoking a smile of derision." He justified his proposal by using his favorite analogy of the fleet as a sea army. Battleships, like the infantry, he explained, were the foundation of a navy, but the United States had tried to build up a fleet without battleships. This he scornfully rejected as no policy at all, declaring: "In the absence of anything and everything that might resemble a naval policy, we have reversed the usual order of naval development. The battleship being the very foundation of a navy, and the United

49. Luce, "Our Future Navy," *North American Review, 149* (1889), pp. 54–65.

States having no battleship, it is plain that in a military sense
. . . she has no navy." Indeed Luce could only discover one
idea behind the development of the new Navy—to run away
from the problem altogether. "If there is any one fact made
clear by the history of the past, it is the true function of our
navy. The role of a navy is essentially *offensive,* as contrasted
with sea-coast fortifications, which are *defensive.*" Luce concluded with a powerful plea for immediate action: since battleships could not be built overnight, the United States should
at once embark on a program of construction that would provide the United States with the twenty battleships Luce regarded as the minimum required.[50]

Luce's article made an impact where it mattered most. He
had become President of the Naval Institute and had arranged
for a meeting at which his paper would be discussed. The
article was circulated to the officers who attended and it was
reprinted in the *Proceedings of the Naval Institute;* a résumé
of the discussion that had followed the reading of the paper
was also printed. Of particular interest are Mahan's remarks.
He accepted Luce's views: "I have only to express my entire
concurrence in the general tenor of this admirable paper, and
in the principles of naval policy adopted in it." He thus wished
to reinforce the paper by giving those views the largest possible consensus of professional opinion. If he understood Luce
correctly, a war directed against an enemy's commerce was
utterly insufficient. It followed, he went on, that the United
States was committed to an erroneous and disastrous policy.
Great harm had been done by not building battleships, "which
are undoubtedly the real strength of the navy." [51]

By publishing his views in the *Proceedings,* Luce had made

50. Luce, "Our Future Navy," *Proceedings of the United States Naval
Institute,* 15 (1889), 541–59.
51. Mahan's comments are printed together with Luce's "Our Future
Navy," *Proceedings of the United States Naval Institute,* 15 (1889).

sure that the members of the Policy Board, who were to issue their report in January 1890, would be aware of them. Four of the seven members of the board were also members of the Naval Institute and so received a copy of the *Proceedings* that autumn. Luce's article created something of a sensation in naval circles. He received letters of congratulation from a number of senior officers and a request for a copy from the Chairman of the House Committee on Naval Affairs.[52] There can be no doubt that the article was brought to the attention of Secretary Tracy and that it probably influenced him, the Policy Board, and discussion in the House Committee on Naval Affairs. The outcome of the debate was Tracy's annual report and the report of the Policy Board.[53] In the following spring, Congress began to take the first, if halting, steps toward the creation of a fighting fleet.

To recognize the achievements of Luce and the part he played in the creation of a fighting fleet does not diminish Mahan's stature in any way; it places his contribution in its proper perspective. The services of Luce, the Admiral in politics, proved as vital a factor in the creation of a fighting fleet as did the more spectacular feats of Mahan, who popularized the new Navy, and Dewey and Sampson, who first proved the Navy in battle.

Party politics and personal rivalries played an important and injurious role in the development of an efficient Navy. The existence of the Naval War College was for years jeopardized by the jealousy of Democratic politicians who looked upon it as a Republican institution. The acceptance of technological improvements in the Navy, the debate over capital

52. Boutelle requested a copy of the article in December 1889. Boutelle to Luce, December 1889; Luce to Boutelle, December 28, 29, 1889. Luce Papers.

53. The report of 1890 was printed in full in the *Proceedings of the United States Naval Institute, 16* (1890), 201–77.

ships as against cruisers, and the provision of naval bases were bedeviled by similar rivalries. Fortunately, those men—politicians and naval officers—who recognized that they were dealing with a great national question and not with a party or personal issue triumphed in the end. Luce had contributed powerfully to their victory. Without an efficient Navy, no Administration could conduct foreign policy to meet American needs, for foreign policy is a national and not a party question. But a study of Cleveland's first Administration shows how few politicians were ready to consider the nation before the party.

Chapter Two
Party Politics and Foreign Policy:
Grover Cleveland's
First Administration, 1885–1889

THE "EXCESSIVE SPIRIT OF PARTY" which for years blighted the life of the Naval War College also paralyzed the conduct of foreign policy during the course of Cleveland's first Administration; it distracted the public councils and enfeebled government. In a striking passage of his Farewell Address, Washington had warned his fellow citizens against the effect of party politics in these very words. During Cleveland's first Administration, the Republican-dominated Congress sought to discredit the Democrats by every possible means. Cleveland's inflexible domestic policies at the same time alienated the majority of his own supporters.

The United States still enjoyed such a degree of security that the conduct of diplomacy could be mishandled without permanent harm. This would not always remain true. Thomas Francis Bayard, Cleveland's Secretary of State in the mid-80s, already discerned dangers on the horizon. He foresaw the possibility that the European powers would establish bases for future expansion in the Western Hemisphere. How best to meet this threat became a dominant theme in the formation of American foreign policy. Bayard was no imperialist; nor were his preoccupations purely parochial; but he viewed the problem of American security on a hemispheric scale. The might of Bismarck's Germany was a new factor in the calculations of American diplomats. "Germany," Bayard observed, "has of late years given evidence of a disposition to cherish schemes of distant annexation and civilization in many quarters of the globe." [1] There were rumors that Germany hoped to obtain footholds in Central America and Cuba. To Bayard and others such plans were "utterly inadmissible."

Bayard upheld American rights in Samoa in the face of German pressure precisely because he feared that any show of weakness would encourage the Germans to seek colonies in the West Indies. The growing European influence in Central America and the prospects of an isthmian canal posed another threat. The United States would reject "any arrangement by which vessels could pass through that canal to assail our own Western coast." [2] International rivalry in the Pacific also disturbed Bayard. When the lease of Pearl Harbor as a naval station was under discussion, Bayard affirmed that the islands "could never be allowed to become a menace or source of danger to the United States." [3] While some of these issues still lay in the future, Bayard conceived it as his most urgent task to settle the present problems: to remove the difficulties that impeded good relations with England and with Canada, and to solve by diplomacy the question of Asiatic immigration.

Cleveland had no such grasp of the fundamental needs of American foreign policy, and he exerted only slight influence upon it during his first three years in office. These years witnessed the growth of American imperialism, reflected in the

1. Bayard to Pendleton, Sept. 9, 1885. Charles C. Tansill, *The Foreign Policy of Thomas F. Bayard* (New York, Fordham University Press, 1940), pp. 29–30.
2. Tansil, *Bayard*, p. 670.
3. For the best treatment of the Hawaiian question, see Tansill, *Bayard*, pp. 359–409.

popularity of the inspirational writings of John Fiske and the Reverend Josiah Strong. Cleveland's own approach to problems of foreign relations was dominated by domestic political considerations. He gave little thought to America's role in world affairs and instead interpreted the advice of the founding fathers simply and literally: he sought to avoid foreign complications, to settle existing disputes amicably, and to limit American responsibilities as far as possible. He could see no serious danger from abroad, and he was content to leave the conduct of foreign policy to his Secretary of State.

To understand Cleveland, we must first penetrate the legend that has grown around him, one that Cleveland himself staunchly believed. His supporters in 1884 presented him to the American people as a man of unimpeachable honesty, unbending principle, and high courage. Half a century later, a distinguished American historian saw Cleveland as a political leader who "possessed honesty, courage, firmness, independence and common sense." His honesty "was of the undeviating type which never compromised an inch; his courage was immense, rugged, unconquerable; his independence was elemental and self-assertive . . . he ploughed straight forward, never flinching, always following the path that his conscience approved to the end." Cleveland might have written that passage himself. He used to remark to his friends with (becoming) modesty: "it is no credit to me to do right. I am never under any temptation to do wrong." [4]

4. Allan Nevins, *Grover Cleveland, A Study in Courage* (New York, Dodd, Mead, 1932), pp. 4–5 and 765. Nevins' monumental study, based on a careful investigation of the then available archival material, largely supersedes Robert M. McElroy's *Grover Cleveland, The Man and Statesman* (2 vols. New York, Harper, 1923). Every student of Cleveland's policy is in Nevins' debt. However, Nevins presents Cleveland in the best possible light. Horace Samuel Merrill provides a corrective in his *Bourbon Leader: Grover Cleveland and the Democratic Party* (Boston, Little, Brown, 1957). Merrill's account in turn is partly indebted to Matthew

If Cleveland did not quite live up to his own estimate, there is really no cause to wonder. Until the dawn of the millenium, the White House will be occupied by men who lead their party as well as the nation. By duty, the interest of the nation comes before the party, but the facts of political life do not always present a clear choice. Faced with an opposition ready to use any weapon at hand, the President—especially as an election drew near—could scarcely avoid coming to terms with the attractive belief that he too was justified in making use of national issues to further his own and his party's interests. Cleveland's conduct should be judged within this context of political realities and not by the absolute moral standard which he believed had actuated all his decisions. Cleveland was just as honest as other politicians; his capacity for self-delusion was simply greater.

To steer a wise course through the perplexing political crosscurrents of the decade from 1884 to 1896 would have taxed a president with greater intellectual capabilities than Cleveland's. Cleveland sought simple solutions to complex problems; he believed that America's salvation lay in the maintenance of "sound money" and in tariff reform. Until 1882 his horizon was limited to the comparatively parochial affairs of Buffalo, New York. A respected lawyer and a leading citizen, Cleveland had by industry amassed a modest fortune and gained a reputation for honesty and personal integrity. As this

---

Josephson's caustic comment on American politics in his *The Politicos, 1865–1896* (New York, Harcourt, Brace, 1938). J. Rogers Hollingsworth, *The Whirligig of Politics, The Democracy of Cleveland and Bryan* (Chicago, University of Chicago Press, 1963), provides a penetrating estimate of Cleveland as a party leader during his second Administration and after. For general background, Leonard D. White, *The Republican Era, 1869–1901* (New York, Macmillan, 1958), is extremely helpful. While we must accept responsibility for the views here expressed on Cleveland's general capacities and rise to power, we have relied on the books listed above.

burly and forthright bachelor went about his business in Buffalo, he exuded the quiet, confident air of the self-made man who knew his own worth.

There was more to the picture of Cleveland than that of a worthy and staid citizen, for Cleveland did possess qualities that were extraordinary, not the least of which was his capacity to adapt to the changes of his personal fortunes. He took in his stride the meteoric rise from Mayor of Buffalo to President of the United States within the astonishing short space of three years. If others were responsible for endowing him with a public image that carried him to the White House, Cleveland understood how to live up to it.

His closest supporters believed in "sound finance." This meant for them a rigid adherence to the gold standard. They sternly condemned the silver lobbyists who, they believed, only desired to aid debtors at the expense of creditors. Cleveland was presented to the business leaders as a "sound-money" man worthy of their confidence. They sensed that their chance of victory in the elections of 1884 lay in attacking the graft and corruption of the Republican Administration and attaching to their own party the magic label "reform." But the business interests who supported Cleveland narrowly defined what they meant by reform; aid for the working man in his struggles against the employer, the attack on monopolies, and greater social justice were objectives which did not win their sympathy. Civil service reform and the eradication of financial corruption in the Administration, on the other hand, were causes on which businessmen and the people could happily unite, and these issues sufficed to defeat the Republicans in 1884.

Cleveland owed his rapid rise to power to the help of Charles W. McCune, editor of the Buffalo *Courier,* Edgar K. Apgar, a fervent Democratic state politician, and especially to

Daniel Manning, the powerful Democratic State Chairman for New York. They backed Cleveland for Governor as the anti-Tammany candidate; he won the election by a large majority. A year later, the support of the New York organization, led by Manning and Samuel Jones Tilden, one-time Governor of New York and presidential contender, assured his nomination at the Democratic National Convention.

In a shrewd election campaign, the integrity of James G. Blaine, the Republican candidate, was placed in public doubt. Cleveland's supporters made the most of Blaine's unethical dealings with the Little Rock and Fort Smith Railroad in 1876. The Republicans exposed Cleveland's earlier involvement with the widow Halpin, who had borne him a son. Partisan newspapers vilified the opposing candidate, and neither side could take much pride in the conduct of the election.

Cleveland owed the presidency to the support of Tilden, Manning, and the big business interests they represented. He repaid the debt by unswerving loyalty to their economic policies —with ultimately disastrous results for the cohesion of the party. Tensions between the silver lobbyists and the sound-money supporters was already evident in 1884. Within a decade, the majority of the Democratic rank and file who represented the hard-pressed western farmers and artisans bolted from the business leadership and followed Bryan's crusading banner.

The President's knowledge of fiscal problems was too unsophisticated to enable him to work out his own public arguments in favor of the gold standard. This task he assigned to Manton Marble, a former editor of the New York *World*. He drafted important documents for both Cleveland and Manning, who—on Tilden's suggestion—had entered Cleveland's cabinet as Secretary of the Treasury. Secretary of State Bayard was in close sympathy with their conservative economic views.[5]

Cleveland, Marble, Manning, and Bayard thus formed a closely knit group which sought in every way to further the cause of fiscal orthodoxy. Their attempt to utilize diplomatic means to preserve the gold standard illustrates the dominance of domestic issues in the 1880s, which worked to the detriment of foreign relations. The story of these efforts, the pursuit of the so-called "silver diplomacy," is often overlooked in the broader studies of American foreign relations.

During the months between Cleveland's election and his inauguration, coinage became the principal bone of contention of the last, and troubled, session of the Forty-eighth Congress. The gold reserve had been declining; fears were expressed that unless some action were taken it might fall below the critical $100 million level.

The financial conservatives in both parties saw bankruptcy drawing near. They urged that the Treasury cease purchasing silver in small amounts, as provided for by the Bland-Allison Act of 1878. Cleveland agreed with this point of view. But to suspend the operation of the Bland Allison Act was political dynamite. In the Republican Senate, the sound-money advocates predominated; in the Democratic House where the majority of Democrats reflected agrarian views and continued to press for the unlimited coinage of silver, Cleveland was obliged to rely

---

5. The relationships between Cleveland and Tilden and Manning and Tilden may be studied in John Bigelow's *Letters and Literary Memorials of Samuel J. Tilden* (2 vols. New York, New York Public Library, 1908). See esp. Tilden to Cleveland, Jan. 2, 1885 (2, 665); Manning to Tilden, Feb. 13, 1885 (2, 678). For Marble's relations with Tilden, see Marble to Tilden, Nov. 15 and 21, 1885, and March 26, 1886; Tilden to Marble, Nov. 20, 1885. Marble MSS. Bayard had himself aspired to the Secretaryship of the Treasury. Washington McClean to Tilden. Bigelow, *Tilden Letters*, 2, 669–70.

on his political opponents rather than on the majority of his own party.

The hostility of Cleveland, Manning, and Bayard to free silver was already well known before the inauguration. But it was Cleveland who took the decision to identify his Administration with a minority of the Democrats.[6] Over two thirds of the Democrats in Congress had defended silver for more than six years before Cleveland. The President staked his political future on carrying the dissident silver men with him before his Administration had run its course. He failed. But how had he imagined he could succeed?

Cleveland and his advisers evidently believed that an expedient already tried by previous administrations would now work: they sought to prevent the silverites from taking precipitate action first by holding out hopes of an international agreement on bimetallism. Later the Administration would blunt the arguments of the supporters of free silver by revealing that such an international agreement could not be reached. The blame could then be placed on other countries, especially on England, for refusing to depart from the gold standard. Cleveland thus was ready to use diplomacy to serve domestic political ends despite the harmful repercussions. It became only too easy for the public to believe that America's economic problems were not of the country's own making, that the European powers were to blame and were motivated by malice; Henry Cabot Lodge and other rising young politicians even persuaded themselves that the British government, having failed to diminish American power by military and diplomatic means, was resorting to a hostile financial policy to achieve the same end.

6. *President Cleveland and the Silver Question, Correspondence between the President-Elect and the Friends of Silver in the House of the Forty-eighth Congress* (Philadelphia, 1885), pp. 3–7. Jordan to Marble, Feb. 21, 1885. Marble MSS. Nevins, *Cleveland*, p. 204. Randall to Tilden, Feb. 17, 1885. Bigelow, *Tilden Letters*, 2, 680.

In his Inaugural Address, Cleveland declared his intention to place American finance on "a sound and sensible basis." [7] By the end of April 1885, the President and his Secretary of State had decided to send a special agent abroad, ostensibly to investigate the attitude of European powers toward bimetallism. On Manning's advice, Bayard asked Marble to come to Washington for a conference. From this conference, held early in May 1885, Marble emerged as an agent of the Executive, whose task it was to ascertain the prospect for international bimetallism.[8]

Bayard was on friendly terms with Marble; he was content to allow Manning, with Tilden's support, to direct the silver mission.[9] Bayard, Manning, and Marble were astute observers of domestic politics with a realistic view of the international monetary situation. They all believed international bimetallism impossible; Marble's mission was not to promote international bimetallism, but to obtain evidence that their opinion was correct. This evidence when laid before Congress by the President, they calculated, could then be used to justify a recommendation to suspend the coinage of silver altogether.[10]

The silver mission was conducted on an informal basis. Marble embodied his reports in private letters to Manning and Bayard; they were never published, and much of this correspondence has subsequently been lost.[11] Fortunately the main events of the mission can be reconstructed.

7. James D. Richardson, ed., *A Compilation of the Messages and Papers of the Presidents, 1789–1897* (10 vols. Washington, D.C., 1899), 8, 302.

8. Manning to Marble, April 29, 1885; Marble to Manning, May 3, 1885. Marble MSS.

9. Bayard to Marble, Aug. 22 and Oct. 29, 1885. Marble MSS. Manning to Marble, Sept. 6, 1885; Bayard to Manning, Sept. 25 and Oct. 13, 1885. Manning MSS.

10. See esp. Marble to Manning, May 3, 1885. Marble MSS.

11. See esp. Bayard to Manning, Oct. 23, 1886. Manning MSS. Manning to Marble, April 29, 1885, and Feb. 10, 1887. Marble MSS.

Marble arrived in London toward the end of May. 1885. In mid-July, he approached Lord Iddesleigh, the First Lord of the Treasury. Did the British government, Marble asked him, regard bimetallism in a more favorable light than it had in 1881? After consulting his cabinet colleagues, Iddesleigh rebuffed Marble, saying there was "nothing doing, nor anything in immediate contemplation with respect to the currency and standard of value questions." [12] Marble tried again a fortnight later, as he accosted Iddesleigh on his way to the House of Lords. Iddesleigh would not stop to talk with him, but he sent Marble a letter on July 23, explaining that the British government was ready to reject his suggestion formally. Iddesleigh hoped that Marble would not require a formal reply, since in his view the whole procedure would be just "a waste of time." [13]

The First Lord of the Treasury could not have known that a formal British refusal was precisely what the American hoped to obtain. Marble now explained the situation to Iddesleigh:

I would have inquired of you whether, and explained why it would be desirable that, two notes might pass between us quite in the sense of your favor of the 22nd inst. [saying that further discussion of the metallic question was a waste of time], which I beg to acknowledge with thanks, and *adapted somewhat more precisely to our present occasions in the United States.* This may seem to you impracticable, in which case be pleased to cancel the enclosure. But if the expression of an opinion in which it is obvious that the great mass of all parties in Great Britain concur, could be so couched as *to cast light upon the subject for all parties in the United States next December,* then I would beg leave to suggest the enclosure as a draft of the first note, sub-

12. Iddesleigh to Marble, July 22, 1885. Marble MSS.
13. Iddesleigh to Marble, July 28, 1885. Marble MSS.

ject to every modification which you would kindly indicate.[14]

Marble's frankness in indicating that such an exchange of notes would be used as political ammunition by the sound-money contingent in the United States might have been disarming. But Iddesleigh immediately saw its implications and bearing on the President's position in the silver controversy, sure to break out when Congress convened in December. "It would not become me," he very properly replied, "to offer an informal suggestion bearing on the probable course of the Executive of the United States." [15]

After obtaining such small satisfaction from Iddesleigh, Marble crossed the Channel to France in August. From there he traveled to Berlin and finally returned to London by way of Paris early in October. Marble returned to America convinced that any agreement on an international ratio between gold and silver was out of the question. No other result had been expected in Washington.

The Administration decided not to publish the results of Marble's mission straightaway. Marble released a guarded statement to the press early in November; the newspapers on the following day carried brief accounts of the mission, and Bayard felt that Marble had "timed his action wisely." [16] The true inwardness of Marble's information was meanwhile reserved for use in the President's Annual Message and in the Annual Report of the Secretary of the Treasury.

Marble was asked to assist in the drafting of these two messages. They were considered crucial in the Administration's fight against silver coinage. When Marble visited Tilden, he

14. Marble to Iddesleigh, July 30, 1885. Marble MSS. Italics added.
15. Iddesleigh to Marble, Aug. 3, 1885. Marble MSS.
16. Bayard to Marble, Oct. 29, 1885. Marble MSS. New York *Times* (Nov. 9, 1885). Bayard to Manning, Nov. 9, 1885. Manning MSS.

learned of Tilden's recommendation that no new arguments be introduced in the message to Congress. Marble was also in communication with A. J. Warner, the Democrat and archsilverite, J. G. Carlisle, Speaker of the House, and Perry Belmont, a congressman from New York who supported the Administration. Manning in Washington and Marble in New York meanwhile wrote to each other constantly. For the President's treatment of the silver problem Marble thought a special message essential, but Cleveland decided to treat the matter along with his general report on the state of the nation.[17]

The President and the Secretary of the Treasury sent their messages to Congress when it met in December 1885. Secretary Manning argued that Germany's desertion of silver had upset the European balance; France and the Latin Union had been driven to gold. The only way to retain coins of both metals in use, he believed, was to stop the coinage of the metal unacceptable to other nations. After marshaling the usual anti-inflation arguments, the President summed up the results of the Marble mission: no international agreement was possible. Since the domestic coinage ratio between the two metals was ruinous and an international ratio impossible to achieve, Cleveland concluded: "I recommend the suspension of the compulsory coinage of silver dollars, directed by the law passed in February, 1878." [18]

The President and his advisors had planned to give the coup de grace to silver coinage in the annual message, and they expected to succeed. But the western congressmen were not to be brushed aside so easily. Their attacks on the Administration ushered in the "silver blizzard" of 1886. Secretary Manning's policy of international bimetallism only provoked the opposition to retort that the United States should free herself from

17. For this correspondence during Nov. 1885, see Marble MSS.
18. *Annual Report of the Secretary of the Treasury, 1885*, p. xvii. Richardson, *Messages and Papers*, 8, 344–46.

dependence on Europe. Exclaimed Senator Bowen: "The great question is, shall this Government issue a declaration of financial independence? A declaration not only against Europe, but against the organized enemies at home." [19]

The maneuvering had actually achieved little. Congress merely became hostile to any further attempt to secure international agreement. Cleveland had not succeeded in persuading the majority of his own party to accept his approach to the currency question. Only the support of Republicans in both houses prevented the passage of a bill, introduced in defiance of Cleveland, that provided for a measure of unlimited coinage of silver. But when the President attempted to stop the limited coinage of silver required by the Bland-Allison Act, the Republicans refused to help him. The President was aided during the last two years of his Administration not by political jockeying at home and abroad but by the improvement of business conditions. Unfortunately for him, the respite was merely temporary (as the financial crisis of his second Administration was to show); in the end Cleveland's political fortunes foundered on the silver issue.

His handling of the difficulties raised by Asiatic immigration illustrates even more clearly the unsalutary effects of domestic political considerations on the conduct of foreign policy. The United States possessed two great advantages in her relations with countries beyond the Western Hemisphere: her opposition to European colonialism and her faith in the right of all peoples to their independence. This contrasted sharply with the conduct of the European powers waging wars of conquest in Africa and China, but the United States jeopardized its advantage by discriminating against Asian immigrants. Deeply

19. *Congressional Record,* 49th Cong., 1st sess. (March 8, 1886), *17,* 2182.

wounding to the pride of Asian peoples, this discrimination created emotional obstacles to the long-term development of good American relations with the East.

From the beginning of his presidency, Cleveland realized that Chinese immigration was a question of major political consequence which, unless promptly and effectively settled, would be exploited by the opposition. The discovery of gold in California had led to the first large immigration of Chinese workers; the reactions of the Californians to these new immigrants soon became equivocal. On the one hand, the industrious Chinese were valued as servants, merchants, and, above all, laborers in developing the West. But racial and economic prejudice were also operative, and the 1860s saw the passage of many discriminatory measures by the California Legislature. The measures were, however, not effective. A decade later, the question of Chinese immigration had begun to play a dominant role in California politics. Worsening economic conditions, the completion of the Central Pacific Railroad—largely constructed by Chinese labor—and the increasing number of immigrants with different customs all provided rabble-rousing politicians with the opportunity to inflame mass prejudice.[20]

In the 1870s the congressmen from California began to demand exclusion. "The Chinese are of a sickly white or light yellow colour, with coarse, glossy, lank, black hair, and thin, scanty, black beards," Representative William Piper, a Democrat from California, informed his fellow congressmen in 1876.

> Their eyes are invariably black, and apparently oblique . . . their faces are remarkably round, with high cheek bones and small, much depressed noses, and thick lips. The women are disproportionally small in size, and, with their broad upper face, low nose, and linear eyes, possess little

20. Tansill, *Bayard*, pp. 123–35.

beauty, and in fact are quite the reverse of handsome. These are the characteristics of a subject, servile race.[21]

One root of the trouble lay in the existence of an American–Chinese treaty, the Burlinghame Treaty of 1868, under whose broad provisions the subjects of the Emperor of China and American citizens were to enjoy "the free migration and emigration of their citizens and subjects respectively from the one country to the other." But entry to the United States proved easier and more frequent in practice than the penetration of China.

The rising hostility on the coast inspired attempts in Congress to abrogate the treaty unilaterally by enacting exclusion bills. But Presidents Hayes and Arthur vetoed the measures. The Executive followed the path of seeking to secure the consent of the Chinese authorities to a modification of the Burlinghame Treaty.

An American commission to China in 1880 secured a new convention. In return for promising to extend to the Chinese who were already in the United States all the privileges and rights of citizens of the most favored nation, the American government was now conceded the right to "regulate, limit, or suspend" the entry of Chinese laborers (it being understood that immigration could not be prohibited altogether, that such restrictions should be "reasonable," and that they were not to apply to immigrants other than "laborers"). Unhappily this treaty, which had been so quickly and amicably concluded, proved to be not a settlement but a source of trouble. Congress was in no mood to compromise. Measures intended to exclude all Chinese laborers for ten years were passed by both houses and became law.[22]

21. *Congressional Record,* 44th Cong., 1st sess. (May 18, 1876), 4, 3183–84.
22. Tansill, *Bayard,* pp. 135–38; *Congressional Record,* 48th Cong., 1st sess. (May 3, July 3, 1884), 15, 3777, 5938.

When Cleveland entered the White House, he must have recognized that the party which accomplished most to obstruct further immigration would be able to carry the Pacific states in 1888. In the recent elections, the Democrats had lost California, Colorado, Nevada, and Oregon, with a total of seventeen electoral votes, by relatively close margins. It is therefore to his credit that he pursued a temperate course at the outset. But he was soon faced with a grave crisis: mob violence broke out in the autumn of 1885, a wave of hate spreading from Rock Springs, Wyoming, where twenty-eight Chinese were murdered, to Washington Territory. Cleveland and Bayard took prompt steps to protect the Chinese minority by ordering federal troops to safeguard them. The Chinese, however, continued to live in poverty and perpetual fear.[23]

The President hoped ultimately to solve the problem by diplomacy. The legislation restricting immigration was not effective. Cleveland instructed his Secretary of State to work out new legislation which would be both acceptable to the Chinese and effective. Meanwhile the Administration would ignore congressional attacks and the malice of political opponents. The good name of the United States was not to be jeopardized by unilateral abrogation of international treaties for the sake of political advantage.

In the face of congressional provocation and Chinese procrastination, Bayard conducted negotiations with the Chinese Minister in Washington, Chang Yen Hoon, tenaciously, patiently, and unfortunately in vain. Ultimate authority did not rest with the Minister; the Chinese had only adopted the semblance of Western diplomatic usage. Bayard did not appreciate this crucial fact, and throughout the negotiations he wrongly assumed China's good faith. In March 1888 he actually signed

23. *H. Ex. Doc.*, no. 102 49th Cong., 1st sess., serial 2398. *Foreign Relations, 1886*, p. 155.

a treaty to which Chang also appended his name. It was too late. The attitude of the Chinese court in Peking and Cleveland's political calculations in Washington overrode considerations of mere diplomacy.[24]

Despite the hostility of the Republican majority and many Democrats in Congress, Cleveland kept the Chinese question out of the political arena for three years. But in the summer of 1887, as the national elections drew near, he found it difficult to ignore the pressure from Congress and to maintain his judicious attitude.

In July 1887 a subcommittee of the Senate Foreign Relations Committee composed of Senators Dolph, Morgan, and Sherman heard evidence from five senators and seven representatives from California, Nevada, and Oregon. Senator John T. Morgan of Alabama informed the President of the views and conclusions. Their discussion, he recalled, had been free and fair; they were all agreed that Chinese immigration was increasing and that "ninety per cent of the Pacific coast people insisted that Chinese immigration, of all sorts (except Government officials, etc.) *should be stopped by a resort to any measures that would operate most speedily and effectually.*" Senator Morgan asked the legislators pointedly whether they were willing to forgo commercial privileges secured in the treaties (which China might abrogate in reprisal for summary action by the United States on the question of immigration) for the sake of excluding the Chinese. "I dwelt on the point and asked for a careful answer, one that could be stated to the Senate. Without exception, they answered that 90 percent of their people would abandon all commerce with China, rather than ac-

24. Denby to Bayard, Aug. 4, 1886, U.S. Department of State, *China*, National Archives, Washington, D.C. Bayard memorandum, Jan. 12, 1887; Chang Yen Hoon to Bayard, April 13, 1887; Bayard to Chang Yen Hoon, April 15, 1887; Bayard to Denby, April 18, 1887. Bayard MSS. For the best published treatment of the question, see Tansill, *Bayard*, pp. 123–81.

cept Chinese immigration. Shorthand writers recorded these statements & they will be printed."

With thinly veiled contempt for Bayard's negotiations, Morgan then informed the President that the subcommittee had not yet agreed on a report, but that the "conservative" Senator Sherman wanted "the President & the Senate to have a fair chance to amend the treaties, before inviting the House to join us in an act to abrogate them." [25] The effrontery of this sentence must have struck Bayard like a lash.[26] Absolute exclusion, Morgan continued, "would be immensely & generally popular." China, he added optimistically, might find this solution agreeable; in any case the far West demanded some such action. He went on to warn Cleveland: "If such a conclusion is not readily attainable, the delay of protracted negotiations will be seized upon as a pretext for severe legislation & the whole matter will be exploited for political purposes." [27]

That same summer of 1887, Cleveland was deciding upon the grand political strategy most likely to secure his reelection and a Democratic victory the following year. The growing Treasury surplus was held responsible for many of America's economic ills. The silver lobby called for a policy of inflation; others advocated a program of unprecedented government expenditure. Cleveland found both expedients repugnant. The President instead proposed a reduction of the tariff. He devoted the whole of his annual message of December 6, 1887, to the issue, which instantly became the chief topic of political discussion. As it turned out, the President showed greater political canniness than had many of his supporters who at first

25. Morgan to Cleveland, July 18, 1887. Cleveland MSS. Italics are Senator Morgan's.

26. Bayard looked upon Morgan (nominally a leading Democrat) as an enemy of the Administration. Bayard to Marble, May 9, 1885. Marble MSS.

27. Morgan to Cleveland, July 18, 1887. Cleveland MSS.

believed that the Democrats stood to lose more votes than they would gain on such a platform. But would it be sufficient to rally the Democratic party? Unsure of his ground, Cleveland sought to enhance his popularity by espousing a foreign policy at variance with his and Bayard's earlier intentions.

Two weeks after sending his tariff message to Congress, he urged Bayard to persuade the Chinese Minister to conclude the treaty for excluding Chinese laborers without delay. "The present condition regarding Chinese immigration should be remedied, or an attempt in that direction made at once and by us, that is *our party*," he privately wrote to Bayard. A Chinese treaty was not necessary for its own sake but would be popular with the electorate. "I am fearful almost to conviction that our people in Congress will so botch and blunder upon the tariff question that all the benefits of the stand already taken will not be realized. If my fears should appear to be well founded, a proper movement upon the Chinese question would furnish a compensation in the way of another string to our bow." [28]

The plan misfired; Bayard at once renewed negotiations with the Chinese Minister and warned Chang that if they failed to reach agreement, Congress would in all probability abrogate altogether the existing treaties. Chang at first temporized but finally, in March 1888, signed the treaty whose principal provision was to exclude Chinese laborers for twenty years.[29]

In Peking the signed treaty gathered dust for months. Procrastination was the favorite Chinese method of avoiding undesirable decisions. In Washington the President promptly sent the treaty to the Senate, whose methods of frustrating it were different from the Chinese but equally efficacious. It might be supposed that the Senate would ratify the treaty quickly, since in practice its provisions corresponded to their

28. Cleveland to Bayard, Dec. 18, 1887. Bayard MSS.
29. For the correspondence between Bayard and Chang, see *Foreign Relations, 1888*, pp. 379–88; also Bayard MSS.

demands. But the consideration uppermost in the minds of the Republican senators was that the Democratic Administration should not receive credit for the Secretary of State's labors. They could oblige the Administration to reopen negotiations by insisting on amendments—however immaterial they might be—and made use of this power not as a result of their belief that the modifications were necessary but in an effort to discredit the President. The veil of Executive Session was drawn over the treaty, and Bayard began to fear that the treaty was being abused. To Denby he complained of "the incoherent violence and extreme statements of the Republican leaders." The Republican Senate, he bitterly commented, was denying "comity, courtesy or common justice to the Administration." [30] His doubts were increased by the garbled and misleading statements released to the press on the West Coast. On May 7, the Senate ratified the treaty with two amendments which clarified rather than changed the meaning of the original text. A week later Bayard and the Chinese Minister formally accepted the treaty as amended, Chang inquiring in perplexity why the changes had been made, since the amendments did not alter the original agreement. It looked as if the treaty would be confirmed after all.

Unhappily the Chinese Minister was on the point of leaving the United States for an extended tour of South America and Europe. Bayard now expressed his anger at the attitude of the Senate. They had clamored for the treaty and attacked the Administration for not concluding it more quickly, yet had deliberately delayed the treaty until the eve of Chang's departure for Peru. "So we must wait," wrote the weary Secretary; he hoped meanwhile that the Senate's "petty obstructiveness" would be made known so that the people would realize where

30. Bayard to Denby, March 17 and April 21, 1888. Bayard MSS.

the blame lay.[31] No word from China reached the State Department for four months. The Democrats strove frantically to retrieve some political advantage from the Chinese issue; the Republicans had a golden opportunity to taunt the Administration with accusations of bad faith and weakness. America's good name in international affairs was thus sullied by the actions of the Senate.

In June 1888 the Democratic and Republican Conventions nominated Cleveland and Harrison, respectively. The Democratic platform berated the Republicans for continued Chinese immigration by blocking in the Senate a treaty which provided for effective exclusion. The Republicans blamed the Democrats. Ignoring the treaty already concluded, they called for immediate legislation prohibiting all Chinese labor from America. Paradoxically, partisan politics had left the final decision to the Chinese. Had they now speedily ratified the treaty as amended by the Senate, it would certainly have been finally signed by Cleveland and would thus have become binding.[32] Instead they chose to procrastinate before finally insisting on further amendments which effectively destroyed the treaty.

To unravel the final stages of the tortuous interplay of diplomacy and politics, close attention must be paid to the order of events. A bill introduced by Senator Dolph of Oregon, a member of the Senate Foreign Relations Committee, in July 1888 provided for the enforcement of the Bayard-Chang treaty in advance of ratification. It passed both the Senate and the House and was presented for the President's signature on September 1. That same day, the New York *Herald* published a telegram from London stating that the Chinese had rejected the treaty. Bayard's advice to the President was simple and straightforward: he should not hastily endorse or sign any of

---

31. Bayard to John P. Irish, May 12, 1888. Bayard MSS.
32. Bayard memorandum, July 16, 1888. Bayard MSS.

the measures now put forward by an increasingly hysterical Congress, at least not until a formal Chinese answer had been communicated to Washington. Cleveland chose a different course. His one purpose now was to retrieve his political fortunes. While Bayard sought some definite information from Minister Denby in Peking, Cleveland and a few of his intimates in the Administration tried to steal the thunder from even the most rabid of senators and congressmen by putting forward a bill perpetually excluding Chinese workmen.

In San Francisco, William D. English, Chairman of the Democratic State Committee of California, heard of the rumor that China had rejected the treaty and recognized at once that, unless prompt action were taken, the cause of Cleveland's reelection would be heavily compromised in the West. English at once wired Lamont, Cleveland's sagacious and indispensable private secretary, that rejection of the treaty in Peking made the Chinese question the paramount issue on the West Coast and urged him to confer at once with leading Democrats in the Senate and the House, naming particularly Senator Hearst, Representatives Thompson, Kenna, Belmont, and Carlisle, the powerful Speaker of the House. The Democrats, English urged, must come out squarely for a policy of total Chinese exclusion. The telegram reached Lamont on September 2, a Sunday,[33] the same day that in Washington Representative William L. Scott, a millionaire from Pennsylvania and one of Cleveland's loyal supporters, read the item in the *Herald*. On Monday morning, he hurriedly conferred with Cleveland and Carlisle. The three men agreed that Scott should introduce a measure in the House supplanting the negotiated treaty and providing for the perpetual exclusion of Chinese laborers.[34]

33. English to Lamont, telegram, Sept. 1, 1888. Cleveland MSS.
34. New York *World* (Sept. 6, 1888). See also Senator Sherman's speech on Sept. 6, 1888, *Congressional Record*, 50th Cong., 1st sess. (Sept. 6, 1888), 19, 8328.

Bayard was not consulted. The President ignored his Secretary of State and, on the mere evidence of a newspaper report, authorized the destruction of Bayard's long and patient negotiations. By midafternoon on Monday, Scott had not only introduced his bill but also, with the aid of hints that the Administration approved the drastic measure, had passed it through the House without a dissenting vote. The bill was immediately sent up to the Senate where Stewart of Nevada, Teller of Colorado, and Dolph and Mitchell of Oregon attempted to railroad it through with equal speed. But the Senate was in a speechmaking mood and adjourned before voting—though not before Senator Butler of South Carolina had caustically denounced the proceedings as "a game of politics . . . and not a very seemly one either." But for the coming presidential elections, he surmised, the whole debate would not have taken place.[35]

In an effort to restore dignity to a debate which had descended to mudslinging, Senator Sherman called on the President on September 5 and asked him whether the treaty had officially been rejected by the Chinese. The hapless Secretary of State had himself tried to discover just what the facts were, but he got no firm reply from Denby in Peking. On September 5, Denby cabled Washington that he believed the treaty rejected; on September 7, he cabled that the Chinese had postponed a decision "for further deliberation." On Bayard's advice, the two telegrams were at once communicated to the Senate, where that same day the Scott bill was passed.[36] But it did not go directly to the White House. Opponents of the bill tried to force reconsideration of the vote, and day after day of debate passed while no quorum could be mustered.

Pressure from the Pacific states was mounting steadily. A

35. *Congressional Record,* 50th Cong., 1st sess. (Sept. 3, 4, and 5, 1888), *19,* 8215–26, 8249–56, 8296–97.
36. *Foreign Relations, 1888,* p. 350. Bayard to Cleveland, Sept. 5 and 7, 1888. Cleveland MSS.

mass meeting in San Francisco urgently appealed to the Senate to send the Scott bill to the President for signature. Advice poured into the White House. The delay in the Senate produced something akin to panic among Democratic politicians in California. They warned Cleveland that votes were being lost every day the bill was delayed; the Democrats would be blamed if the bill did not become law.[37] Cleveland knew he had to act, so on September 13 he signed the original Dolph bill, which enforced the provisions of the American–Chinese treaty in advance of Chinese ratification. It was unlikely that the Chinese would ratify the treaty. The President's signature made little sense, except within the context of domestic politics. Four days later, on September 17, the Senate finally sent the Scott bill to the President for signature. This attempt to stultify a law only four days in operation must mark something of a record, even for a capricious Senate. But the President did not sign immediately.

Bayard was incensed to see his negotiations ending in so bizarre a manner. He had lost all patience with the Chinese, but he felt that the dignity of the United States required the President and Congress to wait until the Chinese had actually refused to ratify the treaty before embarking on retaliatory legislation. He had hoped in vain that the Senate would reconsider "the humiliating and disgraceful vote by which the Chinese exclusion bill, in shocking disregard of every conventional and decent restraint, was rushed through." In the depths of his depression he advised Cleveland on September 18 that "international courtesy, good faith and self respect" demanded that he should refuse to sign the Scott bill.[38] In speaking to the distraught Chinese chargé d'affaires, Bayard assured him of

37. English to Cleveland, telegram, Sept. 8 and 16, 1888; Irish to Lamont, Sept. 15, 1888. Cleveland MSS.
38. Bayard to Cleveland, Sept. 18, 1888. Bayard MSS.

his personal good faith, admitting that he had no prior knowledge of the Scott bill. Bayard pointedly informed the President of the words he had used. At this juncture, the Chinese rescued Cleveland and Bayard from their embarrassment. Denby telegraphed Bayard on September 21 that the Chinese government refused to ratify the treaty unless the twenty-year prohibition of immigration were shortened. When this news was confirmed by the Chinese chargé, Bayard finally agreed to draft a message for the President to accompany signature of the Scott bill.[39] Cleveland signed the bill a few days later.

Jubilation in the West was great. The occasion was marked by processions and bonfires; Republicans in San Francisco fired rounds of cannon in an attempt to persuade the public that credit for the exclusion bill was theirs. The Democrats claimed the credit too. But the bill had been delayed too long in the Senate and treated in its last stages too hesitantly in the White House to benefit Cleveland's election campaign. He lost all four western states.

Cleveland had gained nothing. He had signed a bill unilaterally abrogating an international treaty; he had supported the Scott bill while the Chinese rejection of the treaty was still in doubt; in lending his name to this move, he discredited a Secretary of State who had served him loyally.

Bayard's negotiations with Canada suffered a similar fate when party politics and Cleveland's election tactics again influenced the conduct of American foreign policy. To digest the essential documents and all that contemporary authors and later historians have written on the subject of the respective rights of American and Canadian fishermen would tax the hardiest

39. Bayard to Denby, Sept. 18, 1888. U.S. Department of State, *China,* National Archives, Washington, D.C. Denby to Bayard, Sept. 21, 1888. *Foreign Relations, 1888,* pp. 350–55. Bayard to Cleveland, Sept. 26, 1888. Bayard MSS.

scholar.[40] By comparison the Schleswig-Holstein imbroglio—
which they say only three men understood—appears straightforward. The thorny fisheries question had been temporarily
settled in 1871 by the Treaty of Washington. This treaty superseded an earlier one, concluded in 1818, and was more favorable to Americans in Canadian waters. But the United States
paid an annual sum in compensation for the concessions made
in 1871. Twelve years later, Congress denounced the fisheries
settlement, claiming that the price was too high for the privileges accorded American seamen. A crisis was postponed by a
subsequent convention which allowed the provisions of the
Treaty of Washington to remain in force until January 1886.
American vessels would be denied access to the inshore fisheries thereafter, and any ships that defied these stipulations
would be liable to seizure by the Canadian authorities.

The fisheries question was not discussed in Congress as a
legal question, but with impassioned tempers and hostility.
The ancient rights of the sturdy American mariners were not
defended simply on the grounds of the economic value of their
catch of codfish. These rights dated back to the establishment
of the republic; to abandon them now was to some Americans
like abandoning a portion of the national heritage.

Bayard's most determined opponent in the Senate was William P. Frye, the redoubtable Republican Senator from Maine.
His approach to the question was typical of the opposition.
"The Republic itself has a deep and an abiding interest in this
industry. . . . Has it forgotten that its proud position was
largely won by the endurance, skill, courage, and fidelity of
these sailors . . . Can she be unmindful of their conspicuous
services in the war of our independence . . . Who does not
know that in our last terrible struggle for life [1812] there was

40. Fortunately it did not have this effect on Tansill. For his treatment,
see *Bayard*, pp. 185–204, 479–524.

not a deck of our fleet unmoistened by their blood?" And how, he asked, would the United States man its fleet in time of war if the fishermen were deprived of their living? [41] Even more important than such historical sentiment was the attitude of the Republicans in Congress, swayed from the first by domestic political considerations, who sought to stultify the Administration's policy, wrest the control of diplomacy from the President's hands, and use any American–Canadian settlement the Administration might reach as a stick to beat the Democrats with during the elections of 1888.

During 1886 American fishermen offered every sort of provocation to the Canadian authorities and suffered many an indignity. The entire section on Great Britain in the annual volume on *Foreign Relations* for 1886 was given over to correspondence concerning seizures of American citizens and vessels and the denial of American rights. It would be difficult to exaggerate the chaotic and dangerous conditions prevailing in the fishing grounds. The people of Maine and Massachusetts —the majority of American fishermen—were hostile to the Canadians and English for other reasons, and the Irish-Americans, whose vote was critical in New York, were receptive to an anti-British policy. To these anglophobes may be added the growing Populist movement in the West, encouraged by their leaders and their own experience to regard the English as a race of demonic creditors. No one realized better than Blaine, a leading contender for the Republican nomination, that an aggressive policy toward Great Britain was one assuredly popular issue, and he opened the campaign in September 1886 with a denunciation of the Administration's attempts to settle the fisheries dispute. The vehemence of his attack was only matched by its complete lack of justification.

41. William P. Frye, "Our Fisheries," in John D. Long, ed., *The Republican Party: Its History, Principles, and Policies* (New York, Hazen Co., 1888), p. 164.

Cleveland and Bayard had no intention of allowing American rights to be infringed, but they made it plain that they would take no precipitate or thoughtless action: they would investigate each case and judge it on its merits until a just and honorable settlement could be secured. Since many of the hostile acts occurred in remote places, settlement was frequently delayed and tempers, especially in New England, were aroused. Piecemeal treatment of individual cases had broken down that autumn, and a general settlement was manifestly necessary. Accordingly, in November Bayard made overtures to the British government for the formation of a mixed commission to negotiate a treaty. Fifteen months later—on February 15, 1888—a fisheries treaty was actually signed.[42] Bayard had conducted the negotiation dispassionately and without thought of political advantage. It was an eminently wise and just settlement, but it proved abortive.

The Senate, which had already demonstrated its hostility to the Executive's foreign policy, had not awaited the conclusion of the treaty before acting on its own responsibility and according to its own belligerent ideas. On May 20, 1886, Senator Frye sent an open letter to Bayard demanding summary justice for injured American fishermen.[43] During the course of the following months, many unfriendly resolutions insisting on the instant vindication of American rights were submitted to Congress. Senators and representatives were clearly contemplating some plan of retaliation against Canada.[44]

The lame-duck session of the Forty-ninth Congress compen-

42. For two interesting early accounts of these negotiations besides Tansill's, see J. B. Henderson, Jr., *American Diplomatic Questions* (New York, 1901), pp. 451–529, and J. B. Moore, *The Principles of American Diplomacy* (New York, Harper, 1918), pp. 135–47.

43. *Public Opinion*, 1 (May 29, 1886), 121.

44. *Congressional Record*, 49th Cong., 1st sess. (May 10, June 3 and 4, July 10, 23, and 24, 1886), 17, 4303, 4324, 5181–82, 5259, 6722, 7350, 7430.

sated for its shortness by the violence of its legislation. Senator Gorman submitted a resolution on January 18, 1887, to exclude Canadians from American territorial waters. But the Senate Foreign Relations Committee shelved Gorman's proposal and presented its own bill the next day. Submitted by Senator Edmunds, its provisions were simple and comprehensive: it obliged the President to deny American waters to Canadians if he should find the Canadians guilty of practicing any sort of discrimination against American fishermen on their vessels. The bill ostensibly provided for retaliation in kind; its real purpose was to give New England a monopoly of the fishing industry. With the force of the Foreign Relations Committee's support, the bill passed the Senate on January 24, 1887, by a vote of 46 to 1.[45] Two days later it went to the House Foreign Relations Committee, where it remained for three weeks.

Up to this time Cleveland had not circulated his views on retaliation. This accounts for the Senate's nonpartisan vote on the Edmunds resolution, for, in the battle of party politics, the Democrats felt no obligation to support unpopular Administration policies before a public statement had been made. Cleveland now identified himself with a policy of severing all commercial relations with Canada, arguing that the effects of retaliation should not be confined to one section of the community but should be borne by the whole country.[46] But he was only posing as a just and impartial President. Entirely to disrupt American–Canadian relations was the last thing Cleveland wanted. Congress, as he well knew, was bound to oppose such massive retaliation. The Senate would hardly lend a hand in bankrupting the railroads and destroying the immense carrying trade involved in commerce with Canada. Cleveland

45. *Congressional Record,* 49th Cong., 2d sess. (Jan. 18, 19, and 24, 1887), *18,* 748, 793, 952.
46. *Congressional Record,* 49th Cong., 2d sess. (Jan. 26, 1887), *18,* 1047.

was effectively turning the tables on Congress. By now insisting on a complete severance of commercial relations with Canada, he calculated that he could prevent the enactment of any sort of sectional retaliation which would jeopardize the pending treaty negotiations.

To carry out his plan, the President asked Perry Belmont, a congressman from New York and a member of the House Foreign Affairs Committee who was friendly to the Administration, to introduce a bill providing for the total severance of commercial relations with Canada. When the committee balked at endorsing such a measure, Belmont took its members to see the President, who persuaded a majority of them that he would "make good use of the power." Belmont was then able to introduce into the House the Administration bill as a substitute for Edmunds' measure, which had been passed in the Senate.[47]

Now that the President's will was openly expressed, intense partisanship on the fisheries question became more apparent. The behavior of the Republicans was contradictory: they wished to record their support of a retaliatory policy against the Canadians without running any risk of interrupting trade, and so in the House they unanimously supported the Belmont bill while in the Senate they rejected it. Meanwhile the Edmunds measure, providing for retaliation against the Canadian fishermen only, had passed both houses, and it became law with the President's signature on March 3, 1887.[48] But Cleveland had no notion of enforcing an act so alien to his convictions.

Not content with having outmaneuvered Cleveland, the Republican Senator George Frisbie Hoar of Massachusetts in-

47. Nevins, *Cleveland,* p. 411.
48. *Congressional Record,* 49th Cong., 2d sess. (Feb. 16, 23, 24, and 28, March 2 and 3, 1887), 18, 1821, 2149–50, 2166–67, 2452–54, 2387–90, 2562, 2563, 2611.

troduced a resolution involving the most serious attempt by
the Senate to curtail Cleveland's power in foreign relations. It
provided for severe limitation of the Executive treaty-making
power. His plan, submitted on February 24, was to forbid the
Executive, by virtue of congressional power over taxation, to
undertake any negotiation with Canada that would involve the
reduction of duty on fish imported into the United States. Since
free importation of fish had been a cornerstone of the abro-
gated provisions of the Treaty of 1871, and since Canada
would probably have refused a treaty without some reduction
of duty on fish, the Senate's approval of the Hoar resolution
would have been tantamount to prohibiting altogether the
negotiation of a treaty with Canada and Britain. Bayard and
Manning were greatly worried. They exerted the full pressure
of the Executive to defeat the resolution. Senator Beck was
able, finally, with unexpected assistance from John T. Morgan,
to shunt Hoar's resolution to the Finance Committee, from
which it never emerged.[49]

The adjournment of Congress from March until December
1887 brought a temporary cessation of organized partisan attacks on Cleveland's fisheries policy. The Administration now
made every effort to reach agreement on a new treaty which
was being negotiated by two British and two American commissioners in Washington. On February 15, 1888, soon after the
Fiftieth Congress convened, the draft treaty was signed; it
was submitted to the Senate five days later. Cleveland knew
for sure that the treaty would be subjected to partisan attack.
Probably in order to hold up to public censure the workings
of party politics, Cleveland requested the Senate to remove
the customary injunction of secrecy from the discussion of the
treaty.

49. *Congressional Record*, 49th Cong., 2d sess. (Feb. 24 and 25, 1887),
18, 2191, 2235–36. Bayard to Manning, Feb. 26, 1887; Bayard to Senator
Beck, Feb. 26, 1887. Manning MSS.

The treaty was referred to the Senate Foreign Relations Committee, where it was considered until May 7. The majority report, which appeared on that day, was signed by the five Republican members of the Committee, the minority report by the four Democrats. Three days later, the Senate consented to make the reports public. Political motives, which had already greatly endangered the settlement of the fisheries dispute, now prompted the Republican majority to adopt the unprecedented step of forcing consideration of the treaty in open session.[50]

The fisheries question was hotly debated throughout the summer, both sides seeking to derive from it maximum political advantage. The Republicans, ostensibly professing to be in favor of a more aggressive policy toward Canada, got the better of the argument. They branded the Democrats as spineless and pro-British. Bayard, already suspect for his policy of friendship with England, became the favorite target of their attack. The Republicans ignored the merits of the treaty; they only wanted to win votes in the November election. As soon as they felt that they had discredited Cleveland and Bayard, they rejected the treaty in the Senate on August 21, 1888, and then cynically blocked any attempts to amend it.[51]

Cleveland, as a result of his honest attempt to settle the fisheries dispute, had thus become encumbered by a political liability of the first magnitude. In the fierce partisanship of July and August 1888, the treaty, equitable though it was, came to be considered pro-English. To praise it or to defend the President was, in the opinion of an increasing number of voters, to curry favor with England. "England is unanimously Democratic," scoffed Blaine, "and I am inclined to think that Canada

50. *Congressional Record,* 50th Cong., 1st sess. (June 7, 1888), *19,* 4980; *Senate Ex. Jour., 26,* 265–68. See also W. Stull Holt, *Treaties Defeated by the Senate* (Baltimore, Johns Hopkins Press), 1933, pp. 144–49.
51. *Congressional Record,* 50th Cong., 1st sess. (Aug. 21, 1888), *19,* 7767.

feels the same way." [52] Cleveland was perfectly aware, long before the treaty reached a vote on August 21, that the Senate would refuse to approve it. He was equally aware that the Democrats were being worsted in the presidential campaign, of which the fisheries treaty was an incidental victim. Only a dramatic gesture might reverse this unhappy trend. He found it in foreign affairs.

Cleveland chose to strengthen his position and to recapture votes he feared he would otherwise lose by a jingoism alien to his earlier policy and outlook. He drafted a special message to Congress and sent it with dramatic suddenness on August 23. Since the Senate had rejected the original treaty, a just and suitable settlement, he requested Congress to give him the powers necessary to enact measures of general retaliation against Canada, to ensure "the interests of our people and maintain the high standard and the becoming pride of American citizenship." [53]

The immediate response of the Democrats to the retaliation message was one of relief and elation; the congressional reporter in the House recorded "loud applause on the Democratic side"; Calvin C. Brice, Democratic National Chairman, sent his congratulations by telegram. [54] The Irish were jubilant, the Democratic press applauded, and even sober politicians acclaimed the message as a telling rebuke to the Republicans. Cleveland's retaliation message was the climax to a diplomatic affair which had suffered from party politics from the start.

The President knew full well that the business interests supporting the Republicans stood to lose most from any measures of retaliation. The Senate had obstructed the treaty for purely partisan reasons, and political interests effectively prevented

52. Nevins, *Cleveland,* p. 413.
53. *Congressional Record,* 50th Cong., 1st sess. (Aug. 23, 1888), 19, 7900–01.
54. Brice to Cleveland, telegram, Aug. 24, 1888. Cleveland MSS.

the majority of Senators from supporting a policy of retaliation, especially in an election year. In any case, since the commissioners had agreed that the modus vivendi should remain in force until 1890 if the Senate rejected the treaty, American fishermen stood in no need of protection. One must conclude, then, that Cleveland was guilty of playing politics with an explosive foreign issue.

In the course of both the Chinese and the Canadian negotiations, American party politics compromised the dignity of the Senate and impaired the diplomatic prerogatives of the President. Party politics led to delays in concluding the treaty with China and eventually to the adoption of an unjustified policy of unilateral abrogation. Party politics also stultified Bayard's statesmanlike Canadian policy and endangered the good development of Canadian–American relations.

And what of the President's conduct? His most cherished objective was to combat monetary inflation, especially as it was sought through the unlimited coinage of silver. Committed to the repeal of the silver coinage legislation and defeated on the issue by his own party before his inauguration, he turned to diplomacy as a means to achieve the same end. On the Chinese and Canadian issues he was content to support his Secretary of State; his first instincts were sound and even generous. Goaded into action by a partisan Congress and by the fear that Bayard's statesmanlike handling of diplomatic questions would lose him votes, he personally seized the initiative and pursued popular support by jingoistic policies he did not like. These are formidable indictments. They may however be softened by consideration of two circumstances. His political opponents made unscrupulous use of diplomatic issues to further their own purposes, tempting the President to play the same game. It must also be remembered that domestic rather than foreign issues were regarded as vital to the welfare of the United States. Cleveland did not believe he was injuring America's vital interests. Lacking any real understanding of diplomacy, he was faced with a choice: he could either follow the advice of his Secretary of State whom he trusted, or he could move according to political expediency. When the stakes were high enough he chose the latter. The President's behavior justified the observation of foreign diplomats that the gap between the high moral protestations of American principles and the realities of its foreign policy was often wide.

Chapter Three

The Challenge of Latin America:

Harrison and Blaine, 1889–1892

THERE IS NO obvious reason why, as the decade of the 1880s drew to a close, the American people should have given more thought than before to the place of the United States in the world. Such specific problems as the fisheries, Chinese immigration, and Canadian reciprocity aroused only sectional interest. On a few occasions a particular crisis even focused national attention on foreign affairs, and Americans responded with patriotic fervor. The *Virginius* incident in 1873 and German policy in Samoa in 1889 created such excitement; but for the most part the vast majority of Americans were thankful to be spared the conflicts and wars of Europe. They would have been surprised at the very notion that the United States needed a foreign policy.

The early 1890s were a singularly unpropitious time for arousing the American people to an appreciation of world affairs. Their energies were absorbed at home. On the farm and in the city these were the years of protest. Farmers struggled desperately for a livelihood; working men were goaded into violence by the harshness and repression of the employer; the immigrants sought to come to terms with life in a strange urban environment; the rich were getting richer and the poor more destitute. As the depression deepened and the people blindly sought the causes of their misfortune, the danger of social revolution seemed to stalk the land.[1] Many turned to Populism and William Jennings Bryan in disillusionment with the existing parties and institutions. They gave no thought to expanding American influence beyond the confines of the continent. The Populist Platform included no word on foreign policy. The Populists looked suspiciously at a hostile world; they believed capitalists on two continents were pursuing a "vast conspiracy against mankind."[2] To regard the new developments of American diplomacy in the 1880s and early 1890s as having occurred in response to a growing popular demand for national self-assertion is thus something of an illusion.

Politicians found it hard to discern what the people really wanted. Although the Republican and Democratic administrations broadly speaking followed similar objectives in their foreign policies during the 1880s, the two parties struck different public poses. The Democrats in 1888 identified their party with prudence and hallowed tradition; the Republicans were more strident. They condemned the Democrats for conducting a foreign policy "distinguished by its inefficiency and its cowardice"; they also blamed the Cleveland Administration for failing to preserve American interests in Central and South America.[3] Four years later the Republican platform contained a strong foreign policy plank. The Democrats, on the other hand, blamed the Republicans for following a policy of "irritation and bluster which is liable at any time to con-

1. For a good general treatment of the period, see Harold U. Faulkner, *Politics, Reform and Expansion 1890–1900* (New York, Harper, 1959).
2. Kirk H. Porter and Donald Bruce Johnson, eds., *National Party Platforms 1840–1960* (Urbana, University of Illinois Press, 1961), pp. 89–91.
3. Ibid., pp. 76–83.

front us with the alternative of humiliation or war." [4] The attempt to utilize international questions for political advantage does not appear to have been effective. The swing of party fortunes depended on domestic issues.

While it is questionable whether the outlook of the American people had altered very radically during the 1880s, the change of mood in Congress was dramatic. In the 1870s only a few legislators had been concerned with America's security. Twenty years later a number of powerful senators became spokesmen on military and diplomatic questions. They supported the Executive whenever a forceful policy was adopted, whether its purpose was the defense of the Monroe Doctrine or the construction of a naval station in Pago-Pago. Several senators to be sure were recent converts. Randall Lee Gibson, Democratic Senator from Louisiana, stated in 1888 that he believed the day "not far distant when the dominion of the United States will be extended by the free consent of its inhabitants to every part of the American continent—British America, Mexico, Cuba, Central America, and the islands on our coast." [5] Gibson was a typical convert; shortly before this speech he had opposed annexation of Hawaii. It would not be difficult to show that the outlook of Congress toward the end of the 1880s had become aggressive and chauvinistic. The opponents of an active policy, strong though they were, could no longer command a majority in either house. The spirit of national self-assertion was nurtured by politicians, newspaper editors, businessmen, and publicists. These men regarded themselves as the proselytizers of new truths. Much of what they wrote about Manifest Destiny and the supremacy of the Anglo-Saxon race was froth. The change of attitude on the part of the Executive and many senators was based on more

4. Ibid., pp. 86–95.
5. Senator Gibson, *Congressional Record*, 50th Cong., 1st sess. (August 16, 1888), *19*, p. 7633.

realistic and substantial foundations. They feared that the Western Hemisphere was no longer secure from European encroachment. They also believed that America could make it secure again. They were especially alarmed by developments in South and Central America.

The diplomatic and consular reports reaching the State Department during the 1880s from the legations and consulates of Latin America told depressingly similar stories of the growth of European influence, the decline of American influence, and the loss of opportunities. The offices of the United States legations presented a sorry picture of neglect and official parsimony. Patrick Egan reported from Santiago in 1889 that the furniture in his legation consisted of three bookcases, three desks, one office chair, and a worn-out carpet. In reply to his request to purchase a flagstaff "as there is none," one sofa, two armchairs, twelve ordinary chairs, two carpets, and curtains, the State Department noted: "We cannot afford $902 in a single year. Can we not allow Mr. Egan $500 and let him make it go as far as he can—consistent with true economy in the purchase of good substantial furniture and carpets of good quality." [6] Egan's furnishings were princely compared with those of the legation in Bogota, whose unfortunate incumbent complained some years later that no other legation was as shabby as his. There was no gas (for lighting), no carpet to cover the bare boards, no filing cabinet for secret papers, and for the lack of bookcases the legation volumes lay in piles on the floor.[7]

The diplomats who represented their country in these legations were the beneficiaries of a shameless spoils system; they

6. Egan to Blaine, Oct. 21, 1889. U.S. Department of State, *Chile*, National Archives, Washington, D.C.

7. Burdett to Sherman, Aug. 13, 1897, U.S. Department of State, *Colombia*, National Archives, Washington, D.C.

usually were replaced when a new administration came into power. This put them at a disadvantage when dealing with European career diplomats, and mishaps did happen: on one occasion an ambassador lost the secret cypher book. Nor was every diplomat sufficiently well versed in diplomatic usage and the English language to transact routine business satisfactorily. But for all the unfortunate exceptions, the United States was ably served by the majority of her representatives in South America. A few of them, Judge John E. Bacon, Frederick Douglass, the first Negro to head a mission abroad, and Patrick Egan, to name but three, were men of exceptional abilities.

The manner of Bacon's appointment is an interesting illustration of how diplomatic posts were customarily filled. Cleveland had just been installed in the White House when Bacon wrote to the State Department staking a claim: "our state has asked for little and I think she should have at least a small mission." His application was endorsed by a number of prominent politicians from South Carolina. A local paper, the Edge-hill *Monitor*, described the candidate's contributions to the success of his party in direct and simple language: "South Carolina has the largest negro majority of any State in the Union, and consequently her struggle for Democratic success has been continual and desperate against radicals, negroes, carpetbaggers, and scalawags, in which Judge Bacon had always been a constant and indefatigable worker." A clipping from the newspaper was sent to the State Department. In July 1885 Bacon once more pressed Secretary Bayard for an appointment. His claims, he wrote, were small; he would be satisfied with a third-class mission, such as Bogota or Caracas. And so he was appointed Minister to Paraguay and Uruguay.[8]

8. Entry for John E. Bacon. Personnel files, U.S. Department of State, National Archives, Washington, D.C.

While serving in Uruguay Bacon made a special study of the relations between the United States and the South American republics. In January 1888 he sent Secretary of State Bayard an analysis covering more than a hundred pages. He pointed out that the Europeans attached great importance to trade with Latin America, which amounted to $700,000,000. Spain was making energetic efforts to reestablish her former primacy; the Germans were even more energetic and successful. European governments encouraged trade by subsidy, bounty, and investment. American commercial enterprise lagged behind. In 1883 only one American ship had entered Montevideo, as against 407 English, 231 French, 209 German and 90 Italian, whereas before the Civil War, American vessels had conveyed more than three times the trade of all foreign ships together. The market of South America was surely worth having, concluded Bacon, and deserved "a serious struggle." Most of the Latin American countries lay within the tropics. According to Bacon, it "renders them in climate, production, supply and demand the reverse of the United States . . . [but] strange to say," the United States only controlled one fifth of the trade.

Bacon suggested a number of remedies. European business methods should be studied and followed. England had subsidized her merchant marine; the great British steamship lines, the Royal Mail Steam Packet Company, the Pacific Steam and Navigation Company, the Peninsula and Oriental Steamship Company, and the Cunard Line had prospered as a result. The United States merchant marine had dwindled from lack of any but negligible payments for carrying the mail. Bacon next suggested that the United States abolish duties on the primary produce of Latin America and provide adequate credit facilities. He especially stressed the need for trained, intelligent, and energetic consuls.

[79]

There was one remedy for recovering American trade and influence which Bacon believed transcended all others—the construction of an international American railway. Three years of study had convinced him, he wrote, that the railway was not as gigantic an undertaking as the Pacific Railroad; furthermore, it was not an impossible undertaking. Commercially, it would monopolize trade; "politically it would be a matter of fact Monroe Doctrine, that no nation would dare to question as it would unite, in one iron bond, not only materially, but morally, socially and politically the whole of the western hemisphere, and breathe light and life into the struggling republics of South America." He forecast that the railway would transform the present state of affairs in which "day by day, our commercial relations with them [the countries of South America] are becoming less, our sailing vessels few and far between, and not a flag from a single steamer floats at least, in the water of the great La Plata, or south of Rio de Janeiro. Politically we have little to do with them, socially less, and commercially, in comparison with the great European Powers, still less." Bacon closed his notable dispatch with the plea that the United States help the millions of people in Latin America who struggled under the tyranny of church and state: "The railway will break their chains." Why not, he suggested to Bayard, call a conference of the presidents of the South American republics to discuss the problems? [9]

Bacon was not expressing eccentric, personal views. The unanimity of the diplomatic representatives is impressive. They all stressed that American business took little trouble and failed to study the market, that in price and quality European goods were frequently superior, and that the absence of American rail and steamship transportation was a major

9. Bacon to Bayard, Jan. 11, 1888. U.S. Department of State, *Paraguay and Uruguay*, National Archives, Washington, D.C.

impediment to the development of trade. In many South American countries the Germans, who had recently entered the market, were ahead of the United States. Was the United States falling behind through lack of interest? John T. Abbott, the United States Minister in Colombia, suggested that ignorance was really the culprit: "Every mail brings to this Legation numerous letters of inquiry as to exports and imports, the views of the people, the character and standing of the dealers, the climate, the tariff." But, commented Abbott, these remarkable questions merely displayed the "outstanding ignorance of our people." [10] Abbott stressed that trade could not be captured by correspondence or by organizations formed in the United States to promote commerce:

> As long as the individual merchant or manufacturer depends for concrete orders upon these agencies alone, however valuable they may be, he is doomed to wait and wish. That some reliable house will commence to work this field by sending here men of brains, energy and great patience is my hope.[11]

The men on the spot discerned clearly that the United States could not hope to capitalize on any preference of South American merchants for their northern neighbors; such preference rarely existed. By culture, and by long-established habit, the Latin American merchants looked to Europe. A share of the market for American produce could only be won by offering a better product at a better price.

The ministers in Latin America observed the close link between the volume of trade and the degree of national influence. Africa, moreover, provided an object lesson of how Eu-

10. John T. Abbott to Secretary Blaine, Sept. 4, 1889. U.S. Department of State, *Colombia*, National Archives, Washington, D.C.
11. Abbott to Blaine, Aug. 29, 1890. Ibid.

ropean rivalry for trade could lead to territorial partition. Was Latin America exposed to a similar danger? The American reaction to Ferdinand de Lesseps' attempt to construct the Panama Canal reveals how sensitive the Administration and Congress had become to the threat of increasing European influence in South America.

Europe's renewed interest in the isthmus profoundly affected American attitudes and policy. When the French Canal Company secured a treaty with Colombia to build the canal, President Hayes in his annual message of 1880 responded by calling for a canal under American control, and Secretary of State Evarts sought and secured a disavowal from the French government that the canal company was a national enterprise.[12] Many Americans nevertheless regarded the supposedly private nature of the French company as something of a sham. The isthmus was of great commercial and strategic importance to the United States. The attempt to construct the canal under French auspices was widely regarded as an infraction of the Monroe Doctrine. Toward the end of the decade a mere rumor that the French Canal Company was seeking to solve its financial difficulties by securing subsidies from the French government sufficed to throw Congress into a state of frenzied excitement. Senator George Franklin Edmunds of Vermont introduced a resolution expressing the Senate's disapproval of "any connection" of "any European government with the construction or control of any ship-canal across the Isthmus of Darien or across Central America." [13] But although several senators doubted whether the construction of the canal by a private company involved the Monroe Doctrine, only three voted against the Edmunds resolution. The significance of this

12. For a good summary of American reactions, see Walter Lafeber, *The New Empire, An Interpretation of American Expansion 1860–1898* (Ithaca, Cornell University Press, 1963), pp. 39–53.

13. Tansill, *Bayard,* pp. 676–77.

did not escape one distinguished historian, who observed that the senators evidently thought it "undesirable to go on record against any declaration which was connected with the Monroe Doctrine." [14]

The desire to expand trade so as to counter the effects of depression at home contributed to the renewal of American interest in Latin America. But the belief that American influence was declining in this area commercially, politically, and strategically proved to be an even more fundamental stimulus to action. Any extension of European political and military control would negate the advantages the United States still derived from geographic isolation. A European hegemony seemed to endanger the very fabric of American institutions. The separation of American and European affairs would become impossible, and the American people might even be driven to the burden of maintaining a large standing army. The task of diplomacy was to avert such a calamitous chain of events while there was still time. When Benjamin Harrison entered the White House in March 1889 his Administration responded with vigor to both the real and imagined threats.

The record of the Harrison Administration's conduct of Latin American affairs is a particularly controversial chapter in the history of American foreign policy.[15] At the center of the controversy stands Secretary of State James G. Blaine. Historians

14. Dexter Perkins, *The Monroe Doctrine 1867–1907* (Boston, Houghton Mifflin, 1937), p. 107.
15. For comprehensive studies of the foreign policy of the Harrison Administration, see Alice Felt Tyler, *The Foreign Policy of James G. Blaine* (Minneapolis, University of Minnesota Press, 1927). David Saville Muzzey, *James G. Blaine, A Political Idol of Other Days* (New York, Dodd, Mead, 1935). Joseph B. Lockey, "James G. Blaine," in Samuel Flagg Bemis, ed., *American Secretaries of State and Their Diplomacy* (10 vols. New York, Knopf, 1927–29), 8, 109–84. Albert T. Volwiler, "Harrison, Blaine, and American Foreign Policy, 1889–1893," *Proceedings of the American Philosophical Society*, 79 (1938), 637–48.

are as divided in their estimate of him as were his contemporaries. Blaine has been regarded as the apostle of a new Pan-American spirit. He certainly proclaimed lofty ideals to the Latin American delegates assembled in Washington to participate in the first International American Conference in October 1889:

> We believe that friendship, avowed with candor and maintained with good faith, will remove from American States the necessity of guarding boundary lines between themselves with fortifications and military force.
>
> We believe that standing armies, beyond those which are needful for public order and the safety of internal administration, should be unknown on both American continents.
>
> We believe that friendship and not force, the spirit of just law and not the violence of the mob, should be the recognized rule of administration between American nations and in American nations.[16]

American diplomacy in Haiti, Santo Domingo, and Chile and the adoption of a retaliatory economic policy seem to belie these peaceful intentions. Were they all sham? Did Blaine in reality establish the unhappy precedent one historian describes as the "policy of promoting friendly relations with Latin American nations and the concurrent practice of seeking to infringe their sovereignty"?[17] A dispassionate assessment of the available sources does not support so harsh a judgment.

Harrison and Blaine were eager to reestablish American influence in Latin America. They were following in the steps

16. Lockey, "James G. Blaine," p. 169.
17. Rayford W. Logan, *The Diplomatic Relations of the United States with Haiti, 1776–1891* (Chapel Hill, University of North Carolina Press, 1941), p. 411.

of their immediate predecessors and were determined to achieve their ends by winning the friendship and confidence of Latin American governments. Neither jingoism nor ruthlessness characterize their Latin American policy; it simply showed a touch of naïveté. "I am especially interested in the improvement of our relations with the Central and South American States. We must win their confidence by deserving it," Harrison wrote to Blaine when asking him to accept the office of Secretary of State.[18] Two years later Harrison explained to Blaine that he did not intend to embark on a policy of colonization: "You know I am not much of an annexationist; though I do feel that in some directions, as to naval stations and points of influence, we must look forward to a departure from the too conservative opinions which have been held heretofore." [19] Although they limited the objectives of their policy, Harrison and Blaine were firm believers in Manifest Destiny. They cherished visions of union with Canada, control of the Caribbean, and perhaps dominance in the Pacific. But Harrison and Blaine were shrewd men. They knew that none of this was practical politics in 1889. Their modest immediate aims are summed up in a letter from Blaine to Harrison:

I think there are only three places that are of value enough to be taken, that are not continental. One is Hawaii and the others are Cuba and Porto Rico. Cuba and Porto Rico are not now imminent and will not be for a generation. Hawaii may come up for decision at any unexpected hour

18. Harrison to Blaine, Jan. 17, 1889. Albert T. Volwiler, ed., *The Correspondence Between Benjamin Harrison and James G. Blaine* (Philadelphia, American Philosophical Society, 1940), pp. 44–45.

19. Harrison to Blaine, Oct. 1, 1891. Volwiler, "Harrison, Blaine, and American Foreign Policy," pp. 638–39.

and I hope we shall be prepared to decide it in the affirmative.[20]

Harrison's policy on the major diplomatic questions inherited from the previous Administration did not differ, except perhaps in emphasis, from Bayard's. Harrison and Blaine maintained Bayard's firm policy in Samoa and with equal vigor defended the seals threatened with extinction in the Bering Sea. Though Blaine was no admirer of the English in general and Prime Minister Lord Salisbury in particular, his handling of Anglo–American differences was circumspect. He skillfully avoided a confrontation of strength. There occurred no dramatic settlement of these differences in America's favor. The efforts of the Administration in securing Caribbean naval bases also ended in failure. Nor was Hawaiian annexation consummated before the Administration left office. The policy of friendship in Latin America was also largely a failure. The most sensational event of these years was the conflict with Chile which at one time seemed destined to end in war.

If the actual achievements of the Administration appear meager, it has long been recognized that a significant contribution to the development of American foreign policy was made during these years. To contemporary critics it seemed that Harrison had encouraged a spirit of chauvinism and had tried to change the character of American policy. This point of view is brought out by an editorial appearing in 1893 in *Harper's Weekly* condemning the Administration's "entangling alliances and intrigues . . . [and] its series of departures of the gravest nature from the old and fixed traditions of the Government." The journal posed the question: "Are we ready to alter the whole character of the government, with its benef-

20. Blaine to Harrison, Aug. 8, 1891. Volwiler, ed., *The Correspondence Between Harrison and Blaine,* pp. 173–74.

icent traditional policies, to impose upon the people the burdens entailed by the building up and maintaining of immense armaments . . . ?" [21] The changes in the course of American policy, however, evolved more gradually than many of Harrison's contemporaries supposed. That old and fixed traditions had guided policy until the advent of the Harrison Administration was something of an illusion.

The conduct of policy during the years of Harrison's presidency, however, did differ in one important respect. Harrison was the first President since the Civil War who fully recognized the need to coordinate the strategic, diplomatic, and economic factors of policy. Of his successors from Cleveland to Wilson, only Theodore Roosevelt attempted, but did not succeed, in so coordinating policy. Harrison, moreover, was fortunate in being able to rely on sufficient bipartisan support in Congress for his naval and foreign policies. Rarely indeed has there been such harmony in the management of America's foreign relations.

We know little about Harrison beyond the bare bones of his career. The correspondence of the majority of American politicians who were active during the last three decades of the nineteenth century is singularly disappointing. Success in American politics demanded discretion; Harrison was certainly discreet. Contemporaries testify to his coldness and aloofness. He carefully covered the tracks of his path to power. He posed as a man without ambition who reluctantly accepted the burdens of high office and was fond of telling the story of how in 1856 he was "drafted into the service of the Republican party," and how "after having refused, from modesty, to make a speech [he] was carried feet first into the

21. Volwiler, "Harrison, Blaine, and American Foreign Policy," p. 637.

room where the audience was assembled, and compelled to declare his political faith." [22] Harrison was a loyal Republican all his life. The grandson of a President, he rose to prominence at the Indiana bar. His war record was distinguished. In 1876 Harrison unsuccessfully ran for Governor of Indiana. Five years later he was elected to the Senate. Though an able and hardworking senator, Harrison attracted no spectacular attention. Nevertheless in 1888 he reached political heights: with Blaine's help and the usual promises of patronage, Harrison secured the nomination of the Republican National Convention.

During the course of the presidential campaign of 1888, Harrison displayed his customary discretion. He managed to say little about any major issue; President Cleveland said nothing at all. Harrison won no overwhelming vote of national confidence. The election was decided by the geographical distribution of his supporters, and Cleveland had the popular majority. Harrison was not an engaging national leader, but he was a strong President. Forceful, clearheaded, and loyal to his close associates, Harrison grasped the reins of power and, a politician to his fingertips, brought a touch of professionalism to the White House.

The president-elect was deluged with requests for jobs in return for political services rendered and rewarded the faithful. Tenure of fourth-class postmasterships changed hands wholesale—as was the custom. Only a small number of offices were protected by the civil service law. The distribution of the principal Cabinet posts was a more complex matter; political service to the party and the candidate, the claims of important states, past promises and future expectations had to be weighed against considerations of fitness for office.

22. John D. Long, ed., *The Republican Party: Its History, Principles, and Policies* (New York, Hazen and Co., 1888), p. 363.

Ability did not always rank first, and Harrison made some shocking appointments. That a government judged corrupt even by contemporary standards could also bring to the forefront a few men of talent and vision is perhaps surprising but such was certainly the case.

Harrison could not ignore the claims of Blaine, the veteran Republican leader, to the senior position in his Administration; but he did not immediately offer him the appointment of Secretary of State, nor did he consult him about other appointments. He was anxious to show himself as master in his own house. Although Blaine's supporters claimed that he had been slighted, the correspondence between the President and the Secretary of State shows them to have been in perfect harmony during the early months of the Administration. Their estrangement occurred later and for reasons that can only be surmised. The appalling personal tragedies that befell Blaine —the death of his brother in December was followed a few months later by those of his son Walker and his daughter Alice—and the onset of his own mortal illness increased his eccentricity. He was careless about attending Cabinet meetings and said they bored him. He was forgetful, the despair of the State Department; he would carry secret dispatches around in his pocket, and sometimes read them to Henry Cabot Lodge's vivacious young wife Anna, whose slightest whim he sought to satisfy. Blaine's neglect of administrative routine no doubt offended the methodical President. Blaine became increasingly touchy, and Harrison later recalled: "My association with Mr. Blaine covers some of the most pleasant experience of my public life, and some of the most trying." [23] During Blaine's bedridden months, much of the State Department business was conducted in the White House. Long be-

23. Memorandum by Harrison, May 1893. Volwiler, ed., *The Correspondence Between Harrison and Blaine*, pp. 294–303.

fore Blaine resigned in June 1892 his relations with the President had become coldly formal. Neither the breach between the two men nor Blaine's illness, however, significantly affected American diplomacy, for they remained in close agreement on actual questions of policy. Harrison was perhaps the more belligerent of the two and inclined to seek clear-cut decisions. Blaine showed more patience and subtlety. But both men agreed on one major aspect of policy: even when the stakes were high they both shrank from the use of force against a weak neighbor. They sought to conserve American interests and to strengthen the rule of law and international order in the hemisphere; they did not see these aims as incompatible.

Blaine had outlined his view of the proper Latin American policy some years earlier in an article in which he attempted to justify his conduct of foreign policy during the Garfield Administration. He placed equal stress on the needs to increase American exports and assure peace among the Latin American republics, peace being essential to commerce. The balance of trade was against the United States. The drain of gold that resulted, he argued, was in "time of stringency a standing menace of financial disaster." Blaine's stress on the advantages of supporting an active policy in the hemisphere may well have been partly due to his desire to overcome America's lack of concern with foreign relations. Of special interest are those passages of the article which reveal Blaine's ideas about the problems the United States was facing in South America and how they ought to be met.

Threescore years have passed. The power of the Republic in many directions has grown beyond all anticipation, but we have relatively lost ground in some great fields of enterprise. We have added thousands of miles to our ocean front, but our foreign commerce is relatively less, and from ardent friendship with Spanish America we have drifted into indifference if not into coldness. It is but one step further to reach a condition of positive unfriendliness, which may end in what would be equivalent to a commercial alliance against us. Already one of the most dangerous of movements—that of a European guarantee and guardianship of the Interoceanic canal—is suggested and urged upon the foreign Powers by representatives of a South-American country. If these tendencies are to be averted, if Spanish-American friendship is to be regained, if the commercial empire that legitimately belongs to us is to be ours, we must not lie idle and witness its transfer to others.[24]

The first step, Blaine argued, was to call together a Peace Congress of the Americas such as he had planned and President Arthur's Administration had abandoned. "The Spanish-American States are in special need of the help which the Peace Congress would afford them. They require external pressure to keep them from war; when at war they require external pressure to bring them to peace." Blaine did not doubt that the United States was the one country uniquely capable of exercizing this pressure wisely and fairly. He also deluded himself in thinking that the Latin American republics would thank the United States for keeping the peace or that, to use Blaine's words, "though tending for years past to estrangement . . . [they] would promptly respond to any advance made by the Great Republic of the North." Blaine even advanced in embryonic form arguments better known later as the Roosevelt corollary. He pointed out America's duty and the consequences of neglecting it:

24. James G. Blaine, *Political Discussions, Legislative, Diplomatic and Popular 1856–1886* (Norwich, Connecticut, Henry Bill, 1887), pp. 418–19.

Such friendly interventions as the proposed Peace Congress, and as the attempt to restore peace between Chile and Peru, fall within the line of both duty and interest on the part of the United States . . . Our own Government cannot take the ground that it will not offer friendly intervention to settle troubles between American countries, unless at the same time it freely concedes to European Governments the right of such intervention, and thus consents to a practical destruction of the Monroe doctrine and an unlimited increase of European influence on this continent . . . If our Government does not resume its efforts to secure peace in South America some European Government will be forced to perform that friendly office. The United States cannot play between nations the part of dog in the manger.[25]

In 1889 Blaine was still of the same opinions, and Harrison shared them.

It was fitting that Blaine should have presided over the first Conference of American States. He presided, moreover, with tact and distinction. The positive outcome of the lengthy debates proved to be disappointing. The establishment of the Commercial Bureau of the American Republics was practically the only material legacy of this historic gathering. On the other hand, to have secured the attendance of every American republic except Santo Domingo was a remarkable achievement in itself. The importance of the Congress, Blaine predicted, would be acknowledged in future years. The precedent of having brought together the American republics for discussion of their common welfare proved more important than the actual results achieved.

Harrison and Blaine did not believe that the United States would win a commanding influence in the Western Hemisphere

25. Ibid., pp. 414–15.

merely by setting an example of moral and peaceful conduct or even by more vigorous commercial enterprise. They also attached importance to considerations of military power. Possibly the Administration's greatest contribution to foreign affairs was to set the United States on the road to eventual naval supremacy.

Judge Benjamin Franklin Tracy, Harrison's Secretary of the Navy, soon proved his outstanding abilities. In his first annual report of December 1889 Tracy decisively broke with past traditions of naval policy by calling for a powerful battleship fleet. It was characteristic of the new Administration's conduct of affairs to encourage professional advice. Tracy was especially sympathetic to the views of Admiral Luce, who had been ignored by the Navy Department for years. He accepted Luce's arguments on the need for battleships and endorsed his recommendation that at least twenty such vessels were required to give the United States a proper fleet.[26] Tracy also reappointed Mahan as President of the Naval War College. He wished to keep Mahan close at hand to advise on strategy. In a letter to Luce, Mahan later recalled: "Mr. Tracy at one time, in 1890, directed Folger and me to draw up outline plans of operations necessary to be undertaken at once in case of war with foreign nations. I drew up two—that I remember—possibly more; in the case of Britain and Spain. I have had an impression that those, in which Folger concurred, found their way to the Bureau of Intelligence."[27] It is unfortunate that Mahan never described in more detail the nature of his secret employment in the Navy Department. He was undoubtedly closely involved in the search for suitable Caribbean bases for the Navy. It is significant, for example, that among his papers there is a

26. See pp. 35–37.
27. Mahan to Luce, Sept. 3, 1901. Mahan Papers, Library of Congress, Washington, D.C.

pencil draft of the instructions which were dispatched to Admiral Gherardi to secure, if he could, Molé St. Nicholas, Haiti, for the Navy.

The strategic importance of the island of Santo Domingo had long been recognized. The hostility of Britain, France, and Spain during the Civil War stimulated the desire for naval stations in the Caribbean as outposts against possible European aggression. Secretary of State Seward actually negotiated a treaty with Denmark for the cession of the Virgin Islands, and President Grant came to a more dubious agreement with a Dominican President for the annexation of his country, but both treaties failed to be ratified by the Senate. A few years later the projected Nicaraguan canal again directed the attention of the Navy Department to the isthmus and Santo Domingo. The outbreak of a revolution in Haiti in 1888 appeared to provide an opportunity for securing the lease of a naval base there, since the two contenders for power regarded the attitude of the United States as crucial to their own success. The revolutionary party created the impression in Washington that they would prove more accommodating to American wishes, and discussions for the lease of a naval station at Molé St. Nicholas had begun before Blaine took charge of the State Department. Blaine and Tracy eagerly pursued them. A wealthy American shipping magnate, William P. Clyde, a former client of Tracy's law firm, also sought to benefit from a closer association between Haiti and the United States. The full story of the negotiations need not be recounted here. Blaine cajoled and threatened without securing the desired lease. Once the new Haitian President no longer needed American aid, he refused to live up to his earlier promises.[28] Blaine and Tracy then tried to negotiate the lease of Samana Bay with the Dominican

28. Logan, *Diplomatic Relations*, pp. 315–441.

government and were equally unsuccessful, although they appeared to be on the verge of success on several occasions.[29]

The policy of the Harrison Administration in Haiti and the Dominican Republic has been harshly judged as an attempt to take advantage of civil war. It certainly did not conform to ethical standards. But far more extraordinary is the fact that the Administration did not simply seize a naval base; the Dominican president practically invited them to do just that. Harrison, Blaine, and Tracy attached the greatest importance to the possession of a base in the Caribbean, and no single European power would have hesitated in a like situation. Gladstone invaded Egypt for far less cause. The precedent set by the Harrison Administration, moreover, was not followed by his successors, who used force when, in their judgment, national interests demanded it.

Civil war in Haiti provided the opportunity to extend American influence; in Chile it led to the opposite result. The Harrison Administration made a number of imaginative appointments to the diplomatic service. Patrick Egan, minister to Chile, a one time Fenian and a fugitive from British justice, was one of the best known Irish patriots in exile. His qualifications for membership in the diplomatic corps were unusual. Blaine could take for granted that Egan would seek to assert American influence in a country dominated by Britain. But Egan was neither an anglophobe nor a rabid nationalist. A close friend and associate of Charles Stewart Parnell, Egan identified himself closely with nonviolent land agitation. Forced to flee from Ireland where he had helped found the Irish Land League, he settled in Lincoln, Nebraska. He built up a successful business and presided over the Irish National League of America. He belonged to that group of Irishmen, who sup-

29. Sumner Welles, *The Dominican Republic, 1844–1924*, 1 (2 vols. New York, Payson and Clarke, 1928), 444–96.

ported the Republicans and who helped to break the almost solid Irish Democratic vote. Egan was a man of integrity, ability, and courage; a good fighter for any cause he believed in, he also possessed undoubted charm. His main failing was lack of discretion.

The appointment of Egan, one of Blaine's Irishmen, immediately aroused fierce criticism. On his arrival in Chile, Egan was cold-shouldered by the Chilean government and the pro-British newspapers. Baron Gutschmid, the German Minister, derived much satisfaction from this state of affairs, adding, in a report to his government that President José Manuel Balmaceda did not approve of the American representative and on one pretext after another had postponed receiving him in formal audience.[30] Egan patiently worked to overcome the personal prejudice against him. He saw as his principal mission the reestablishment of good relations between Chile and the United States. At first he succeeded, but in a sense he succeeded too well. He became closely identified with the government of Balmaceda and aroused the hatred of the opposition party, which came into power when Balmaceda was overthrown. The United States has often followed a similar pattern toward Latin America in the twentieth century. There seems to be no solution to the dilemma of how to foster a friendly Pan-American spirit without seeming to side with the ruling party in each country, thereby earning the hatred of the opposition, the rulers of tomorrow.

The conduct of Harrison, Blaine, and Egan during the Chilean revolution poisoned the relations between the United States and Chile for many years. The facts are well established and need only to be briefly touched upon here. When in Janu-

30. Gutschmid to Bismarck, Aug. 12, 1889. Microfilm of the German Foreign Ministry Archives, G.F.M. 21/245, Public Record Office, London.

ary 1891 President Balmaceda sought to set aside the power of Congress because it had been used to frustrate effective government, the leaders of Congress declared the deposition of the President. They proclaimed to the people that they were fighting for liberty and parliamentary government and were joined by the Chilean navy, which raised the standard of resistance in the northern provinces. The revolutionaries established their headquarters at Iquique and defeated a small government force there. The army, however, remained loyal to the President, who, without a navy, could not come to grips with the weaker Congress forces in the north. The choice of Iquique by the Congress party, moreover, had been shrewd, for it was from this port that nitrate, Chile's main export, was sent to Europe. Despite the protest of the Balmacedist government, the British, French, and Germans continued to trade in Iquique, paying their taxes to the insurgents, who used these funds to build up an army equipped with weapons imported mainly from Europe. In August 1891 the Congress party was ready to strike. Their army landed a few miles from Valparaíso and defeated the Balmacedists on August 28 at the battle of Placilla. Balmaceda's family sought asylum in the American legation; a few days later Balmaceda shot himself.[31]

The specific charges against the United States were that Egan had openly sided with Balmaceda, that the American admiral in Chilean waters had done the same, and that the United States Navy had wrongfully seized arms, purchased in the United States and carried on the *Itata* to Iquique, which were intended for the Congress party. As far as the *Itata*

31. For a sound and brief account, see Luis Galdames, *A History of Chile,* Isaac Joslin Cox, ed. and trans. (Chapel Hill, University of North Carolina Press, 1941), pp. 400–11. In a despatch to Blaine dated Aug. 31, 1891, Egan pointed out that the English legation alone had refused to admit any refugees.

affair was concerned, an American court concurred in the view taken by the Congress party and eventually ordered the release of the arms.

The European and American archives now permit the historian to gain a better perspective on this quarrel. They also illuminate Egan's behavior and exonerate him personally and the United States generally. American conduct was no more reprehensible than that of the interested European powers. Space does not permit a full treatment of the question, but this much can be said. It would be wrong to look upon the struggle in Chile as one between a constitutional party and a dictatorship, with the United States backing the latter. Egan characterized the conflict as one "between two elements of the oligarchy." [32] The British minister, after mature reflection, was of the same opinion. In a private memorandum for the Foreign Office, John Gordon Kennedy wrote that Europe had been misled about the revolution: "Balmaceda was an able and honest man, but he was deficient in firmness, sincerity and elevation of character." In short, he was not the stuff dictators are made of. "The Chilean revolution may be described as an interested movement of political parties for obtaining power. The question of principle found little place in the struggle," [33] so concluded Kennedy.

That history may become the story of the victor is illustrated by the customary condemnation of the Harrison Administration. The Administration was adjudged at fault in the *Itata* affair, but, it should be noted, by an American court. Egan did openly and indiscreetly show preference for Balmaceda and believed that the President was bound to win ultimately. Nevertheless, Egan was perfectly sincere in his efforts to medi-

32. Egan to Blaine, Jan. 12, 1891. U.S. Department of State, *Chile*, National Archives, Washington, D.C.
33. Kennedy to Sanderson, Sept. 24, 1892. The Records of the British Foreign Office, F.O. 16/280, Public Record Office, London.

ate between the two warring parties, though this was used in evidence against him later. Apart from the *Itata* incident, the United States had given Balmaceda purely moral support.

The European governments, on the other hand, provided material support for the Congress party. They continued the nitrate trade with the port of Iquique, threatening to use force if the Chilean government attempted to interfere. At the request of the Chilean minister in Paris, the French government on various pretexts refused to hand over two warships built for the Chilean navy.[34] Kennedy thought at the time that if Balmaceda could have obtained the warships belonging to Chile he would have won easily.[35] The support rendered to the opposition by the English community and by the Royal Navy, moreover, was substantial, and Kennedy admitted after the battle of Placilla: "We Britishers are now in tremendous favour with all classes. No doubt the naval officers and the British community in Valparaiso and all along the coast rendered material assistance to the opposition and committed many breaches of neutrality. This made my position at the Moneda very difficult and I was obliged to be strictly neutral with an apparent leaning to Balmaceda." [36] There can be little doubt that a victory for Balmaceda would have discredited the European governments just as his defeat discredited the United States.

Egan's subsequent conduct in granting asylum to the Balmacedist refugees, his courage in the face of insults, his handling of the Baltimore incident, Egan remaining calm amid the passion it aroused, and his efforts to establish good relations with the new government (two of whose members he

34. Whitelaw Reid to Blaine, March 18, 1891. U.S. Department of State, *France*, National Archives, Washington, D.C.

35. Kennedy to Sanderson, June 9, 1891. British Foreign Office Records, F.O. 16/265.

36. Kennedy to Sanderson, Sept. 15, 1891. Ibid., F.O. 16/265.

had protected in the legation during Balmaceda's tenure of power) excited the grudging admiration of the other foreign diplomats. The last word may well be left to the British Minister who was not particularly well disposed to Egan: "Egan has been steadily supported and approved by the President and Secretary of State; and he certainly deserves credit for the firmness and ability which he has displayed under circumstances of unusual difficulty." [37]

The United States came very close to war with Chile during the winter of 1891. Harrison demanded an apology from the Chileans and compensation for the murdered sailors of the *Baltimore*. When faced with an ultimatum, Chile agreed to pay an indemnity. If Harrison had behaved highhandedly it must also be remembered that the provocation had been extreme.[38]

It would be misleading to judge the Administration's attitude toward Latin America by the Chilean episode alone. The President and the Secretary of State were anxious to convince the Latin American republics that the United States was their true friend. That they were motivated by good will is evident in their unspectacular day-to-day dealings in Latin America. They nevertheless reacted with unnecessary severity whenever they felt the United States had received a slight. Their sensitivity was due in part to their apprehensions over Europe's growing influence in Latin America. Harrison and Blaine were constantly looking for ways to decrease this power, and they sometimes overcompensated with belligerence in countries where American influence was particularly weak. This helps to explain why Harrison contemplated the use of force in Chile, but not in Haiti and the Dominican Republic.

Blaine hoped that one day all the people of the Western

37. Kennedy to Sanderson, Dec. 31, 1891. Ibid., F.O. 16/266.
38. For the best account see, Volwiler, "Harrison, Blaine, and American Foreign Policy," pp. 639–48.

Hemisphere would come to share the American outlook and that national differences would cease to play an important role. But in meeting the problems of his time Blaine did not always succeed in reconciling Pan-American ideals with America's national interests. Harrison and Blaine were searching for a constructive, not a purely negative, hemispheric policy, and this is to their credit. At home they achieved a remarkable co-ordination of policy. Abroad they earned distrust and suspicion. Their foreign policy was not framed in response to a public demand for national self-assertion; on the contrary, their policies stimulated such sentiments. During the closing weeks of the Administration, the debate over the future of Hawaii was to reveal the strength of the expansionists.

Chapter Four
An Administration in Search of a Policy:
Hawaii and Latin America, 1893–1895

PARTY POLITICS HAD SERIOUSLY IMPEDED the conduct of American foreign policy during Cleveland's first Administration. When Cleveland returned to the White House in 1893, Congress (and the nation) had become increasingly aware of the importance of foreign affairs and seemed less inclined to utilize such questions of national importance for political advantage. The Democrats and Republicans were giving bipartisan support to naval expansion and the acquisition of bases necessary for defense. The broad issue of expansion overseas, although heatedly debated, had not divided Congress along party lines in the past. It need not have done so in 1893, when the question over the future of Hawaii focused the attention of Congress and the nation on America's "manifest destiny" once again.

Leading politicians of both parties favored annexation: Republican Senators Henry Cabot Lodge, William E. Chandler, and William Pierce Frye endorsed it; Senator John Tyler Morgan, the senior Democrat on the Foreign Relations Committee, and Thomas F. Bayard, Cleveland's former Secretary of State, concurred. Senator Orville Hitchcock Platt sensed the fundamental issue when he told a newspaper reporter that " a policy of isolation did well enough when we were an embryo nation, but today things are different . . . We are sixty-five million of people, the most advanced and powerful on earth, and regard to our future welfare demands an abandonment of the doctrines of isolation." [1] But Carl Schurz spoke for those Americans who believed that a policy of annexing dependencies beyond the shores of the continent was alien to the character of the republic and threatened its institutions. The United States appeared to be at the crossroads; the nation debated whether national security and welfare could be maintained without abandoning traditional tenets of foreign policy.

The incoming Administration might have been expected to declare its own policy and provide the nation with leadership. But Cleveland and his new Secretary of State, Walter Quintin Gresham, waited many months before they announced their course. They did so eventually in language forceful enough to belie their earlier uncertainties. The President proclaimed in December 1893 that "national honesty" precluded a "desire for territorial extension." [2] He further blamed the Republican Administration for its unpatriotic handling of foreign affairs. Thus the acquisition of overseas dependencies became a political issue. The course of American foreign policy was probably not much affected by the postponement of Hawaii's annexation; but the manner of Cleveland's rejection of annexation insured that the conduct of foreign policy would be handicapped by political strife for years to come. Here lies the historical importance of Cleveland's 1893 Hawaiian policy.

Cleveland leaned heavily on his Secretary of State for ad-

1. Ernest R. May, *Imperial Democracy, The Emergence of America as a Great Power* (New York, Harcourt, Brace, 1961), pp. 19–20.

2. James D. Richardson, ed., *Messages and Papers*, 9, 461. See also Cleveland's statement to the Associated Press in January 1898 that the "extension of American sovereignty was opposed to our national policy . . . a perversion of our national mission." Allan Nevins, ed., *The Letters of Grover Cleveland, 1850–1908* (Boston and New York, Houghton Mifflin, 1933), pp. 491–92.

vice on questions of foreign policy. Consequently the personality and outlook of the Secretary played a crucial role in the shaping of policies. In 1893, Cleveland found the task of choosing his Cabinet particularly difficult: "I cannot get the men I want to help me." He offered the State Department to Judge Gresham, who accepted the assignment with reluctance. And well he might, for Gresham, a former Postmaster General and candidate for the presidential nomination, had all his life been a Republican. The choice surpised Democrats and Republicans alike. But Gresham's fitness for the post in other respects was not questioned. Gresham had proved himself to Cleveland as a man of principle and independence when he announced his intention to vote for the Democratic candidate because he disagreed with the Republican tariff policy. Cleveland evidently admired men who committed political suicide, scorning party loyalties when they believed the national good was at stake. Gresham's reward was not oblivion but the position of Secretary of State.

Despite some personal eccentricities and the informality of his behavior, Gresham was a man of intelligence and ability. He displayed cool judgment and considerable finesse in handling the Brazilian troubles and the Venezuelan boundary dispute. Unhappily, he assumed office in the midst of a problem for which his previous experience had not equipped him—the treaty for the annexation of Hawaii.

The revolution in Hawaii and the arrival in San Francisco on January 28, 1893, of the Hawaiian representatives of the new provisional government, en route to Washington to negotiate a treaty of annexation to the United States, became headline news. A majority of the newspapers favored annexation, a sentiment which the New York *Tribune* summed up tersely and forcefully: "The popular verdict is clear, unequivocal, and

practically unanimous. Hawaii is welcome." Much play was
made of Britain's supposed designs on the islands, as the
Washington *Star* dramatically asked: "Shall we take Hawaii
and thereby prosper and magnify ourselves, or shall we let
England take it, and thereby enfeeble and humiliate us?" But
a few important papers, including the New York *Evening Post*
and the Boston *Herald,* and the influential liberal weeklies *The
Nation* and *Harper's Weekly* expressed their opposition to
hasty annexation.[3] There can be little doubt that those in favor
of annexation had the stronger argument. They vilified the
Queen of Hawaii and extolled the virtues of the revolutionary
party. Washington was showered with petitions from missionaries, members of Congress, and state legislators, all calling
for American control over the islands.

The revolution had occurred during the last weeks of the
Republican Administration, and its sudden outbreak took President Harrison and Secretary of State Foster by surprise. Although he and the President were inclined to accept annexation at the request of the new Hawaiian government, Foster
had, a few days prior to the revolution, advised the revolutionists to postpone action. It was Foster's belief that the incoming
Democrats were as favorably inclined toward annexation as
were the Republicans, and so nothing was to be lost by the delay.

Foster had all along assumed that the Hawaiians would
make their own revolution. If it succeeded, and the new government received de facto recognition, the question of annexation could be taken up by the two governments. As soon as
Foster discovered that Minister Stevens had on his own authority proclaimed Hawaii an American protectorate, he dis-
avowed the actions of the Minister, which, however, did not

3. Sylvester K. Stevens, *American Expansion in Hawaii* (Harrisburg,
Archives Publishing Co. of Pennsylvania, 1945), pp. 234–39.

stop the Administration from negotiating a treaty of annexation with the Hawaiian commissioners who had come to Washington. A treaty was concluded on February 14, 1893.[4]

One day later the annexation treaty was rushed to the Senate. Senator John T. Morgan of Alabama and Senator Gorman of Maryland, both Democrats, had already pledged Foster their support. It was taken for granted that the Republicans in the Senate would also support annexation, and it was favorably reported in the short time of two days. With the support of a number of Democrats, the treaty thus appeared to be sure of speedy ratification—had not Cleveland intervened at this late stage.[5]

Cleveland, who up to this time had given no inkling of his opinion on the annexation of Hawaii, in February sent John Griffin Carlisle, Secretary of the Treasury–designate, to Washington. Carlisle, on behalf of the incoming Administration, persuaded the Democratic senators to block any hasty action and postpone a Senate decision on the treaty.[6] No one inferred from Cleveland's action that he was opposed to annexation; there was no reason to believe this possibility. In a message to Congress of seven years before, Cleveland had spoken of his "unhesitating conviction that the intimacy of our relations with Hawaii should be emphasized"; he had also recommended—and obtained—a seven-year extension of the rec-

4. For the best and most recent treatment, see William Adam Russ, *The Hawaiian Revolution* (1893–94) (Selinsgrove, Susquehanna University Press, 1959). But two accounts that remain valuable are Stevens, *American Expansion in Hawaii*, and Julius W. Pratt, *Expansionists of 1898: The Acquisition of Hawaii and the Spanish Islands* (Baltimore, Johns Hopkins Press, 1936), pp. 1–187 passim.

5. J. W. Foster, *Diplomatic Memoirs* (2 vols. Boston and New York, Houghton Mifflin, 1909), 2, 168. *Journal of the Executive Proceedings of the Senate of the United States* (Washington, D.C., Government Printing Office, 1901), 28, 397–98.

6. Matilda Gresham, *Life of Walter Quintin Gresham* (2 vols. Chicago, Rand McNally, 1919), 2, 684–85. Foster, *Diplomatic Memoirs*, 2, 168.

iprocity treaty, in order to preserve America's "paramount interests" in the islands.[7]

Cleveland's blocking ratification in the Senate at this time, right before the inauguration, was generally interpreted as a wish to reserve credit for the Democrats. Three days after Cleveland's inauguration, Gresham granted an hour-and-a-half interview to Rear Admiral George Brown, the details of which Brown made known to Lorrin A. Thurston, the Hawaiian Commissioner, the following day. Gresham told the Admiral of his suspicion that the revolution in Hawaii and the annexation movement were inspired by financial interests; however Gresham also assured the Admiral that "the President was in favor of retaining the advantage gained by the United States at the islands"; Cleveland, Gresham had said, was not sure whether this could best be done by annexing Hawaii or by proclaiming a protectorate over the islands; the President wanted more time to study the question and would therefore probably withdraw the pending treaty from the Senate.[8]

Whatever Gresham might have felt so soon after assuming office, he was not ready to commit the President to any decided policy. The eventual annexation of Hawaii certainly had not been ruled out. Gresham informed the Russian Minister that although the Administration was inclined to conservatism in foreign affairs and did not favor a policy of acquisition of foreign territory, "so far as the Hawaiian Islands were concerned, the attitude of the Administration would be consistent with the past policy of the United States." [9] On a later occasion, he claimed that he had not been opposed to annexation as such. He was, rather, opposed to the annexation of remote

7. Richardson, *Messages and Papers*, 8, 149–50.
8. Thurston to Dole, March 10, 1893, Lorrin A. Thurston, *Memoirs of the Hawaiian Revolution* (Honolulu, Advertiser Publishing Company, 1936), p. 561.
9. Gresham memorandum of conversation with Prince Cantacuzene, March 16, 1893. U.S. Department of State, *Memoranda of Conversations*.

territory and to annexation by force or fraud.[10] There is ample reason for believing, however, that Hawaii was no longer regarded as "remote territory" in 1893.

Even when, five days after his inauguration, the President withdrew the treaty from the Senate "for the purpose of reexamination," it was still widely belived that Hawaii would become American in due course. Some delay could be expected; on March 11 Cleveland had appointed James H. Blount of Georgia as a Special Commissioner to investigate firsthand the causes of the revolt and the political situation in Hawaii. Blount was told that the treaty had been withdrawn for reexamination and that the subject of annexation was "in abeyance" (therefore not dead). He was also instructed to assure the Hawaiians that the withdrawal signified no American unfriendliness, that on the contrary the Administration felt "earnest solicitude" for their "welfare, tranquility, and progress." [11] No action could be expected until Blount had made his report to the President.

We may gather something of Cleveland's feelings about Hawaii from a letter he wrote to Carl Schurz in March 1893. He disabused Schurz of the idea that reexamination of the treaty was equivalent to killing it: "I do not now say that I should hold annexation in all circumstances and at any time unwise, but I am sure we ought to stop and look, and think. That's exactly what we are doing now." [12] Of the two alternatives, Cleveland seems to have inclined toward annexing rather than making Hawaii a protectorate, although the latter would have assured American paramountcy without necessarily involving the disadvantages of outright annexation.

It is a mistake to assume that Cleveland was opposed to es-

10. Gresham to Noble C. Butler, Nov. 23, 1893. Gresham MSS.
11. Gresham to Blount, March 11, 1893. *Foreign Relations, 1894*, appendix II, pp. 467-68.
12. Cleveland to Schurz, March 19, 1893. Schurz MSS.

tablishing a closer relationship with the islands from the outset. Hesitate he did, and for good reason. Thoughtful opinion in the country criticized the indecent haste of the Harrison Administration in attempting to push through annexation. To incorporate the multiracial peoples of the islands into the Union entailed a radical departure from previous American policy. What complications might it not involve, once the excitement had passed away, for Southern Democrats who stood for white supremacy? Only too acutely aware of the economic difficulties which faced the country and threatened a split within Democratic ranks, Cleveland was, not unnaturally, afraid of the political and financial consequences of any opposition to American authority by a majority of native Hawaiians. In making a decision on Hawaii he had every reason to be cautious. From a short-term point of view, Cleveland recognized the immense popularity of annexation. At the outset of his Administration, however, the more distant perspectives carried greater weight with him. In any case, there was no reason for haste.

Cleveland and Gresham—who had gained access to the records of the Department of State—were able to reassure themselves that foreign intervention in Hawaii was not to be feared. The importance they attached to this aspect of the question can be deduced from the fact that although the answers Foster had elicited from the European powers and Japan were wholly satisfactory, Gresham repeated Foster's inquiries. He summoned the European and Japanese Ministers to the State Department on March 16 and made it clear to them that America would brook no foreign interference in the islands.[13] In reality, the attitude of England alone was of

13. Gresham memoranda of conversations with the Japanese, Russian, and British Ministers in Washington—Gozo Tateno, Prince Cantacuzene, and Sir Julian Pauncefote—March 16, 1893. U.S. Department of State, *Memoranda of Conversations.*

major importance. Foreign Secretary Rosebery in London had already decided that pedantic insistence on Britain's treaty rights should not jeopardize the development of good Anglo–American relations. If Sir Julian Pauncefote, the British Ambassador in Washington, when writing his dispatches home, caustically derided annexationist sentiment in the United States, he went out of his way to appear conciliatory in his conversation with Secretary Gresham. The United States, he intimated, should do in regard to Hawaii whatever it deemed to be in its best interests.[14]

Historians have been inclined to accept Cleveland's explanation for withdrawing the treaty: he had been motivated by considerations of justice and honor alone. But the path of virtue was not so clearly marked when Cleveland first considered the implications of the Hawaiian question. Indeed, there is evidence contradicting the President's claim that he had always opposed the annexation of Hawaii.

Justice and honor weighed heavily with Cleveland and Gresham. Their suspicions, already aroused by the haste in which Harrison pushed for annexation, were further strengthened when Paul Neumann, agent in Washington for the Queen of Hawaii, produced evidence showing that the revolution had been accomplished by force and fraud and with the connivance of the American government.[15] Nevertheless Cleveland did not at once reject the possibility of annexation. He desired to bring it about honorably and in conformity with the long-term interests of the American people and the Democratic party. He further wished to consider other alternatives, such as proclamation of Hawaii as a protectorate.

14. Rosebery to Dufferin, Jan. 30, 1893; Rosebery to Pauncefote, telegrams, Jan. 30, 31, 1893; Pauncefote to Rosebery, Feb. 7, 1893; Wodehouse to Rosebery, telegram, Nov. 2, 1892; Rosebery to Wodehouse, Nov. 11, 1892. *Foreign Office Records*, 534/55, Public Record Office, London.
15. *Foreign Relations, 1894*, appendix II, pp. 638–40, 848.

While awaiting the results of Blount's Hawaiian investigation, Cleveland and Gresham maintained open minds. Blount's painstaking and thorough report was finished in Honolulu on July 17, 1893; it reached the State Department some time later. On the whole a reasonable appraisal of the situation, the report supported the case of the native Queen rather than that of the revolutionists. Gresham's two chief questions were answered: the American Minister *had* conspired with the revolutionists to overthrow the Queen, and without his aid in landing American troops, the revolution could not have been undertaken; the Hawaiian people were opposed to annexation. If people of all nationalities who could read and write were allowed to vote, annexation would, Blount calculated, be defeated by a majority of two to one.[16] Gresham accepted the report. The Hawaiian Commissioner insisted to the last that the American Minister had not conspired with the revolutionists, but the Secretary of State had made up his mind.[17] By the middle of September 1893, he had determined to right the wrong by restoring the Queen to her throne.[18]

Gresham's plan was fantastic. Attorney General Olney heard of it at a cabinet meeting early in October, and although he agreed with Gresham on the moral issue, he immediately saw that the Secretary was rapidly getting out of his depth. He sent Gresham a memorandum pointing out the obstacles this new policy would have to overcome. An insuperable difficulty would arise if the Hawaiian people had come to favor the revolutionary regime by this time, in which case the use of force would be necessary to restore the Queen to power. He reminded Gresham that while a mere show of force was

16. Ibid., pp. 567–605.
17. Gresham memorandum of conversation with Thurston, Aug. 14, 1893. U.S. Department of State, *Memoranda of Conversations*.
18. Carl Schurz wrote to Gresham expressing his approval, Schurz to Gresham, Sept. 24, 1893. Gresham MSS.

permissible (Stevens had used force to insure the success of the revolution in the first place), any act amounting to war would first have to secure the approval of Congress. In any case, before restoring the Queen, the Administration would have to obtain a promise of an amnesty for the revolutionists.[19] One wonders whether Gresham had considered the morality of bringing about the resignation of the revolutionary leaders who were members of the provisional government so that the Queen might possibly behead them; perhaps he did not entertain this possibility at all.

Olney thought that he had restrained the Administration from making a serious error, but in fact Gresham persevered with his ill-fated plan. He reported his conclusions officially to Cleveland on October 18, and on the same day, with the President's concurrence, sent instructions to Albert S. Willis, who had succeeded Blount as the American representative in Hawaii. Willis was to express regret for the conduct of Minister Stevens, to tell the Queen that the United States would do her justice, and to exact from her a promise of amnesty for the revolutionists. The provisional government would then be requested "to abide by the President's decision," that is, to resign in favor of the Queen. The Queen refused to promise an amnesty until it was too late; naturally the provisional government declined to relinquish its power at the request of the American President.[20]

Cleveland admitted that his plans were blocked, and on December 18, 1893, he submitted the whole question and correspondence "to the broader authority and discretion of Congress," whatever that meant. In his December message, Cleveland declared that he had withdrawn the treaty because he

19. Olney to Gresham, Oct. 9, 1893. Henry James, *Richard Olney and His Public Service* (Boston and New York, Houghton Mifflin, 1923), pp. 212–16.

20. *Foreign Relations, 1894*, pp. 459–64, 1189, 1270–73, 1276–82.

believed that the American "mission" precluded the annexation of the islands. This put an end to any possibility of annexing the Hawaiian islands during Cleveland's Administration. The debates which followed were therefore largely
confined to mutual defense and vilification. The unseemly,
partisan mudslinging has been well reviewed by Julius Pratt
in his *Expansionists of 1898* and need not be discussed in detail here. The President's restoration plan was repudiated by
resolutions in the House on February 7, 1894, and in the
Senate on May 31. Congress endorsed nonintervention in
Hawaii and, for the moment, nonannexation of the islands.
Cleveland gave the coup de grace to his own policy of intervention to restore the Queen on July 5, 1894, when he grace-
fully recognized the government of the Hawaiian Republic.[21]

At the close of a year of disappointment and abuse, the
President had admitted to Congress his failure to resolve the
Hawaiian question. He adopted a righteous and slightly hurt
attitude in abdicating to the legislature his initiative in diplomacy. He announced that, unless he misunderstood the character of his government and the conscience of the people,
"national honesty" precluded a "desire for territorial extension"; he then proceeded to accuse the Harrison Administration of fraud. Cleveland left his hearers with the impression
that he thought his failure was due to the "wrong" perpetrated
by the Republicans and the "public misrepresentations." They
were so heinous that "Executive mediation" was powerless to
right the situation. The President's bland and somewhat self-
righteous assumption that the restoration of the Hawaiian
Queen was the only course consistent with international morality and American honor deserves scrutiny.

21. Richardson, *Messages and Papers*, 9, 460–72. Pratt, *Expansionists
of 1898*, pp. 171–87.

Cleveland appears not to have thought of such a plan; Gresham only discovered it in September or October.[22] He had told two Hawaiian representatives in the previous April that he had no intention of reinstating the Queen.[23] If, as Cleveland and Gresham later maintained, they had immediately suspected foul play, it is remarkable that the idea of restoring the Queen was not considered seriously until the autumn. This suggests that Gresham, as well as Cleveland, had been considering other plans. What if Blount's investigation confirmed the claims of the Hawaiian commissioners that annexation was the wish of the Hawaiian people? Cleveland and Gresham knew that annexation would be popular, and Cleveland, at least, had been willing to establish American control over the islands in March 1893. Whatever policy the Administration finally adopted, annexation or protectorate, it would have been shaped so as to identify it with the Democrats. When it became certain that the pre-annexation revolution in Hawaii had been effected through the collusion of American officials, the Administration evolved a plan, once rejected, that was in every way the antithesis of Republican policy. Withdrawal of the treaty was a slap in the face of the Republicans; to denounce annexation as fraudulent and to restore the Queen was tantamount to calling Harrison and his advisers international brigands. Neither Cleveland nor Gresham was willing to carry out this policy quietly and without recrimination. Gresham's letter to the President and instruction to Willis on October 18 and Cleveland's message two months later were both packed with gratuitous insults to Foster and Stevens and contained thinly veiled reflections on Harrison. Commented the Republicans—and with justification—"The

22. Olney first heard of the plan at a Cabinet meeting early in October 1893. James, *Richard Olney*, p. 85.
23. Smith to Dole, April 6, 1893; Carter to Dole, April 17, 1893. Spaulding MSS, cited by Pratt, *Expansionists of 1898*, p. 138.

Administration had blackguarded the foreign policy of its predecessor before the world." [24]

It was Cleveland and Gresham who made Hawaiian annexation the violently partisan issue it was after December 1893. The Republicans were forced to defend their last President, his advisers, and their party. Even Minister Stevens, whom few seriously believed to be innocent of conspiracy, became "patriotic" and "truthful," in the words of Republican Senator Frye of Maine.[25]

The unseemly and profitless debate wore on for years. It, more than any other factor, caused the Republican party to become identified with expansionism. A curious by-product of the partisanship and debate was that Cleveland was forced to adopt his uncritical and unhistorical policy of denouncing all annexation—a position far indeed from his considered statement to Schurz in March 1893. Whether one judges it from the political or the diplomatic point of view, Cleveland's and Gresham's handling of the Hawaiian question was maladroit.

The public reaction in early November 1893 to the publication of the Blount report and to Gresham's advice that the Queen of Hawaii should be restored must have convinced the Secretary of State that his Hawaiian policy was highly unpopular. The thoughtful people who approved of it were a minority—even if a distinguished one. Gresham comforted himself with the hope that the American people would, in time, come around to his point of view. He wrote to Carl Schurz: "I have enough confidence in the patriotism and intelligence of the American people to feel that they will support the position taken." [26] Meanwhile Cleveland's Administration, already

24. James, *Richard Olney*, p. 94.
25. *Congressional Record*, 53d Cong., 2d sess. (Dec. 13, 1893), 26, 190 ff.
26. Gresham to Schurz, Sept. 23, 1893. Gresham MSS.

beset by domestic troubles, had to face the charge that its foreign policy was cowardly and weak. "Oh for one day of Blaine," sighed the Republican press. But Cleveland was moved neither by these outbursts nor by the growing disarray within his party. Ignoring all counterindications, he nailed his standard to the cause of repealing the Sherman Silver Purchase Act as a cure for the business depression. On October 30, 1893, the Senate finally repealed the act. Cleveland now confidently expected that his diagnosis of America's economic ills would be vindicated before the three and one-half years left to his Administration had elapsed. With the return of prosperity, the Populists and Silver Democrats would be vanquished. He therefore felt that there was no need to add a popular foreign stand to his general program. He fully endorsed Gresham's policy, which he believed to be founded on principles of honor and justice. Gresham, on the other hand, appears to have felt some misgivings. This provides one explanation for his active Latin American policy, begun in the autumn of 1893. He may well have sensed the danger of allowing to go on unchecked the impression that the Administration was pursuing a weak foreign policy. This would prove damaging not only at home but also abroad, as it might encourage other nations to follow adventurous policies in the Western Hemisphere. There was no need to look for trouble in South America, where political conditions were perennially unsettled. Ever since Chile's success during the War of the Pacific, Chile's neighbors anxiously watched her growth of power; Colombia and Costa Rica were involved in a boundary dispute; tension between Nicaragua and Honduras flared into open hostilities in January 1894, and the Nicaraguans had meanwhile been attempting to abrogate the self-government treaties assured to the Mosquito Indians, treaties for whose observance England had made herself responsible. An insurrection broke out in Brazil in September 1893, and it was widely believed that the insurgents planned to restore the monarchy. Seen within this context, the old quarrel between England and Venezuela over the Guiana frontier was one among several problems, any of which might lead to serious complications with the European powers. The Venezuelan question certainly did *not* appear to be the most urgent of Gresham's problems as he grappled with the affairs of Colombia, Brazil, and Nicaragua.

The Secretary of State had inherited a substantial Latin American policy from Blaine. Gresham began by intervening in the frontier dispute between Colombia and Costa Rica, which the Colombians resented. The Colombian government negotiated directly with the Costa Rican government without reference to the United States legation in Bogota, although it ostensibly accepted Gresham's offer of his good offices. The United States Minister McKinney thereupon warned Gresham, "there is a good deal of prejudice among a large class of people in Colombia against the United States." The remedy he suggested was to keep a gunboat within easy reach of the isthmus to protect American interests in case of a revolution: "I am not writing this under excitement, but after a full and thorough investigation of the condition and feelings of the people." [27] Gresham, however, had his way, and the dispute was referred to arbitration in Washington. Even so, the unsettled state of affairs on the isthmus and the financial collapse of the New Panama Canal Company remained matters of grave concern to the United States. The control of the future canal was a question that for decades had been recognized as vital to the United States.

In his dealings with Brazil, Gresham achieved spectacular

27. McKinney to Gresham, Jan. 12 and April 2, 1894. U.S. Department of State, *Colombia*, National Archives, Washington, D.C.

success. A revolt led by the Brazilian Navy had broken out in September 1893. It laid siege to the harbor of Rio de Janeiro, threatening to disrupt all foreign trade. American, English, French, and German merchants called upon their respective governments to intervene. American trade with Brazil was certainly not inconsiderable, and Gresham no doubt wished to protect it, but the possibility of European interference was even more disturbing to him. England, he wrote to Ambassador Bayard in December 1893, would need to be watched in case its government were disposed first to recognize the insurgents as belligerents and then to aid them. Gresham concluded: "The consistent views of the Government of the United States touching non-intervention of the powers of Europe in the domestic questions of the American hemisphere have become well known abroad, and are firmly noted here." [28] By taking the lead in Rio de Janeiro, Gresham forestalled any possibility of European intervention. He refused to treat the insurgent naval commanders as anything but pirates; the American squadron under the command of Admiral Benham was reinforced until it became the strongest in the harbor. In January 1894 the insurgent Brazilian admiral fired a blank shell across the bow of an American merchantman seeking to unload its cargo, a warning to which the escorting American warship retaliated by firing a real shell into the side of the Brazilian vessel. The revolt collapsed a few weeks later. Gresham's policy had undoubtedly contributed to its failure.

Of course Gresham realized that he could not deal in such a cavalier fashion with the dispute between Nicaragua and England over the status of the Mosquito Indians. The British case was based on an arbitral award handed down by the

28. Gresham to Bayard, Dec. 18, 1893. U.S. Department of State, *Instructions, Great Britain,* National Archives, Washington, D.C. See also Walter Lafeber, "American Depression Diplomacy and the Brazilian Revolution, 1893–1894," *Hispanic American Historical Review,* 40 (1960), whose conclusions somewhat differ in emphasis from ours.

Emperor of Austria in 1881. While the award recognized the sovereignty of Nicaragua over the Mosquito Reservation, it also guaranteed the right of self-government to the Mosquito Indians. As an act of defiance, President Zelaya attempted to establish Nicaraguan control over the area in November 1893. When hostilities broke out between Nicaragua and Honduras two months later, Zelaya utilized the situation to send his troops into the reservation, declare martial law, and depose the Indian authorities. Thereupon, Great Britain and the United States each ordered a warship to Bluefields. Unhappily, the American ship sank on the way. (A fine commentary on the state of the United States Navy.) The British Consul at Bluefields was consequently able to have things his own way. At his request, British sailors were landed on March 2, 1894. The Nicaraguans were obliged to withdraw their troops and a British–Nicaraguan administration was set up. Gresham strongly mistrusted Britain's motives; his reaction was vigorous. He instructed Bayard in London to insist on the maintenance of Nicaraguan sovereignty over the reservation. Fortunately for the United States, the British government was at this critical time faced with grave international difficulties in Siam, Africa, and Turkey. As Bayard quite rightly commented, a quarrel with the United States was the last thing the British government desired just then. Accordingly, Foreign Secretary Kimberley's language to Bayard was sweet reasonableness. When the Mosquito Indians revolted against the provisional administration in July 1894, the Americans took charge of the situation by landing sailors from a warship hastily ordered to Bluefields. By autumn, Gresham had induced the British to abandon their claims and to recognize unrestricted Nicaraguan sovereignty over the reservation. This, for a time, satisfactorily settled the question from the American standpoint.[29]

29. Tansill, *Bayard*, pp. 665 ff.

Considering Gresham's active Latin American policy, one should not be surprised by the fact that the Secretary of State also began to look into the Venezuelan boundary dispute. In doing so he certainly did not anticipate that the United States would become involved in diplomatic differences that could not be settled.

The Venezuelans had appealed to successive American administrations for help, but with little success. Blaine had contemplated a more positive American involvement in the autumn of 1891, but he did not pursue such a policy. Venezuelan hopes were raised two years later by Gresham, when the Secretary asked for information about the boundary dispute in October 1893. The Venezuelan legation hastily sent him a memorandum. But Gresham did not treat the matter with any urgency, for he only vaguely assured the Venezuelans that he recognized it was "for the general interests of the United States to take some steps in the matter."[30] He did nothing more for another eight months. Even then, he followed the time-honored American policy of advising the disputants to resume diplomatic relations (broken off in 1887) and urging both sides to negotiate an agreement that would refer their differences to arbitration. The President, Gresham instructed Bayard on July 13, 1894, was "inspired by a desire for a peaceable and honorable adjustment of the existing difficulties between an American state and a powerful transatlantic nation." Gresham, however, left it entirely to the anglophile Bayard in London to do what he could, whenever he considered it opportune, to further the case of amicable adjustment.[31]

No wonder the Venezuelans remained dissatisfied with America's attitude. Their civil war of 1892 had brought Gen-

30. Gresham to Haselton, Nov. 15, 1893. U.S. Department of State, *Venezuela,* National Archives, Washington, D.C.
31. Gresham to Bayard, July 13, 1894. Tansill, *Bayard,* p. 663.

eral Joachim Crespo to power, and the foreign affairs of the country came under the control of Dr. P. Ezequiel Rojas, a man of rare ability. To supplement their entreaties to the State Department, appeals that had proved so ineffectual, Crespo and Rojas decided to attempt to bring the pressure of the American public and congressional opinion to bear on the Executive. For this purpose they retained the services of a William Lindsay Scruggs. In October 1894, Scruggs published and distributed his philippic, entitled *British Aggressions in Venezuela, the Monroe Doctrine on Trial.* Scruggs' campaign to arouse the American people, already stimulated by the events in Nicaragua, soon bore rich dividends. Newspapers all over the country began devoting attention to Britain's supposed designs and to the Monroe Doctrine.

During the fall and winter of 1894, Gresham, his State Department aides in Washington, and Bayard in London did their best to keep the lid on the situation; if it had not yet begun to boil over it was at least starting to simmer. To pursue a strong policy in Latin America was one thing, but it was quite another to plunge headlong into a complicated dispute involving a great European power. The evidence we possess suggests that Gresham attempted to resist the rising tide of American bellicosity during these months.

Gresham's Latin American policy now became more circumspect than it had been a year earlier. He refused an appeal on the part of Uruguay to help maintain its neutrality and independence, if, as its foreign minister feared, that country should become the first victim of a conflagration involving Chile, the Argentine, and Brazil.[32] Relations with Colombia improved, although Gresham's reluctance to assert too overtly

32. Stuart to Gresham, Jan. 25, 1895; Gresham to Stuart, April 10, 1895; Secretary Day also rejected the same appeal in 1898, Day to Finch, July 14, 1898. U.S. Department of State, *Uruguay,* National Archives, Washington, D.C.

the interests of the United States in Panama provoked Admiral Meade, in command of the North Atlantic Station, to advocate occupation of the isthmus: "The only way to protect this transit, if protect it we must, is to do as I advise—at the next revolution, seize it and send two regiments of coloured troops to hold each end of it—with a ship of war at convenient reserve to add to the security of our possession." [33] Nicaragua, too, discovered that the United States could not be counted upon—in all circumstances—to support their country against a European power. In this particular instance, the Nicaraguans were resisting British demands to pay compensation for imprisoning and expelling the British Consul from Bluefields. Gresham advised the Nicaraguans to pay. They did not pay at once, so in April 1895 the Royal Navy landed some armed sailors. When the Nicaraguans agreed to pay compensation in May, the forces were withdrawn. Gresham's reticent and legalistic approach to these questions was sharply criticized by the newspapers. European gunboat diplomacy offended the sensibilities of the American people, who considered such behavior irreconcilable with the Monroe Doctrine. American gunboat diplomacy was acceptable as being in the interests of hemispheric peace and prosperity. Gresham, on the other hand, had become cautious of Latin American politics. For all its pains on their behalf, the United States appeared to be heartily disliked by its sister republics. And so it was with considerable caution that Gresham took up the Venezuelan question.[34]

The Secretary of State was certainly suspicious of British diplomacy. He was even more skeptical of the good faith of the Venezuelan government, whose policy toward the United States for years had been, despite appeals for American help, anything but friendly. If America intervened, it would not be

33. Admiral Meade to Secretary of Navy, April 19, 1895. U.S. Navy Department, R.G. 45, area 8, National Archives, Washington, D.C.
34. Tansill, *Bayard*, pp. 664–65.

for the sake of Venezuela, but in order to sustain the interests of the United States. Gresham did not welcome the prospect of quarreling with England, but he was afraid that Britain's obduracy might force his hand. Instructions to Bayard remained nevertheless extraordinarily mild in tone. On December 1, 1894, he once more urged arbitration and placed on record the Administration's wish that an honorable settlement might be reached; but as far as American interposition was concerned, he merely requested Bayard to exert his influence discreetly to secure such a solution. By the end of March 1895, however, he privately warned Bayard—more in sorrow than in anger—that Britain's attitude was "contradictory and palpably unjust" and that if it were maintained the United States government would be bound to "call a halt." His official instructions to Bayard, however, remained temperate.[35] He continued to press for a resumption of diplomatic relations between England and Venezuela as a necessary preliminary to any form of American intervention.

Dr. Rojas understood the implication perfectly; Gresham insisted that the two principals in the dispute were Venezuela and Great Britain—not the United States and Great Britain. But Rojas saw no hope of Venezuela gaining any advantage from negotiations conducted directly between Venezuela and England. He therefore decided to wait until the success of Scruggs' efforts might oblige the President to adopt a more friendly policy toward Venezuela.

Pressure on the State Department to alter its judicious Venezuelan policy was mounting during the spring of 1895. To Gresham's intense irritation, Scruggs' campaign to mobilize

35. Walter Lafeber, "The Background of Cleveland's Venezuelan Policy: A Reinterpretation," *American Historical Review*, 66 (1961), 947–67. Professor Lafeber argues, "there are good reasons to believe that Gresham's note would have been nearly as blunt and boastful," as Olney's, but the authors are not entirely convinced of this.

Congress and the press on Venezuela's behalf was succeeding all too well, and Gresham knew that Scruggs was largely responsible for the change in American opinion. He received Scruggs coldly in February, and speaking to Andrade, the Venezuelan Minister, some weeks later, the Secretary of State bitterly complained about the activities of the Venezuelan legation in Washington: "We were aware of the efforts which his Government and certain Americans here had made to manufacture a sentiment through the American press which would force this administration to espouse Venezuela's side of the controversy: that Mr. Scruggs, our late Minister to Venezuela, and now employed by his legation here, had been exerting himself in that line." But Gresham warned Andrade that such pressure carried no weight with him. "The controversy was one between Venezuela and Great Britain . . . we sustained no such relation to his Government as made it our duty to take its place in the dispute"; American policy "would depend upon future developments." [36] A week after he recounted this conversation to Bayard, Gresham fell mortally ill and became incapable of shaping American diplomacy any more. President Cleveland, however, had been taking a personal interest in the Venezuelan question some weeks before Gresham's death. It was William Lindsay Scruggs who persuaded the President to adopt a more forceful attitude.

36. Gresham to Bayard, April 23, 1895. Tansill, *Bayard,* pp. 695–96.

Chapter Five

The Diplomat as Propagandist:

William Lindsay Scruggs,

Agent for Venezuela

A HANDFUL OF United States diplomats played a large and still controversial role in the shaping of American foreign policy during the last two decades of the nineteenth century. Paradoxically, these influential posts were not always missions to the great world powers. Until the eve of the Spanish–American War, the dispatches sent home from Paris, Berlin, Vienna, and Rome make dull reading for the most part. The United States stayed aloof from the international controversies of the 1890s—the rivalries in the Balkans, in Africa, and in the Middle East. American politicians showed little interest in either the Triple Alliance of Germany, Italy, and Austria or the Dual Alliance of France and Russia. American diplomats in Europe avoided discussing in their reports home practically every major question of international diplomacy; ostrichlike they avoided even an intellectual entanglement with the Old World. Their dispatches were instead confined to reporting the progress made in negotiations of specific American interests, which were largely economic.

At a time when the Anglo–French conflict in Siam posed the threat of war, the American minister devoted his dispatches to the prospects of increasing the export of American pork. The American ambassador in Berlin sent home a long dispatch on the subject of the German prohibition of the importation of American beef cattle on May 9, 1896; he ignored the Kaiser's Kruger Telegram. By way of contrast, in St. Petersburg both Andrew White and his successor, Clifton R. Breckinridge, took an intelligent interest in Russian foreign policy, and, more especially, in Russia's ambitions in the Far East. Only in London, however, was the United States consistently well served. But the influence of men such as Thomas Francis Bayard, John Hay, Henry White, Andrew White, and Clifton Breckinridge on the general course of American foreign policy was small. The diplomats who most affected the conduct of policy generally served in minor missions. In the early 1890s, Valparaiso and Honolulu figured more in American diplomacy than Berlin and Vienna. Santo Domingo was more important to the State Department than the whole continent of Africa. Diplomats were most influential in these regions of special interest to the United States. That accounts for the significance of Patrick Egan in Chile, of John L. Stevens in Hawaii, of Charles Denby in Peking, and of William Lindsay Scruggs in Caracas. No one would claim that either Egan, Stevens, or Scruggs conformed to the popular notion of the ideal diplomat. They nevertheless proved themselves highly effective diplomats—indeed, in some respects too effective.

They did not hesitate to exceed their function, nor were they content to act as mere ears and mouthpiece of the State Department. These men pursued their own policies and objectives with extraordinary self-confidence; they stirred up public debate on issues of foreign policy; they obliged the Executive to formulate precise policies; they fervently believed in the need for change. In a decade of internal political strife, they helped sustain a concern for America's foreign relations that was rarely equaled in intensity during the following four decades.

Although historians have paid little attention to William Lindsay Scruggs, his impact on American foreign policy was at least equal to if not greater than that of Egan and Stevens. The full story of Scruggs' labors as a diplomat, propagandist, and employee of the Venezuelan government throws new light on the origins of the Venezuelan crisis and provides an extraordinary commentary on the formation of America's foreign policy in the mid-1890s.

Scruggs was born in 1836 on a plantation near Knoxville, Tennessee.[1] There are few remarkable facts to be recorded about the first 56 years of his life. Knoxville, where he grew up, was strongly Unionist in sentiment, and Scruggs accordingly gravitated toward the Republican party. During the Civil War he moved to Georgia. He was admitted to the local bar, but instead of practicing law he accepted the editorship of the Columbus *Daily Sun* in 1861. In the following year he made his home in Atlanta and founded a newspaper, the *New Era,* which was later to win fame under its new name, the Atlanta *Constitution.* Scruggs utilized this early training in law and journalism to the full in his diplomatic career. During the years following the Civil War, he supported moderate Republican policies designed to reconstruct the South and heal the breach with the North. His ability and service to the Republican party were duly recognized in 1872 when he was rewarded with an appointment as Minister to Colombia. He spent the greater part of the next twenty years in the diplomatic service, twice as Minister to Colombia, as Consul General in Canton, and finally, from 1889 until 1893, as Minister to

1. There are no adequate studies of William Lindsay Scruggs, since his private papers have not hitherto been used. For some details of his career and early life, see T. D. Jervey, "William Lindsay Scruggs: A Forgotten Diplomat," *South Atlantic Quarterly,* 27 (1928), 292–309; the brief entry in the *Dictionary of American Biography* is largely based on this article.

Venezuela. His knowledge of South American affairs and his earlier success as arbitrator in a British claim against Colombia predisposed Harrison and Blaine in his favor when, in 1889, they chose Scruggs for the Venezuelan mission. The disputed frontier between Venezuela and British Guiana had already invested the post at Caracas with international importance, and Scruggs was regarded as something of an expert on Latin American boundary questions.

Scruggs' subsequent advocacy of Venezuelan claims might lead one to suppose that his sympathies had been aroused when he was in Caracas, but Venezuelan politicians would have received a rude shock from reading his comments on Venezuelan domestic affairs. During Scruggs' tenure, Venezuela was plunged into civil war by the bitter struggle for power between rivals for the presidency. The United States Minister had nothing good to say about either Venezuelan politician. It appeared that each side was trying to establish a dictatorship and suppress political liberty. "There has not been an honest and clean administration of government in Venezuela for thirty years," he confidentially wrote to the Secretary of State in June 1892; "Guzman, Crespo, Paul and Andueza each, in turn, plundered the public treasury, and common honesty had no existence among the subordinates either. The moral sense of the country seems hopelessly debauched." Of the Venezuelan President (who later commissioned Scruggs as his special agent and legal adviser), he wrote: "Crespo is a half educated mulatto, but a man of military genius and large political following." [2] At no time while in Caracas did Scruggs press the State Department toward a policy of siding with Venezuela against Britain in the boundary dispute.

2. From Scruggs, separate and confidential, June 28, 1892. U.S. Department of State, *Venezuela,* National Archives, Washington, D.C.

American interest in the Guiana boundary was certainly not stimulated by sympathy for Venezuela. Indeed relations between the United States and Venezuela worsened during the years when the United States was cautiously moving toward a policy of intervention in the Anglo–Venezuelan dispute. There were two principal reasons for this: private American citizens claiming compensation from the Venezuelan government for injustices suffered—often decades earlier—had been a constant irritation. The pressure of the United States ministers on behalf of such American claimants exacerbated the relations between the United States and most of Latin America. More fundamental was the fear engendered by Blaine's vigorous policy of increasing American influence. Venezuela felt threatened by Blaine's demand to reduce import duties on American goods and sign a reciprocity treaty. A Venezuelan refusal to comply, it was made clear, would lead to the imposition of high duties on Venezuelan exports to the United States.

To Scruggs fell the thankless and difficult task of implementing such policies as he pressed the claim of an American concern, the Venezuela Steam Transportation Company, in the so-called "Hancox Case."[3] Some twenty years earlier, three ships belonging to the firm had been impounded by the Venezuelan government. Blaine now demanded that the Venezuelans consent to arbitration of the case, but Scruggs met with no success in his efforts to settle the matter.

Scruggs also attempted for more than two years to negotiate a reciprocity treaty.[4] On the face of it, the position of the United States was strong. It was the best customer for coffee,

3. See esp. Blaine to Scruggs, May 20, 1890. U.S. Department of State, *Venezuela.*

4. Blaine to Scruggs, Dec. 22, 1890; Wharton to Scruggs, July 25, 1891; Blaine to Scruggs, Jan. 2 and 12, 1892. U.S. Department of State, *Venezuela.*

Venezuela's principal export. Indeed, during the year 1888–89, the value of Venezuela's exports to the United States was greater than its exports to the rest of the world combined.[5] Blaine therefore found it all the more galling that American exports to Venezuela amounted in value to less than half the American imports from Venezuela; they appreciably lagged behind Britain's. The Venezuelans met Scruggs' pressure with procrastination. By the summer of 1892, the outbreak of civil war in Venezuela made further negotiations useless. Scruggs reported that the President and the Venezuelan people were opposed to reciprocity; in any case they simply did not believe that American duties would ever be levied on coffee.[6] Nevertheless he made one interesting bid to get both disputes out of the way.

For all their fear and dislike of American policy, successive Venezuelan administrations were always ready to seek American help in persuading the British to adjust the Guiana boundary in a manner favorable to Venezuela. In the autumn of 1891, Blaine was ready to contemplate a diplomatic intervention—though only on terms, as it turned out, entirely unacceptable to Venezuela. He confidentially informed Scruggs of this possible change of attitude.[7] Scruggs used this knowledge in an interview with the President of Venezuela in November 1891 and suggested that if the differences between Venezuela and the United States could be resolved, the United States would be ready to change her policy on the Guiana boundary dispute. He later reported to Blaine:

I pointed out the inconsistency and possible futility of any advanced and decisive step by the United States in the mat-

5. For a statistical analysis of Venezuelan imports and exports 1888–89: from Scruggs, March 3, 1891. U.S. Department of State, *Venezuela.*
6. From Scruggs, June 3, 13, 27, 1891; Jan. 27, 1892. U.S. Department of State, *Venezuela.*
7. Blaine to Scruggs, confidential, Oct. 28, 1891. U.S. Department of State, *Venezuela.*

ter of the Guayana boundary dispute, as requested by Venezuela, so long as grave differences between the two Republics remained unadjusted. I intimated, however, that with these differences well out of the way I would then be in a position to pledge the active co-operation of my Government with that of Venezuela to the end that the boundary dispute with Great Britain be promptly adjusted on some just and honorable basis.[8]

The Venezuelans rose to the bait with great caution. In subsequent conversations, the Foreign Minister tried to discover exactly what "advanced and decisive step" the United States had in mind. Scruggs replied that that was a matter for mutual agreement; but he gave his opinion that the British proposal of the frontier made by Lord Aberdeen in 1844 would form a suitable basis for discussions on the boundary. This would have given the Venezuelans far more territory than England was ready to concede half a century later. As soon as Blaine heard this, he rebuked Scruggs for exceeding his instructions.[9] Blaine was not ready to tie his policy in advance to any particular boundary and so wrongly give the impression that America had sided with Venezuela. In any event, the prospect of reciprocity was so repugnant to the Venezuelans that they allowed the discussions that Scruggs had initiated to peter out.

Scruggs' elaboration of instructions probably was not motivated by a desire to support the Venezuelan boundary claims but rather by his wish to settle the "Hancox Case" and secure the reciprocity treaty. The technique of letting United States help depend on Venezuela's acceding to demands having nothing to do with the boundary seems to have occurred to Scruggs rather than to Blaine. Scruggs would certainly have denied that

8. From Scruggs, Nov. 21, 1891. U.S. Department of State, *Venezuela.*
9. From Scruggs, Dec. 5, 1891; Blaine to Scruggs, Jan. 21, 1892. U.S. Department of State, *Venezuela.*

the proposal was a quid pro quo, and though he was reproved, Scruggs was not recalled.

His downfall came about in a curious way a year later. Scruggs was involved in a dubious transaction of a kind not unusual in Latin American politics: he had taken up a private American claim against the Venezuelan government, the so-called "Seixas Case." Unlike the "Hancox Case," the Seixas claim for $50,000 was not well founded; Blaine was therefore not prepared to press it. The claimants, however, took active steps to secure a large sum from the Venezuelan government; they retained Gilbert R. Hawes, a New York attorney, and another attorney in Venezuela to pursue it. Although Scruggs had merely been instructed to use his good offices discreetly, he suggested to Hawes that power of attorney be transferred from the Venezuelan lawyer to himself. It was further agreed that Hawes would accept on behalf of his clients a settlement of $10,500 and that Scruggs and the former Venezuelan attorney should pay themselves "out of the balance." Scruggs announced to Hawes on April 29, 1892, that he had secured settlement, that the sum agreed upon would be transmitted to New York, and that he had not paid himself anything. But when Hawes discovered that the claim had been settled for $25,000 he demanded the balance. Scruggs replied that his client was lucky to get any money, since the claim had been dubious. Hawes thereupon sent copies of his correspondence with Scruggs to Secretary of State Foster.[10] This placed Scruggs in an extremely delicate position. He now had to explain what he had done with the balance of $14,500. The Venezuelan lawyer had not been paid so large a sum. Scruggs revealed to the State Department that most of the balance had been paid as a bribe to the Venezuelan President, Dr. Andueza

10. See esp. Hawes to Scruggs, July 22, 1892; Scruggs to Hawes, Aug. 9, 1892. U.S. Department of State, *Venezuela*.

Palacio. He protested moreover that not a penny had found its way into his own pocket and that "such transactions have been the rule rather than the exception here for two years." [11]

Secretary Foster was shocked. After consulting the President he decided that Scruggs should be dismissed. On November 12, 1892, he instructed Scruggs to return to the United States. The facts, he wrote, had been laid before the President. "I am directed by him to say that such conduct on your part, involving the bribery of the President of the country to which you are accredited, is unworthy of a diplomatic representative of the United States and he cannot consent that you should continue to exercise the duties of your office." [12] Scruggs was to depart from Caracas at once and was granted a one-month leave of absence on the understanding that he would hand in his resignation when that time was up.

So ended Scruggs' career as an American diplomat. A year later he accepted an appointment from the government to which he had so recently been accredited. In Venezuelan employ, Scruggs secured for himself a sure place in the history of American foreign relations—an achievement which had eluded him in almost twenty years of service. Scruggs had, of course, until very recently been privy to the secrets and confidences of his own country. Yet the propriety of a former American diplomat's placing his knowledge at the disposal of another country seems to have caused concern to no one, least of all to Scruggs himself. Perhaps the State Department had long before de-

11. From Scruggs, confidential, Aug. 9, 1892. U.S. Department of State, *Venezuela.*

12. Foster to Scruggs, Nov. 12, 1892. U.S. Department of State, *Venezuela.* Scruggs later vainly appealed to Foster to remove the correspondence from the State Department files, but Foster declined, writing, "it does not lie within my discretion to mutilate an official record." Foster to Scruggs (addressed to Atlanta, Georgia) Feb. 4, 1893. U.S. Department of State, *Venezuela.* The secret of his dismissal was nevertheless well kept down to the present day.

spaired of preserving its secrets; it was fortunate for the conduct of American foreign policy that others did not follow Scruggs' example. The Venezuelans, for their part, were lucky to have obtained the help of the one man in a unique position to know exactly how to present their case in America.

Scruggs, as an American citizen, was able to roam the committee rooms of Congress from which an alien official would have been excluded. As a former lawyer, journalist, Republican politician, and diplomat, he was extraordinarily well equipped for his new occupation of lobbyist. He understood how to rouse American public opinion on behalf of Venezuela and move the American political machine to action. His acquaintance with the intricacies of the boundary dispute was of no great import to the Venezuelans; Scruggs had never sent any enlightening dispatches to the United States on the matter when he was Minister in Caracas. At no time did he appear to take an interest in the boundary question for its own sake. But any deficiency in this respect was made good by the Venezuelan Foreign Minister, who, through Dr. Andrade, the Minister in Washington, supplied Scruggs with all the information needed to support the case. It would certainly be a mistake either to conclude from Scruggs' activities that he was solely moved by a passionate desire to redress a wrong or to suppose that he apprehended a real danger to the United States. The Venezuelan Government paid him the handsome retainer of $227 a month. And they got good value for it, a fact which the Venezuelan Foreign Minister generously acknowledged by doubling Scruggs' stipend a year later.[13]

13. Scruggs kept three volumes of a journal containing copies of his correspondence, his comments on it, and press cuttings. They are denoted here as Scruggs MSS I, II, and III. Rojas to Scruggs, June 18, 1894, Scruggs MSS I. They were in the private possession of the family when the research was undertaken.

Scruggs deserves far more credit for focusing the attention of newspapers and Congress on the Anglo–Venezuelan dispute than has so far been given him. The debate accompanying the buildup of a fighting fleet, the need preached by Mahan for the United States to make herself strategically secure in the Pacific and the Caribbean, the Chilean embroglio, the controversy over American relations with Hawaii, and latent suspicion of British policy—all produced an explosive climate of opinion in Congress and in the editorial offices of the newspapers. Scruggs was not responsible for this general feeling; his genius lay in the ability to direct, channel, and exploit it into a powerful movement that would ultimately demand intervention in the Anglo–Venezuelan dispute to preserve vital American interests. An issue that the State Department had handled cautiously and discreetly for a decade thus became a national question of high importance for the Administration. Scruggs achieved more in a few months than the Venezuelan ministers in Washington, working through more orthodox channels, had been able to effect over a period of years.

Ezequiel Rojas, the Venezuelan Foreign Minister, conceived the campaign; early in August 1894 he instructed Scruggs to cultivate good relations with the press, Congress, and the political leaders of both parties. Scruggs was to emphasize that no mere boundary was in dispute, but a question of deep significance, the defense of the South American continent from European encroachment.[14]

Scruggs began his labors by preparing a statement of Venezuela's case for submission to the Senate Foreign Relations Committee. He then went to Washington to confer with Andrade and "informally but confidentially with one or two of the Cabinet ministers with whom I am in social relations." [15]

14. Rojas to Scruggs, June 18 and Aug. 10, 1894. Scruggs MSS I.
15. Scruggs to Rojas, June 30, Aug. 28, 1894. Scruggs MSS I.

Scruggs expanded his statement of Venezuela's case into the famous pamphlet *British Aggressions in Venezuela, the Monroe Doctrine on Trial.* Andrade had contributed the historical information and Scruggs the polemic. The pamphlet was printed in Atlanta and was ready for its educational role in October 1894. With Andrade's assistance, Scruggs embarked upon an immense propagandist venture: he sent copies of his pamphlet to the President, to the Cabinet, to senators and representatives, to the leading newspapers and learned journals, and to all the Venezuelan diplomatic representatives abroad.[16]

From the date of its publication until the early months of 1896, the pamphlet played a key role in the development of American policy. Scruggs masqueraded as an impartial friend of both parties. The facts of the dispute were taken from the historical account put together by Andrade. This held the field, for the British government denied that American interests were involved and therefore disdained to present its side of the case until the spring of 1896. American opinion was thus formed on incomplete and one-sided evidence.

The pamphlet backed up Venezeula's boundary claims "by an unbroken chain of historical and documentary evidence extending back over a period of more than two centuries." Venezuela's historical title to the land was based on a principle "now universally accepted." Were this not the case, the territorial integrity of nearly all the Latin American republics and "the title of the United States to the territory of many of our present commonwealths, and to more than one-half of our public domain in the northwest" would be destroyed. Scruggs sought to demonstrate that Britain had expanded the territory of her colony Guiana by "aggression" against Venezuela. In this and in her refusal to arbitrate the disputed area, England

16. Andrade to Scruggs, Oct. 23, Nov. 7, 18, and 29, 1894. Scruggs MSS I.

had not only taken advantage of her weaker adversary but also contravened the Monroe Doctrine. A further argument put forward by Scruggs should be particularly noted: England had now pushed her claims to the mouth of the Orinoco river as a step toward the fulfillment of her plan to dominate the trade of the vast region of that river system.

These facts carry their own comment. Studied in connection with any good map of the country, they have a startling significance. The South American continent, by its peculiar configuration, is naturally divided into three immense valleys— the Orinoco, the Amazon, and the Plata. Each of these valleys is, in itself, a complete network of fluviatile navigation, open from the sea to the remote interior. Those of the Guayaquil, Atrato, and Magdalena are of but little consequence in comparison; for the chain of the Andes, extending from Patagonia along the Pacific, and thence eastward along the Caribbean to the Gulf of Paria, constitute a natural barrier to the interior. But there are no mountain chains traversing the continent from east to west; no such barriers to communication between the valleys of the Orinoco, Amazon, and Plata; and those three great rivers communicate by distinct bifurcations. Hence, the dominion of the mouth of either by such a power as England, would, in the course of time, and almost as a natural consequence, open the way to pretensions over the others. . . .

Let it be borne in mind also that the country which is being thus ruthlessly despoiled of its territorial sovereignty is not in some remote and inaccessible corner of the earth with which we neither have, nor hope to have, any very direct political or commercial relations. It is nearest of all our South American neighbors. Its political capital, one of the most beautiful and attractive on the continent, is less than six days' journey from Washington. Its commercial marts, second to none on the Caribbean shores, are directly opposite to ours on the South Atlantic and Gulf coasts, and distant less than five days' sail. Even the harbors and inlets of Guayana and the Orinoco delta are only about five days' sail from New York. It is the only South American republic with which we are in direct and regular weekly communication by an American line of steamships. Its people are among the most intelligent and progressive of all Latin America. And our commerce with it is now about double, in volume and value, our trade with any of the other trans-Caribbean free States. These conditions alone, even if others were wanting, could hardly fail to inspire our sympathy and enlist our active interposition.[17]

How by any stretch of the imagination the Venezuela of 1894, under the dictatorship of Crespo, could be described as progressive, is difficult to understand. The State Department on the basis of Scruggs' earlier dispatches could have harbored few illusions on that score. We cannot question Scruggs' skill as a propagandist, whatever doubts may arise about his sincerity. His purpose was to persuade his fellow countrymen that on moral grounds as well as for reasons of self-interest the United States was bound to intervene in the Anglo–Venezuelan dispute; such intervention should be not merely as a neutral and impartial friend of both sides but as a principal in the controversy.

Scruggs chose a felicitous title for his pamphlet which, in the best tradition of the journalist, packed a punch in nine words. British aggression in Venezuela was coupled with the notion that it placed the Monroe Doctrine on trial; if that doc-

---

17. Scruggs, *British Aggressions in Venezuela, the Monroe Doctrine on Trial,* see esp. pp. 7, 14–15, 24–25, 28–31.

trine were to mean anything in the future, then America must act now. He based his contention on the broadest possible grounds. To the anti-imperialists he held up the maintenance of the Monroe Doctrine as belonging to the conservative tradition of American foreign policy. The jingoes seized on the argument that the United States must stand up to the British in the Western Hemisphere. In consequent congressional debates, the (supposed) British scheme to control the trade of vast areas of Latin America by establishing itself on the mouth of the Orinoco was earnestly stressed. As the British archives now show, this was a red herring. The confrontation of the weak and progressive Venezuela and the powerful British bully, intent on extending its colonial system, finally added a moral flavor which particularly appealed to President Cleveland. Scruggs knew that not one American in ten thousand had even heard of the boundary question. At the time of publication, he had already been busy lobbying in Washington, although with discouraging results. "I have had several conversations with some of our most influential public men on the subject of the boundary dispute, and have been surprised and disappointed at their ignorance and indifference in regard to it," he reported to Rojas. He was confident that he could change all that: "There will have to be a campaign of education . . . [When] the people of this country understand the real issue involved, they will be aroused to a reassertion and maintenance of the Monroe Doctrine of 1823." [18]

In November, Scruggs began to note a distinct change in the tone of the press. An article which a prominent New York magazine had rejected a few weeks earlier was now solicited and paid for. American newspapers throughout the country were becoming interested in the dispute and were beginning to comment approvingly on Scruggs' pamphlet. By December

18. Scruggs to Rojas, Oct. 20, 1894. Scruggs MSS I.

1894, Scruggs found that he could not keep up with the vast number of clippings sent to him by the newspaper bureaus.[19] More significant than the number of lines of newsprint was the fact that the Monroe Doctrine was receiving more publicity than at any time since the Civil War.[20] But much still remained to be done when Congress reconvened that December.

Scruggs was aided in his single-handed campaign of 1894 and 1895 by sentiment in the United States which was becoming receptive to a more active diplomacy. The hesitant policy of mediation gradually began to alter course. In his annual message to Congress, the American President usually referred briefly to foreign relations. Harrison and Cleveland had for several years expressed the hope in the paragraphs devoted to Venezuela that the boundary dispute would be settled amicably. In his message of December 1894, Cleveland transferred the perennial reference to the unsatisfactory state of the boundary dispute from the section on Venezuela to that on Great Britain.[21] Scruggs noted this significant change with satisfaction. It indicated that Cleveland now regarded the British attitude as the obstacle to a settlement and intended to proceed on that assumption.

Historians have generally been at a loss to account for Cleveland's decision to embark on a new policy toward the Anglo–Venezuelan quarrel during the closing months of 1894. The Scruggs papers suggest that American intervention had been imminent for some years; the precipitating agent was public and private sentiment, which Scruggs had so aptly stimulated. Cleveland and Gresham both possessed copies of *Brit-*

19. Scruggs to Rojas, Oct. 20, 1894; notes by Scruggs, Oct. and Dec. 1894. Scruggs MSS I.
20. Dexter Perkins, *The Monroe Doctrine, 1867–1907* (Baltimore, Johns Hopkins Press, 1937), p. 136.
21. Richardson, *Messages and Papers, 8,* 526.

ish Aggressions in Venezuela, and Cleveland had probably read his, possibly Gresham too.[22] The tone of Scruggs' correspondence indicates that he was in communication with the President and the Secretary of State, although he may have found them inattentive. Andrade and Rojas, in any case, assumed that Cleveland's new advocacy of Venezuela's cause was due to Scruggs.

Although Cleveland's message of December 1894 encouraged the Venezuelans, it did not presage immediate action by the United States in Venezuela's behalf. Nor was the American public sufficiently exercised about Venezuela's plight to satisfy Scruggs. In order to repair these two deficiencies, he embarked on the bold course in which he planned to coerce the Executive through Congress.

Scruggs arrived in Washington from Atlanta on January 2, 1895; he was determined to see Cleveland and Gresham. At the Capitol he proceeded tirelessly to canvass members of both Houses, among them Senator Henry Cabot Lodge. He tried to get support for the President's message by the adoption of a joint resolution which would encourage Cleveland by convincing him that a more active American policy was fervently desired by Congress, but Scruggs discovered to his consternation that domestic affairs absorbed members of Congress to the almost total exclusion of foreign policy. America lay in the grip of a deep economic depression; Cleveland had lost the support of Congress; the anti-Administration forces, none more bitter than the Silver Democrats, were charging the President with betrayal. Both houses were divided into numberless factions, the majority hostile to the Administration. "I never saw such indifference, and such demoralization among members," Scruggs noted. The Senators and Representatives he ap-

22. Scruggs note, Jan. 1895. Scruggs MSS I.

proached were sympathetic in varying degrees but none appeared to be ready to do what Scruggs wished.[23] Scruggs' undertaking seemed almost hopeless. In the end, he turned to his own Congressman, Leonidas Livingston of Atlanta.

Livingston was no shining light. He had never played an active role in Congress. He knew little of foreign affairs, and he was no avid reader—he had neither heard of the boundary dispute nor troubled to examine the Scruggs pamphlet. But Scruggs finally overcame Livingston's apathy by alternatively playing on his vanity and bombarding him with information. Livingston agreed to submit a resolution on the Venezuelan boundary to Congress. Scruggs thereupon wrote out the draft of the resolution on a scrap of paper in Livingston's office. It supported the President's appeal, made in his last annual message, that Britain and Venezuela submit their dispute to arbitration. On the following day, Livingston offered the resolution, exactly as Scruggs had written it, to the House. On January 10, 1885, it was referred to the Foreign Affairs Committee.[24]

Scruggs diligently kept track of the resolution throughout its course in Congress. A member of the House Foreign Affairs Committee, Representative Robert R. Hitt of Illinois, confided to Scruggs that a Dr. Suarez was lobbying against him. Scruggs speedily discredited Suarez. He discovered from Andrade that Suarez, a Cuban by birth and a Venezuelan by adoption, was acting out of personal spite. He had been employed by the ousted Venezuelan President, Blanco Guzman, as a special agent in Washington, and he had lost his post under Crespo.[25] More serious was the fortuitous appearance on the scene of an

23. Scruggs note, Dec. 1895. Scruggs MSS I.
24. This account is based on a lengthy note by Scruggs, Feb. 1895. Scruggs MSS I. See also *Congressional Record,* 53d Cong., 3d sess. (Jan. 10, 1895), 27, 837.
25. Scruggs note, Jan. 1895. Scruggs MSS I.

English Member of Parliament, William Randal Cremer, the Secretary of the International Arbitration League, who had brought with him a memorial signed by 356 members of the House of Commons recommending the signature of an Anglo–American arbitration treaty—a laudable objective dear to Cleveland's heart. Scruggs went at once to the hotel where Cremer was staying, but the Englishman was suspicious of lobbyists and found excuses for not receiving Scruggs. This offended Scruggs who, with characteristic petulance, dismissed the bearer of the noble document as a "novice." [26] Nevertheless Scruggs hastened to see Cleveland before Cremer could call at the White House. Evidently Scruggs thought his schemes were endangered by the possibility of a genuine Anglo–American rapprochement.

The first meeting between Scruggs and Cleveland occurred on January 15, 1895. The only account of this important occasion appears in the Scruggs papers, and it is regrettably brief. "The President seemed deeply interested. He said he had already read my Pamphlet, and intended to study the question thoroughly. Before I left him, he requested me to send him one or more extra copies." [27] What Scruggs said to the President about the arbitration treaty does not appear. It is implied, however, that the President wanted another copy of the pamphlet in order to confront the English M.P. with it. The argument Scruggs employed with the President against the conclusion of such a treaty can be deduced from a letter he sent to Cremer, in which he claimed that an Anglo–American arbitration treaty would endanger the maintenance of the Monroe Doctrine and bind the hands of the Administration in any dispute between England and a Latin American state. It was not difficult to attribute to the British a cunning and clever policy.

26. Correspondence with Cremer and note by Scruggs, Jan. 1895. Scruggs MSS I.

27. Scruggs to Cleveland, Jan. 16, 1895, and note. Scruggs MSS I.

The expression "perfidious Albion" had, after all, gained wide currency in Europe and America. When, some days later, the innocuous British M.P. called on the President and appeared before the House Foreign Affairs Committee, he was asked some very awkward questions—as Scruggs noted with glee.

Scruggs meanwhile kept a careful watch on the progress of his joint resolution. He wrote a report on the boundary which accompanied the resolution to committee. He then appeared in person before the committee, and he explained the scope of the resolution and the relevance of the boundary dispute to the Monroe Doctrine. Through Livingston, he engineered the appointment of a subcommittee. The subcommittee then referred the question to Gresham. The Secretary of State saw no objection to the passage of the resolution; Scruggs was once more summoned to appear before the subcommittee and was asked to write its report. The report was adopted by the whole committee and sent, with the resolution, back to the House.[28]

Here again Scruggs provided for every contingency and wrote out a stirring sponsoring speech for Livingston. The Congressman had asked him to write it. Scruggs' speech was printed in the *Congressional Record* as a contribution to the debate on February 6, 1895. The Representative from Atlanta assumed paternity and received the credit. He repeated all the arguments for intervention which the readers of his pamphlet already knew; phrases and sentences were borrowed from the pamphlet. He went over the ground once again—British aggression, the danger to the independence of Latin American republics, the threat to the legal title of sovereignty over land now forming a goodly part of the United States, the Monroe Doctrine, the importance of the Orinoco, and national honor.

28. *House Report*, Feb. 1, 1895, no. 1748, 53d Cong., 3d sess., serial 3345.

No sir, the United States cannot afford to yield this point. There is no longer any territory on the American continent open to occupancy and conquest by European powers . . . There is but one honorable course before us. Come what may, we have no choice but to resolutely maintain our self-respect and our honor and prestige as a nation.[29]

The speech, so one member of the House who had guessed its authorship later told Scruggs, was a "clincher." After little debate and some languid opposition, the resolution was adopted by the House without a dissenting vote.

Scruggs chaperoned his resolution through the Senate with equal care. He had already sounded out a number of influential senators, including Morgan, Walsh, Gordon, and Lodge. On February 13, 1895, the resolution was favorably reported from the Foreign Affairs Committee; it was passed unanimously by the Senate on the same day. This rare unanimity of Congress in supporting the President cannot have failed to make a great impression on Cleveland. The course on which Cleveland was setting out was not only judged by Congress to be the right one but also likely to prove popular. He approved the resolution on February 20.[30] Scruggs later regarded its passage as marking the turning point in American policy. Even making allowances for Scruggs' natural tendency to magnify his contribution, it would be difficult to dispute that conclusion.

Gresham and the State Department were not so easily carried away by Scruggs' oratory. They felt no particular sympathy for the tyrannical Venezuelan government, which was do-

29. *Congressional Record,* 53d Cong., 3d sess. (Feb. 6, 1895), 27, 1832–34. Scruggs note, Feb. 6, 1895. Scruggs MSS I. For another view, see Walter Lafeber, "The Background of Cleveland's Venezuelan Policy: A Reinterpretation," *American Historical Review,* 61 (1961).

30. *Congressional Record,* 53d Cong., 3d sess. (Feb. 13, 16, and 23, 1895), 27, 2113, 2297, 2642.

ing its best to reduce the political and economic influence of the United States in Latin America. Nor did they look forward to the possibility of a serious Anglo–American crisis. Gresham accordingly continued to insist on exploring the possibility of settling the matter by means of direct Anglo–Venezuelan discussions before a more active policy on the part of the United States could be contemplated. To this end, he advised the Venezuelans to resume diplomatic relations with England and to send a minister to the Court of St. James's. On the evening before he left Washington, Scruggs called on Gresham at his apartment in Arlington and found him "tired, fagged out, worried and cross." Scruggs thought that Gresham had not studied the details of the controversy and resented being pushed. Gresham replied that he possessed information that the Venezuelan government had granted concessions to American citizens in the disputed territory apparently in the hope of involving the United States in the controversy; he had done all he could, Gresham added, until diplomatic relations between Venezuela and England were restored. In the midst of their discussion, the President summoned Gresham to the White House. As Scruggs was taking his leave, the Secretary of State petulantly exclaimed: "Damn it, I'm not made of iron, I must have sleep." He then invited Scruggs to call on him in the State Department after the weekend.[31] Scruggs felt that he could expect little from Gresham. As for the State Department, he thought that it would do everything to hinder him.

Scruggs vented his spleen on anyone who placed obstacles in his way. He credited the much respected Alvey Adee, the Assistant Secretary, with launching a campaign against him. During the spring and summer of 1895 the State Department did in fact make an effort to correct Scruggs' gross distortion

31. Scruggs note, Feb. 1895, and a memorandum, Feb. 1895, "The Gordian Knot," submitted to Andrade. Scruggs MSS I.

of the Monroe Doctrine. It printed an authentic text of President Monroe's message and circulated it to the press. The State Department freely handed out to interested newspapermen copies of an article on the nature and limits of the Monroe Doctrine that had appeared in the New York *Evening Post* of May 4, 1895, above the signature of the noted authority on public international law, John Bassett Moore.[32] In all this, Scruggs saw the hand of Adee, whom he depicted in his journal as an "insignificant fellow . . . a foreigner who scarcely speaks the English language, who crept into the service as a sort of clerk many years ago; just how nobody seems to know. He is now Second Assistant Secretary of State! He is a person of limited intelligence, narrow mind, and hypocritical and false in character." [33] Scruggs believed Adee hated him and was attempting to counteract his influence by issuing distorted information to the press. Scruggs excited himself needlessly, since neither Adee nor the State Department exerted any perceptible influence on the formation of American policy in the Venezuelan dispute.

Scruggs had returned to Atlanta in February 1895. He suggested to the Venezuelan Foreign Minister that he follow Gresham's advice: the Venezuelans should offer to resume diplomatic relations as a preliminary to an agreement on arbitration. If England rejected the Venezuelan overtures, then blame for preventing a settlement would fall on England. Rojas did not agree with this analysis. He calculated cynically that any improvement in Anglo–Venezuelan relations would make American intervention less likely. He therefore refused to entertain the resumption of diplomatic relations with England unless the British government first agreed to arbitrate the ex-

32. Scruggs obtained the information from Andrade, who based it on the authority of Seckendorff of the New York *Tribune* that the State Department was distributing Moore's pamphlet.
33. Scruggs to Rojas, March 23, 1895. Scruggs MSS I.

treme Venezuelan claims. He knew, of course, that the British government would not consent to unlimited arbitration merely at the behest of the Venezuelans. Only forceful American intervention might induce the British government to agree to the arbitration of territory they had occupied for close to a century. Instead of approaching England directly (a method which had failed for fifty years), Rojas preferred the oblique method of stirring up the United States to demand of the British government that the dispute be arbitrated. He therefore urged Scruggs to continue his campaign.[34] Scruggs soon found an opportunity to do just that.

Rumors were circulating in the press of April 5, 1895, that Bayard had telegraphed to the State Department news of the British refusal to go to arbitration on the territory east of the Schomburgk line.[35] Scruggs seized this news and had it published the next day in the Atlanta *Constitution*. The report was worded to imply that an English rebuke had been delivered to American interests in the settlement of a South American dispute. This was the signal for the renaissance of interest in the American press. Virtually every newspaper, from the Concord *Statesman* to the San Francisco *Bulletin*, at some time during April carried reports (no doubt furnished with details by Scruggs) of the controversy and the rebuke to America.[36] British arrogance seemed all the more plausible when the news reached America that British marines had landed on April 27 at Corinto in Nicaragua to secure payment of British claims against the Nicaraguan government. A storm of protest raged in the press, the Assembly of New York State, and the Senate

34. Scruggs to Rojas, Feb. 23, 1895; Rojas to Scruggs, March 11, 22, 1895. Scruggs MSS I.
35. Bayard to Gresham, telegram, April 5, 1895. U.S. Department of State, *Great Britain*, National Archives, Washington, D.C.
36. Clippings, April–May 1895, Scruggs MSS I.

of the State of Connecticut condemning the Administration for its lack of vigor and patriotic spirit. The clamor drowned John Bassett Moore's counsel of restraint.

As early as the previous December, Scruggs had seen the bearing of the Anglo–Nicaraguan dispute on the Venezuelan boundary controversy. In an article robustly entitled "An International Cancer," he pointed out the dangers of European intervention in Latin America.[37] To help the clamor along, he issued a new edition of his *Monroe Doctrine on Trial* and was gratified by the space the press devoted to the pamphlet.[38]

Thus in the four months since Cleveland's message of December 1894, Venezuela had become an issue of national importance. Congress was besieged with petitions demanding arbitration by England. The Monroe Doctrine League sent a petition to the State Department to the effect that the American people would demand action.[39] The San Francisco Chamber of Commerce warned Cleveland to permit no absorption of American territory by a European power.[40] At Caracas, meanwhile, Livingston was being toasted for his resolution and his *discurso magnifico* in the House.[41] When Admiral Meade touched at La Guaira, the port of Caracas, on April 2, 1895, he was feted by crowds demanding a statue of Monroe. The visit of the fleet was interpreted by Venezuela as a warning to England. News of the accolade to Livingston and of the welcome given Meade was reported in the American press.[42]

37. Scruggs' article in the Atlanta *Constitution* (Dec. 31, 1894) was commented on by many newspapers during the spring of 1895.

38. The Scruggs journal is filled with such press cuttings. Scruggs MSS I.

39. *Congressional Record,* 53d Cong., 2d sess., see index entries: "International arbitration," miscellaneous letters, March 26, 1895, D.S.

40. April 16, 1895. Cleveland MSS.

41. Rojas to Scruggs, March 22, 1895. Scruggs MSS I. Livingston's speech was translated and published in the Caracas press. Washington *Star* (April 6, 1895).

42. Atlanta *Constitution* (May 11, 1895).

At the same time General Crespo appointed a Venezuelan cabinet with more radical views on defiance toward England and reliance upon the United States. In Congress, Senator Morgan, a member of the Foreign Relations Committee (perhaps the most powerful Democrat in the Senate), announced on April 10 that he had no doubt of England's aggressive intentions. The United States should take positive and immediate steps to stop this clear violation of the Monroe Doctrine. He even threatened to bring about the impeachment of Bayard unless the American Ambassador in London adopted a more aggressive attitude toward England.[43]

The clamor of the press and the inflammatory speeches in Congress doubtless influenced Cleveland's attitude to the Venezuelan question. He was in any case predisposed to favor Venezuela, having been assiduously fed the "facts" of the case by Scruggs. But his Secretary of State, although increasingly suspicious of Britain, held the President to a cautious and circumspect policy. Two events soon changed all that: the return of Scruggs to Washington toward the end of April, and the death of Gresham on May 28, 1895.

When Scruggs discovered that Gresham was too ill to take any further part in the formation of policy he decided to approach Cleveland directly. What follows is revealed in the Scruggs papers and indeed marks something of a dramatic climax to the story of Scruggs' influence on the shaping of American foreign policy.

It was publicly known that Donald McDonald Dickinson, a middle western politician who had been Postmaster-General in Cleveland's first Administration and was a friend of the President, had visited Cleveland for several days and discussed the Venezuelan question with him. A few days later, on May 10, Dickinson unleashed a tirade against England in a speech

43. Washington *Star* (April 11, 30, 1895).

to the Loyal Legion at Detroit. He denounced British policy in Nicaragua and Venezuela and stressed America's economic need for markets there. He also warned his countrymen against supposing that any ties of Anglo–American kinship would guarantee America protection from harm; England's only concern was to become wealthier and more powerful at the expense of others. The importance of Dickinson's speech lay in the fact that it was widely interpreted as reflecting Cleveland's views, since their previous meeting had been well publicized.[44]

In his discussions with the President, Dickinson was struck with Cleveland's preoccupation over the Venezuelan boundary dispute. When he came into the study, he found Cleveland examining a large map of the controversial boundary. The President was especially disturbed by the British Foreign Secretary's remarks to Bayard not only that England would refuse to go to arbitration on the territory to the East of the Schomburgk line, but also that they claimed a small area of land on the mouth of the Orinoco. That, according to Cleveland, was a most important aspect of the whole question, for if the English claim on the Orinoco were left undisputed, Britain would control the rich trade of the interior and would threaten the political independence of three Latin American republics.

How are we to account for Cleveland's sudden attention to the details of the dispute and his efforts to master the geographical facts of the controversy? Why, above all, this attention to the Orinoco, a river Cleveland, in common with almost every other American, had surely never heard of six months

44. Scruggs note, May 1895. Scruggs MSS I. Washington *Post* (May 11, 1895) and New York *Times* (May 15, 1895). Dickinson to Scruggs, May 15, 1895, and note by Scruggs. Scruggs MSS I. See also Walter Lafeber, "Cleveland's Venezuelan Policy," *American Historical Review*, 61 (1961); Nevins, Cleveland, p. 631; and Perkins, *The Monroe Doctrine, 1867–1907*, p. 147. They err in stating that the visit took place in April. For Cleveland's subsequent endorsement of Dickinson's speech, see Cleveland to Dickinson, July 31, 1895, Nevins, *Letters of Cleveland*, p. 402.

earlier? Cleveland certainly now knew more about the Orinoco than the Prime Minister of England, who had neither privately nor publicly expressed any views on the advantages of possessing portions of the world's most impenetrable jungles. The point needs no further elaboration—the prominence of the Orinoco in American debates on the question was due to Scruggs.

Scruggs had made much of the Orinoco in his *Monroe Doctrine on Trial*, and Cleveland had received a copy of the pamphlet. But it seems unlikely that Cleveland had suddenly taken a second look at Scruggs' pamphlet in May 1895 and was struck by the passages concerning the Orinoco. Scruggs had in fact called on the President *before* the meeting with Dickinson. Historians have misdated the Dickinson interview. It occurred not in late April, but early in May. Scruggs had seen Cleveland at his country home on May 1, but this important confrontation has passed unnoticed.

Scruggs had somehow gained admittance, despite the President's injunction that he was not to be disturbed. We possess a newspaper account of the discussion, and Scruggs has vouched for its accuracy in his journal. It is further confirmed and supplemented by two brief notes in the Scruggs journal dated May 1895 and January 1896.[45] Scruggs was anxious to hide his activities from public view, fearing his influence would be diminished by personal publicity. He was therefore annoyed when the news of his interview with the President leaked out to the press.

The discussion appears to have lasted for a full two hours.

45. A report dated Atlanta, June 16, 1895, appeared in the New York *Morning Journal* and the New York *World* on June 17, 1895. Abbreviated versions were printed on June 17 in the Pittsburgh *Times*. The Boston *Post* and the Cincinnati *Enquirer* carried the report on June 18, 1895. In the Scruggs MSS I, Scruggs added, "Moral: Never tell anything even to your closest and most trusted friend, unless you want the world to know it. I have been caught napping it seems." See also note by Scruggs giving a brief and similar account ·of the interview, May 1895 and Jan. 1896. Scruggs MSS I.

Scruggs went over the whole ground of the dispute. He used two arguments which he hoped would persuade the President to look upon the Anglo–Venezuelan dispute as one of great importance and requiring United States intervention. The first was political: could the President and the Democratic party afford to stand against public opinion? He pointed out that public interest in the problems of America's foreign relations had greatly increased during the years of his presidency. If Cleveland vigorously espoused the Monroe Doctrine, Scruggs went on to say, his popularity would be enhanced, and the people might call on him for a third term—although Cleveland disclaimed any desire to serve again. Scruggs' second argument in favor of intervention was to stress the importance of the Orinoco to *American* interests. From the very first, Scruggs had regarded British claims to the Orinoco as his trump card.

The President was evidently much impressed by what Scruggs told him. He called for maps and detailed information and promised Scruggs that he would look into the whole question personally. Scruggs departed feeling that he had succeeded, confident that the President would act along the lines he had suggested; and Cleveland did. Of course, once the President had taken up the whole question, the main objective of Scruggs and the Venezuelan lobby had been attained. How Cleveland and his new Secretary of State, Richard Olney, plunged the United States into the Venezuelan crisis will be related in the next chapter; as far as Scruggs was personally concerned, the rest of the story is one of his bitter disillusionment with the Venezuelans.

Scruggs ceased to play a key role in shaping American policy after May 1895, for he had succeeded all too well. The strategy of his campaign had been to stress the involvement of American interests. When Cleveland and Olney finally came to grips with the question, they were principally concerned with American—and not Venezuelan—interests. Nor did they even bother to consult Andrade, the Venezuelan Minister in Washington, as to how England might be brought to arbitration on the disputed territory. The Anglo–American settlement did not satisfy the Venezuelans, for apart from some land on the Orinoco their claims were rejected. Since Cleveland and Olney negotiated with the British government mostly in the greatest secrecy, Scruggs was unaware of what exactly was afoot in the beginning.[46]

At first Scruggs was pleased with the apparent success of his campaign to educate the President, Congress, and the American people. He interpreted Olney's appointment on June 8, 1895, as an indication that the President had decided to adopt a more vigorous policy. Scruggs at once sent Olney a flattering letter.[47] He sensed that when Congress reassembled in December 1895 the Venezuelan question would be placed in the forefront of debate. "From the tone of letters I have received from several of the leading Senators, and from confidential utterances of others with whom I have conversed," he privately informed the Venezuelan Foreign Minister, "the indications are that the next Congress of the U.S. will be likely to take some still more advanced and decided stand on this boundary dispute." [48] Scruggs relentlessly continued his campaign throughout the year, seeking out politicians and bombarding the press with information. In December 1895 he found himself a recognized authority on Venezuelan matters. Senator Chandler even asked him to call at his house to "help him cram for a speech." Senator Lodge, too, relied on material furnished by Scruggs.[49] The great event of that December was

46. See chap. 6.
47. Scruggs note, June 1895; Scruggs to Olney, June 17, 1895. Scruggs MSS I.
48. Scruggs to Lucio Pulido, July, 1895. Scruggs MSS I.
49. Scruggs note, Dec. 26, 1895. On Jan. 24, 1896, Scruggs noted that Senators Burrows of Michigan and Cullom of Illinois had asked him to draft speeches for them. Scruggs MSS II.

the President's special message insisting on settlement of the boundary dispute on terms that seemed just to the United States. When the Venezuelan Foreign Minister read it he did not doubt that it was Scruggs who had brought about the American intervention—an opinion which Scruggs shared. Nevertheless a new note of bitterness is noticeable in his private journal.

Scruggs was vain and intensely ambitious, and it irked him that he could not receive full public recognition for his work. He complained that senators used his material without the slightest acknowledgment. He was jealous of the acclaim accorded Olney, noting "credit is seldom given where credit is done. That's been my life's experience." [50] Worse was to follow. Scruggs soon began to doubt whether Cleveland and Olney really intended to follow the aggressive policies that they had proclaimed to Congress.

On January 28, 1896, a month after Cleveland's special message, Scruggs called on Judge Brewer, President of the American commission to delimit the boundary. He was surprised to discover that the Judge was acquainted neither with international law nor with the facts of the dispute. Brewer had no delusions about the importance of the commission, for he told Scruggs that he somehow felt that there would be no war and that "some settlement would be arrived at before the Commission could be ready to make their report." [51] Brewer was quite right, as it turned out, and it is reasonable to conjecture that he may have received some hint not to hurry. Scruggs was not reassured when he called on Cleveland and Olney on March 4, 1896, to present his credentials as Venezuelan counsel to the boundary commission. Olney received him rather coolly and left Scruggs with the impression that he would

50. Scruggs note, Dec. 1895. Scruggs MSS II.
51. Scruggs note, Jan. 28, 1896. Scruggs MSS II.

work for a compromise and that Cleveland hoped Venezuela would moderate her demands.[52]

Scruggs soon discovered why Olney had not been more approachable: the Secretary of State was attempting to replace Scruggs as Venezuela's counsel with someone more pliable and ready to accept whatever settlement Olney could reach in negotiation with the British. Behind Scruggs' back, Olney put pressure on the Venezuelan government to appoint his Boston friend, James Jackson Storrow, a well-known patent lawyer who had taken some interest in the boundary dispute, as counsel. The Venezuelans, not wanting to alienate the United States, gave in and accepted Olney's nominee. When Scruggs expressed his resentment, he learned from the Venezuelan Foreign Minister that Storrow had been foisted on them. Scruggs considered that Olney's intriguing did the Secretary little credit.[53] Nevertheless Scruggs continued to do most of the work of preparing Venezuela's case. His relations with Storrow soon became strained. He suspected Storrow of being little more than Olney's stooge. In fact he was very much afraid that the Secretary of State and Storrow would between them renounce Venezuela's cause altogether. A remark Olney made to him in October 1896 that "a half a loaf would be better than none" confirmed his suspicions.[54]

Scruggs' personal standing soon began to decline. In the spring of 1897 he felt that Olney and Cleveland had treated the Venezuelans badly and that now the Venezuelan government was behaving shabbily towards him. In May he noted that the Venezuelans had not paid him. In the spring of 1898 they dispensed with his services when they still owed him some $3,000. Scruggs was now on bad terms too with José Andrade, the Venezuelan Minister in Washington, and he attrib-

52. Scruggs note, March 4, 1896. Scruggs MSS III.
53. Scruggs note, May 1896. Scruggs MSS III.
54. Scruggs note, Oct. 24, 1896. Scruggs MSS III.

uted his fall from favor to Andrade's treachery and jealousy. Andrade's brother had become President in February 1898, succeeding Crespo, and Scruggs believed that José Andrade had persuaded his brother to cause his dismissal.[55] By then Scruggs was disenchanted with the Venezuelans he had so ardently championed in public. The Venezuelan case was now before an arbitration tribunal sitting in Paris, and Scruggs confided to his journal: "I sincerely hope they may win their suit, although they little deserve success, aside from the intrinsic merit of their case. They have a strong case indeed; but even a strong case in the hands of a false and treacherous people, unable to govern themselves, and incapable of appreciating the efforts of their friends, is sometimes doomed to defeat." [56] Fourteen years after writing this, Scruggs died in comparative obscurity. He never again enjoyed influence, and his work was soon forgotten, rating at best a passing reference in the history books.

The Venezuelan crisis was a milestone in the emergence of the United States as a world power. The evidence points to the labors of Scruggs as a significant contribution to American involvement in the dispute. A boundary dispute of relatively small international import had turned into the notable Venezuelan crisis; it was largely due to Scruggs that the press, Congress, and the President were persuaded that vital American interests were at stake. In this extraordinary manner did the Washington lobby of a Latin American republic—a republic enjoying little international prestige and certainly no power—influence the mainstream of American foreign policy. That lobby was conducted virtually singlehandedly by an American, a discredited diplomat in foreign employ, a man of tireless energy and astonishing political gifts, William Lindsay Scruggs.

55. Scruggs notes, May 1897, April 1898, and April 28, 1898. Scruggs MSS III.
56. Scruggs note, May 14, 1898. Scruggs MSS III.

Chapter Six
Grover Cleveland, Richard Olney,
and the Venezuelan Crisis

AT NO MOMENT during his eight years as President could Grover Cleveland have used a diplomatic diversion to better advantage than in 1895. All the evils of Populism were present in that unhappy year, and Democratic ranks were already split. Repeal of the Silver Coinage Law in 1893 had served only to outrage the now powerful Silverites. The depression showed little sign of abating; the Treasury was being steadily drained of its gold; public discontent with the President's policies had manifested itself in the autumn of 1894 in the shape of a crushing congressional defeat. 1895 was the President's last full year in office; the Fifty-fourth was the last Congress before the nominating conventions and the election of 1896. If he were to save the country from Bryanism and bankruptcy, Cleveland had no time to lose.[1]

Historians have displayed considerable diversity in their explanations of Cleveland's foreign policy. Some find the answer to the problem in Cleveland's sterling character;[2] others have more cynically suggested that the President used "the

1. For an excellent recent account of Cleveland's domestic policies, see J. Rogers Hollingsworth, *The Whirligig of Politics, The Democracy of Cleveland and Bryan* (Chicago, University of Chicago Press, 1963).
2. Allan Nevins, *Grover Cleveland, A Study in Courage* (New York, Dodd, Mead, 1932).

diplomacy of the war-like gesture" to distract the American people from their economic ills.[3] These very economic difficulties have also provided historians with another set of explanations: the argument that the phases of the business cycle of slump and boom are closely related to the ebb and flow of imperialist policies. Cleveland's policy has been described as an example of "negative imperialism"; Cleveland appeared "eager for rule but not for gain."[4] More recently, the influence of the domestic depression on the foreign policy of Cleveland and Gresham has been stressed. Their diplomacy, so one historian suggests, was largely shaped by economic considerations, and their Latin American policy was designed to find markets for American goods.[5] No doubt the historical debate will continue; Cleveland's own letters reveal little of his thoughts on foreign policy.

At least one further alternative appears worth considering. The evidence, or rather the lack of it, suggests that Cleveland pursued no consistent foreign policy, that his approach was pragmatic, that he took only a sporadic interest in foreign affairs and generally let his two Secretaries of State, Gresham and Olney, conduct diplomacy. It was their task to discover the facts and lay them before him. Once he was convinced of the rights and wrongs of a particular problem, the President then generally gave his advisers full backing for their policies.

Cleveland was inclined to avoid the study of foreign policy. Even a dogma as fundamental as the Monroe Doctrine had for many years not received his close attention. "I was quite willing, if possible within the limits of inflexible duty, to escape

3. For example, Charles A. Beard, *The Open Door at Home* (New York, Macmillan, 1934).

4. Alfred Vagts, *Deutschland und die Vereinigten Staaten in der Weltpolitik* (2 vols. London, Dickson & Thompson, 1936).

5. Walter Lafeber, "The Latin American Policy of the Second Cleveland Administration," (Doctoral Dissertation, University of Wisconsin), microfilm.

its serious contemplation," he wrote to Ambassador Bayard (his former Secretary of State) after delivering his Venezuelan special message; he also referred to his inclination "during my former incumbency of this office, to avoid a doctrine which I knew to be troublesome and upon which I had nothing like your clear conception and information." [6]

If this interpretation of Cleveland's attitude is correct, it would tend to dispose of the hypotheses that ulterior political motives or economic considerations played a significant role in the formation of his foreign policy. The Administration's rejection of Hawaiian annexation had clearly not been popular; nor did Cleveland's handling of Cuban affairs gain him general approbation. A careful examination of Cleveland's and Olney's Venezuelan policy reveals, moreover, that the public acclaim this stand received in December 1895 was an incidental result, and not a primary objective, of their diplomacy.

Sometime in the autumn of 1894—there is no evidence to show precisely when—the President had begun to take an interest in the Venezuelan question. He had, by then, received a copy of Scruggs' pamphlet. He must have become aware of the increasing attention devoted by the newspapers to Latin American affairs and to the Monroe Doctrine. By December 1894 he had probably assumed that Venezuela had legitimate grounds for complaint and that England's attitude was preventing settlement.

On January 15, 1895, as has been related, Scruggs called on the President. Cleveland was evidently impressed by Scruggs. Venezuela became an issue of national importance during the succeeding weeks. The passage of the Livingston resolution and the tone of the newspapers were indications that the Administration would be expected to take a stronger line in

6. Nevins, *Letters of Cleveland*, p. 417.

regard to Venezuela. Gresham's letters to Bayard in England at this time vividly illustrate the Secretary of State's dilemma. He was aware of the delicacy of the boundary question; but Cleveland now required some sort of action. It appears that on March 20 there was a Cabinet meeting attended by the President, the Secretary of State, John Griffin Carlisle, Secretary of the Treasury, Attorney General Olney, and Secretary of War Daniel Lamont. As far as we can tell, they decided that the dispute did fall within the purview of the Monroe Doctrine, and Gresham undertook to prepare a report on the controversy.[7] But Cleveland was becoming impatient with Gresham's conciliatory policy toward England. When Scruggs called on him on May 1, the President was ready to listen to new ideas and to study the question for himself. The month of May was a critical time in the formation of Cleveland's attitude. He had become receptive to the Venezuelan complaints just at the time when Gresham, whose advice had hitherto restrained him, fell ill and died.[8]

Before Gresham's death, Cleveland had turned to Olney and requested that he examine the ailing Secretary's files on the boundary dispute and make a report. Olney undertook this task with no predisposition to censure England and with no instructions except to determine "what the facts were and where the right of the matter and the true interests of the United States lay."[9] On June 8, Cleveland appointed Olney Secretary of State. The appointment was regarded as indicating that Cleveland and Olney were both agreed on the need to follow a more aggressive policy toward England.

Before his appointment, Olney had taken the trouble to

7. The New York *Times* (March 21, 1895) listed those present as Cleveland, Gresham, Olney, Carlisle, and Lamont.

8. See chap. 5.

9. Account by Walter Wellman, dated Jan. 22, 1896, in the Chicago *Times-Herald*. Scruggs MSS II.

acquaint himself with the major questions of foreign policy facing the Administration. Gresham's handling of the Hawaiian problem, it will be recalled, had not been to Olney's liking. He regarded Gresham as something of an impractical idealist, and he took it upon himself to hold a watching brief over Cleveland's foreign policy so as to save the Administration from serious blunders. Olney was a man of resource, courage, and strength; he was also single minded in the pursuit of his goals. But it is a mistake to cast him in the role of the bellicose, barrack-room lawyer. Sir Julian Pauncefote, the British Ambassador in Washington, who had every reason to be cautious in his estimate of Olney's character, privately wrote to Prime Minister Salisbury in November 1895: "I have found Mr. Olney a most able, large minded, and honest negotiator." [10] Olney was essentially pacific in outlook, a quality without which Cleveland would not have appointed him to the position of Secretary of State. The objectives of Olney's policy did not differ markedly from Gresham's; their views diverged in their estimates of the means of conducting diplomacy. Olney was out of sympathy with the docile language Gresham had employed in his official instructions to Bayard. The British government had for years politely ignored America's offers to act as a mediator in the Venezuelan dispute. Something different was required to bring Lord Salisbury to the point of actually taking notice of the American point of view. Olney supplied it when he penned his instruction of July 20, 1895, to Bayard in London.[11]

Olney's dispatch gave the appearance of prejudging the

10. Pauncefote to Salisbury, Nov. 8, 1895. Salisbury Papers, Christ Church, Oxford, England.
11. Olney to Bayard, July 20, 1895. *Foreign Relations*, 1895, pp. 562 ff. For a detailed analysis see George B. Young, "Intervention under the Monroe Doctrine: The Olney Corollary," *Political Science Quarterly*, 57 (1942), 250–55.

rights and wrongs of the Venezuelan boundary issue, something his predecessors had been careful to avoid. It will be remembered that Blaine, who was not inclined to concede anything, had reproved Scruggs in 1892 for expressing his opinion on the justice of Venezuela's claims. Olney now concluded that Venezuela, out of moderation and prudence, "contented herself with claiming the Essequibo line, the line of the Essequibo River," as the true boundary between Venezuela and British Guiana. Yet it was certainly not Olney's purpose to champion Venezuela; he merely had his facts wrong. His categorical assertion of impartiality in other parts of the dispatch sincerely expressed his intentions. The British, of course, may be pardoned for not appreciating this at the time. Later that year Cleveland explained his and Olney's attitude in a private letter to Bayard. The Monroe Doctrine was being applied, Cleveland wrote, "for its importance to our government and welfare." Though the dispute of another country had provided the occasion, "we are, I suppose, not looking after *its* interests but *our own.*" [12]

If Olney's dispatch of July 20 is to be correctly understood, we must remember that Olney was pursuing American, not Venezuelan, objectives. Although Olney conceded that the dispute primarily concerned England and Venezuela, he claimed that the United States was also involved; he appealed to the Monroe Doctrine and the disparity of the two contestants as sufficient justification for American intervention in the Anglo–Venezuelan controversy: "Those charged with the interests of the United States are now forced to determine exactly what those interests are and what course of action they require." Olney clearly implied that British pretensions in Latin America menaced the United States. If the British harbored any illusions about the Monroe Doctrine, Olney was deter-

12. Cleveland to Bayard, December 29, 1895. Nevins, *Letters of Cleveland*, pp. 417–20.

mined to dispel them; he therefore sought to define in his dispatch "the history, the precise nature and scope of the Monroe Doctrine," reaching the conclusion that "any permanent political union between a European and an American state [was] unnatural and inexpedient." The Prime Minister of the British Empire was hardly likely to take the Secretary's arguments seriously.

It looks very much as if Olney had been carried away by his own eloquence. Olney, who had boasted of America's strength and condemned British policy, ended with a threat: if Britain did not speedily consent to submit the Venezuelan question "in its entirety to impartial arbitration," American policy would be determined "by another branch of the Government," and this was bound to "greatly embarrass the future relations between this country and Great Britain." Olney was suggesting, in other words, that Salisbury would find it easier to negotiate with the President in secrecy and an atmosphere of relative calm than to face a belligerent and anglophobe Congress. This gave Salisbury until December—when Congress would reconvene—to decide upon his policy. It moreover left plenty of time for further negotiations and discussions which Olney confidently expected to follow the delivery of his dispatch. British refusal to negotiate or indeed even to reply before December entirely and unexpectedly wrecked Olney's diplomatic strategy. When he consulted Cleveland early in July, Olney must have explained his strategy. The President, inexperienced as ever in foreign affairs, saw no danger in the scheme. He modified Olney's language here and there, and his approval of the Secretary's plan was enthusiastic. He had enjoyed going over Olney's "deliverance on Venezuelan affairs," as he aptly called the dispatch, and complimented Olney for writing "the best thing of the kind I have ever read." [13] He later christened Olney's missive "the twenty-inch gun." Olney had convinced him that America was on the side of the angels. Cleveland and Olney were not concocting a grandstand play for votes as they consulted together on the sands of Cape Cod that summer; they adopted what they believed to be an effective method of settling a stubborn dispute. Their plan, if not their language, was prudent. American intervention, epitomized in Olney's note of July 20, was to be kept a secret until December. The President would then be able to report to Congress in his regular summary of the year's diplomacy that the question was settled and that England would arbitrate. There were to be no vote-catching pyrotechnics. The President's wish to treat the matter in his annual message and not in a special message suggests that his intentions were peaceful. The culmination of Cleveland's Venezuelan policy was thus not the later and much publicized message of December 17, 1895, but the secret note of July 20. In July, Olney evidently thought he had sufficient command of the facts to demand, without further question, that Great Britain agree to arbitration.

Despite the spread-eagle effect of his language, the Secretary of State dangled some alluring bait before the British government. The dispute was to be treated as one between England and the United States. Olney had neither consulted the Venezuelan government nor notified it of the United States action. Never in his wildest diplomatic gestures did Theodore Roosevelt actually go so far in assuming responsibility for the welfare of another American state. The Roosevelt corollary has been more widely publicized, but it was not more sweeping than Olney's policy when he simply assumed a proprietary interest in Venezuela's affairs. He hinted

13. Nevins, *Cleveland*, p. 634.

that the British government might find the American Executive more accommodating than Venezuela. He suggested, in the dispatch of July 20, that if Britain would submit the title to the whole disputed territory to arbitration, the United States might be prepared to concede that certain prescriptive rights, acquired by the encroaching British settlers, were not null and void, but at least arbitrable. This was a handsome concession. But it was also a concession of Venezuelan rights which were not at the disposal of the United States. Salisbury, however, was prepared neither to bow to American pressure nor to respond to enticing promises. In his two studiously polite—but negative—dispatches of November 26, 1895, he refuted Olney's arguments and rejected the proposition that the United States had any standing in the matter.[14]

Cleveland and Olney awaited Salisbury's reply with increasing anxiety and impatience. Sent by steamer, it did not arrive in America until December 7, 1895, three days after Cleveland delivered his annual message. Salisbury had not deliberately delayed his reply. He had personally revised the draft at Hatfield in order that a copy be transmitted to the American Embassy in good time. On November 30, Francis Bertie, the Assistant Secretary who was in charge of American affairs at the Foreign Office, learned to his consternation and surprise that Bayard did not intend to cable the contents to Washington. We can only surmise Bayard's intentions. The Ambassador was bitterly critical of Olney's diplomacy, and it is possible that he deliberately delayed informing the President, fearing that it would induce him to make some reckless

14. For the British Cabinet's policy see J. A. S. Grenville, *Lord Salisbury and Foreign Policy: The Close of the Nineteenth Century* (London, Athlone Press, 1964), pp. 54–73.

statement in his annual message. If so, he miscalculated badly.

Cleveland and Olney were shocked by Salisbury's rejoinder. Pauncefote correctly assessed their feelings when he wrote to the Prime Minister: "Your Lordship's most powerful and irrefutable Despatch on the Monroe Doctrine has hit the President and the Jingoes very hard . . . Mr. Olney seemed very anxious when I read your Lordship's despatches to him." [15] But Pauncefote underestimated Olney's resourcefulness. Olney decided that a special message would be necessary to present the reply.

While Cleveland was enjoying himself on a ten-day hunting trip starting on December 5, Olney was laboring over the draft of the special message which he wrote out five times before he found it satisfactory. It was a most skillful piece of work; it satisfied even the wildest jingoes without, in fact, involving the United States in any real danger of conflict. Salisbury's refusal had left Olney with three unpleasant alternatives: resorting to force, beating an ignominious retreat, and just temporizing.

He chose the last. Judging from the plain words of the previous note, one would have supposed that if England refused to arbitrate the United States would force it to do so. But now that Salisbury refused arbitration, the President and the Secretary of State decided to postpone the decision by setting up a commission of investigation. The commission was to decide on the true boundary between Venezuela and British Guiana. "When such report is made *and accepted* it will, *in my opinion,* be the duty of the United States to resist by every means in its power, as a willful aggression upon its rights and interests, the appropriation by Great Britain of any lands

15. Pauncefote to Salisbury, Dec. 20, 1895. Grenville, *Salisbury*, p. 65.

or the exercise of governmental jurisdiction over any territory which *after investigation* we have determined of right belongs to Venezuela." [16]

The qualifying words betray the anticlimactic character of the message of December 17, 1895; Pauncefote was not slow to note that, despite the fine phrases about upholding national honor, the message was in reality "very pale and washy." The creation of an American commission he regarded—accurately —as a fine safety valve.[17] The past July, Olney had said categorically that there was sufficient suspicion of British aggression to justify a demand that the dispute be arbitrated; six months later, Cleveland said there was sufficient suspicion to justify more investigation.

Cleveland did not contemplate war. He had no intention of letting a commission go so far as to delimit a frontier the United States would actually try to force Great Britain to accept. The American people, by now in an aggressive and restless mood, naturally paid more attention to the warlike phrases than to the careful qualifications and caveats, and the message was filled with gratuitously reckless phrases. Cleveland was inclined to justify his actions on broad grounds, as he had done in his previous fisheries and Samoan messages. When the President declared "I am fully alive to the responsibility incurred, and keenly realize all the consequences that may follow," the phrase was mistakenly interpreted as meaning that Cleveland was prepared, if necessary, to go to war.

The President's chauvinistic stand was greeted on the following day, a Wednesday, with almost unanimous approval. No part of the country, apparently, was critical or hostile. But on Thursday, as the stock market sagged under foreign selling of American securities, leaders in financial circles became

16. Richardson, *Messages and Papers*, 9, 655–58. Italics added.
17. Grenville, *Salisbury*, p. 67.

alarmed and, when call money rose to eighty per cent on Friday, they recognized the symptoms of a financial panic. The Chaplain's prayer in the Senate for peace among English-speaking peoples that morning was included, without objection, in the pages of the *Congressional Record*. Congress on the same day enthusiastically appropriated $100,000 to set up the fact-finding commission asked for by the President. Eastern markets were demoralized over the weekend, and in New York alone five brokerage houses were forced to close. Yet it is safe to say that, even with the knowledge that war might result, the majority of Americans supported the President and Congress.

Given the mood of the British Cabinet a month earlier, in November, a serious Anglo–American conflict seemed inevitable. The Cabinet had then supported Salisbury's refusal to negotiate with the Americans over the Venezuelan boundary question. When in mid-December news of Cleveland's special message was received in London, Salisbury was still of the same mind. Cleveland's message, he argued, was addressed to Congress and not to the British government and therefore required no reply. On January 6, 1896, Salisbury minuted that the best way to deal with the crisis was to play a waiting game: let the commission report, maybe the Venezuelans would make a blunder; something might still turn up. His Micawberlike attitude was a good example of his belief in the efficacy of "masterly inactivity" when the occasion called for it. Meanwhile Goschen, the First Lord of the Admiralty, had decided on the organization of the Flying Squadron, and Salisbury (who supported this move) wrote to the Chancellor of the Exchequer (who was troubled by the expenses of naval expansion), "recent events have introduced a new element into the calculation. A war with America—not this year but in the not distant future—has become more than a possibility." [18] None of Salisbury's letters or remarks at this time indicate that he had the slightest intention of making any real concessions to the United States. The most he would do was to suggest to George Earle Buckle, editor of *The* (London) *Times* (for communication through private channels to Olney), that the Secretary of State might consider calling a conference on the Monroe Doctrine. This of course would have interminably delayed any adjustment of the Venezuelan boundary. But although Salisbury remained firm, his Cabinet did not. They fairly turned tail.

In November they believed that Britain held all the trump cards. When the Cabinet met on January 11, 1896, the mood was no longer confident. The Cabinet was now inclined to cut Britain's losses in a world which appeared to have become suddenly hostile. The Jameson raid and its failure had thrown Britain's South African policy into turmoil; the Kaiser's celebrated Kruger Telegram was regarded as proof of Germany's malevolence; Russia continued to menace India and Constantinople. The Cabinet would have been further alarmed had they known that the Russian chargé d'affaires in Washington had on December 23 offered the United States Treasury a large loan of gold; the Russian ministers were doing all they could to strengthen the United States and to make trouble for England.[19] British relations with Russia's ally, France, were also strained in Africa and in Siam. And now to crown it all,

18. Salisbury to Hicks Beach, January 2, 1896. Hicks Beach MSS, cited by Grenville, "Great Britain and the Isthmian Canal," *American Historical Review, 61* (1955), p. 51.

19. Olney was inclined to accept the loan on condition that Russia acknowledged "that negotiations for the purchase of gold by this Government [U.S.] were initiated by Russia partly for the sake of investment and partly for political considerations." Olney to Somow, December 28, 1895. Olney MSS. But Secretary Carlisle deprecated the loan on the grounds that it would be regarded as a virtual alliance with Russia. See Charles S. Hamlin, *Index-Digest to the Manuscript Diary* (Library of Congress), 1, 5.

the Venezuelan boundary had added the United States to the list of England's potential enemies. The Cabinet first concluded that an effort must be made to reach some agreement with France. It then reversed Salisbury's policy toward the United States and decided that negotiations should be opened with Olney, thus implicitly recognizing America's right to a voice in the Venezuelan settlement. Salisbury complained bitterly and even exclaimed that if unconditional surrender to America was being contemplated, the country would have to find a new Prime Minister. In the end, however, he submitted to the wish of his Cabinet. The very next day, January 12, Lord Playfair brought Bayard the first British suggestions for the settlement.[20] If the English Cabinet had been aware that the United States was militarily completely unprepared for war, their actions might have been different. The United States South Atlantic Squadron (of three vessels) was wintering thousands of miles away in Montevideo; the Atlantic coastline and the Great Lakes lay exposed to attack. At the suggestion of Captain Henry C. Taylor (President of the Naval War College), Commander Charles B. Gridley, a lighthouse inspector of Buffalo, New York, was instructed in January 1896 to make plans to organize four squadrons of ships on the Great Lakes; he was also to obtain the information Captain Taylor required for the perfecting of a war plan. Commander Gridley was warned that his mission was to be kept absolutely secret: "the political situation might be seriously disturbed should these preliminary preparations become public." He was to conceal the fact that he was a naval officer and take care to do nothing to "excite suspicion or comment." [21] Gridley succeeded in keeping his mission secret.

20. Grenville, *Salisbury*, pp. 65–73.
21. Secretary of Navy to Commander Gridley, Jan. 23 and 24, 1896: V.I. *File, Venezuelan Crisis*, Navy Department, National Archives, Washington, D.C.

The United States did not possess sufficient warships on the lakes. The Navy Department now hoped to improvise a fleet of 130 vessels by arming steamers and merchant ships with guns. Gridley's task was to find out if there were suitable ships plying the lakes that the United States government could take over in an emergency. Gridley found only wooden ships and reported that few of them were entirely satisfactory; because of the sharp winter, many ships were laid up in small harbors, and Gridley found it difficult to make sketches of them without being noticed. He persevered and sent several reports to Taylor.[22] They were depressing, holding out no hope that a fighting force could be brought together quickly. In mid-March 1896, Taylor was ordered to Washington by the Secretary of the Navy. The war scare, Taylor informed Gridley, had subsided, but he anticipated that it would be renewed in April. While in Washington, Taylor worked out plans for an expedition to surprise the Canadians who would be guarding the Welland Canal at the outbreak of any war; the purpose of this attack was to destroy the canal and to deny the Canadians its use. We have no means of knowing whether any more was done after April 1896. The last document in the file is dated—perhaps appropriately enough—April 1, 1896. One fact must have been accentuated: the United States could not hope to match England's strength on the high seas. It possessed no warship capable of meeting even a single battleship of the powerful British Flying Squadron.[23]

The British strategists were also studying the military implications of a war with the United States, happily with no more reassuring results than those reached by the Americans. Lieutenant Colonel Lake, Quartermaster-General of the Ca-

22. See esp. Gridley to Taylor, February 21, 1896. *V.I. File, Venezuelan Crisis*, Navy Department, National Archives, Washington, D.C.
23. Grenville, *Salisbury*, p. 106, for British naval preparations.

nadian Militia, in March 1896 did not think that the Canadians could with certainty keep the St. Lawrence waterway and Welland Canal open for the passage of ships. Canada could not undertake her own defense; the help of British imperial troops would be essential. In June 1896, when the Joint Naval and Military Committee on Defence met in London, it decided to dispatch two officers to the coasts of Maine and Massachusetts to examine suitable areas for landing a British expeditionary force. But despite all these active preparations for the defense of Canada, Sir John Ardagh, the British Director of Military Intelligence, viewed war with the United States as a calamity. He compared the resources of Canada and the United States in 1897 and calculated that America could raise two and one-half million men in a war with England, although Britain would be better prepared at the beginning of the conflict. Any early British success would prove only temporary:

> We should eventually be swept out of the country by mere superiority of numbers, and Canada would be overrun and occupied . . . That such a struggle may be forced upon us, it is impossible to deny: but that this country would enter upon a war with their kindred beyond the sea with any feelings but of most sincere reluctance and sorrow, is equally certain . . . a land war on the American Continent would be perhaps the most hazardous military enterprise that we could possibly be driven to engage in.[24]

When Ardagh wrote his memorandum, the diplomats had already resolved the Venezuelan dispute. By April 1896, Olney's diplomacy and the pressure of his colleagues on Lord

24. Ardagh to St. John Broderick, June 13, 1896; memorandum by Ardagh on the Defence of Canada, Dec. 12, 1897. The Records of the War Office Intelligence Division, 106/40, Public Record Office, London.

Salisbury had made a pacific adjustment of Anglo–American differences possible. Salisbury cared more for the rights of British settlers then for the mineral wealth of the disputed area; he tenaciously resisted any agreement that would force British subjects, who had settled on the land for generations, to choose between abandoning their possessions and accepting Venezuelan rule. He regarded the Venezuelan government as arbitrary and unjust, and he accordingly felt that he would be failing in his duty as Prime Minister if he handed these British subjects over to such a government. Chamberlain, the Colonial Secretary, also fought fiercely for every inch of the Empire. Sentiment tied him to the United States; moreover he consistently worked for the development of Anglo–American friendship though his first loyalty remained always to British imperial interests. Any show of weakness in British Guiana might have serious consequences elsewhere, for Britain was being pressed hard in other parts of the world by Germany, France, and Russia; the Canadians, Chamberlain also feared, would be disheartened and the American jingoes encouraged, and so he wrote to Salisbury in February 1896: "While I should regard a war with the States as the very worst thing that could possibly happen to us, I should equally deprecate anything like showing the white feather to them. They are great people for bluffing and bad to run away from." [25] Salisbury's and Chamberlain's firmness eventually yielded results, after many months of negotiation, with the signing of an Anglo–Venezuelan treaty on November 12, 1896. It provided for unlimited arbitration, though fifty years of occupation of territory was held to be a good title of possession, and Britain, in practice, thereby was able to make good her title to almost the whole of the land in dispute. While there is no

25. Chamberlain to Salisbury, Feb. 1, 1896. Salisbury Papers.

need to describe the details of these negotiations—for they have been ably analyzed elsewhere—one point needs to be stressed.

Olney did not champion Venezuela; that is clearly brought out by his behavior during the negotiations. Scruggs' suspicions were well justified. Once Britain had conceded that her boundary dispute legitimately involved the United States and the Monroe Doctrine, Olney felt he had gained the principal point. He now went out of his way to reassure the British government and to smooth the way to settlement. To one British emissary Olney said, "If only you had agreed to our arbitration the President and I would have favoured you in every way we could as against the Spanish-Americans—all our predilections were English." "Venezuela," he added, "has got to do exactly as we tell her." Olney was not overly concerned with the intrinsic merit of the dispute. Only one conclusion can be drawn from his further remark: "If you will accept arbitration you can keep the arbitration going on for ten years if you like." [26]

The Secretary of State had been sensitive about Britain's treatment of America before January 1896, as he complained to Chamberlain of "the seeming, if not intentional, contumely with which the statement of our position on the Venezuelan boundary question was received by the British Foreign Office." [27] He did not show such sensitivity toward Venezuela. He reached an agreement with the British Ambassador on the principles by which the boundary dispute was to be arbi-

26. Sir Henry Stafford Northcote to Salisbury, March 16, 1896. Salisbury Papers.

27. Olney to Chamberlain, Sept. 28, 1896. A. E. Campbell, *Great Britain and the United States, 1895–1903* (London, Longmans, 1960), pp. 23–24. Campbell's study analyzes public opinion on both sides of the Atlantic exceedingly well.

trated without consulting the Venezuelan government. Acting on Venezuela's behalf, Olney abandoned her claim to a historical title to land that was not his to concede, and the Anglo–American draft of the treaty permitted the Venezuelans no part in the choice of arbiters. If anyone had been treated with contumely, it was the Venezuelans. Not until the end of the negotiations, when it became apparent that Venezuela would have to be cajoled or coerced into signing the treaty, did Olney take the Venezuelan Minister in Washington into his confidence. Andrade was persuaded, probably with reason, that the Anglo–American draft treaty was the most favorable settlement his country could obtain.[28] He was urged to return to Caracas, where he was to prevail upon his government to accept the treaty.

Immediately after Olney and Pauncefote had reached agreement, Storrow, the counsel for Venezuela, and Andrade took the treaty to Caracas. It was published in the Venezuelan press as a "memorandum" on December 7, 1896, together with a letter from Cleveland, recommending to the President of Venezuela that the treaty be signed in the form agreed upon by the United States and Great Britain. An outcry arose immediately. "Many and discordant were the opinions published in the press of the Republic," reported the Venezuelan foreign secretary. Tomás Michelena, the foremost international lawyer of Venezuela, published an inflammatory letter arguing that the fifty-year clause was outrageous and that the signature of the protocol would convert his country into a protectorate of the United States. Scruggs confided to his diary that Olney was attempting to "over-awe and bull-doze Venezuela." From Venezuela it was reported that private citizens were ordered to deposit their arms at the Ministry of the In-

28. Storrow to Olney, Oct. 22, 1896. Olney MSS.

terior lest President Crespo precipitate a revolution by accepting the treaty.[29]

Storrow and Andrade were forced to postpone their return to Washington from December 10 to 20. At the height of the uproar, the Venezuelans apparently approached the British government with a proposal to negotiate a direct Anglo–Venezuelan settlement, thus putting the United States aside. Salisbury rejected the proposal and tactfully did not mention the subject to Olney. One concession was made to Venezuela: the United States and Great Britain agreed to allow the Venezuelan government to name one of the arbiters. Andrade returned to Washington with the treaty, where it was signed on February 2, 1897, by him and Pauncefote. On the next day, the press of Caracas again pronounced its opposition to the treaty, warning that the United States wished to turn Venezuela into an American protectorate. The Venezuelan Congress, which convened on February 20, deliberately made difficulties. It insisted on its constitutional right to receive a signed copy of the treaty in Spanish. As the delays continued, Scruggs was next sent to Caracas, where he found the treaty lying in the Foreign Affairs Committee of the Venezuelan Senate. After several adjournments for fast days, the Congress reluctantly ratified the treaty on March 30, 1897, and ratifications were exchanged between Venezuela and Great Britain in Washington on June 14, 1897. A tribunal of arbitration was then instituted without delay. Its decision, rendered on October 3, 1899, fixed the boundary of British Guiana and Venezuela; except for some territory on the mouth of the Orinoco, Britain's possession of nine tenths of the land in dispute was confirmed.

29. Young, "Intervention under the Monroe Doctrine: The Olney Corollary," *Political Science Quarterly*, 57 (1942), 276–78, relates Venezuelan reactions.

That the arbitral award possibly favored Britain's claim was, from the point of view of the Americans, immaterial. In the glow of his retirement, Cleveland hailed the control Venezuela gained over the Orinoco as a great victory, although the arbitral award had favored Britain in all other respects. For Olney the actual delimitation of the frontier had all along been a secondary consideration, although he worked hard to insure an impartial, judicial settlement of the dispute. Olney's main concern was to reassert the validity of the Monroe Doctrine and to serve notice on European and Latin American states alike that the United States claimed the right to intervene in any dispute in the Western Hemisphere if it considered its interests to be involved. Moreover, Olney took it for granted that America's power entitled it to a predominant voice in any settlement.

Whether historians describe these objectives of policy as negative imperialism or deny that they represent true imperialism matters very much less than the fact that European governments accepted American claims to a voice in Latin America even though they regarded these claims as unjustified. In the majority of Latin American republics, American pretensions confirmed suspicions of "Yankee imperialism" and hindered the realization of the complementary idealistic conception of Pan-American cooperation. The fact that the majority of articulate opinion in Latin America during the Spanish–American War sympathized with Spain rather than with the United States and Cuba strikingly reveals the depth of anti-American feelings.

Chapter Seven
The Dangers of Cuban Independence,
1895-1897

CUBA HAS BEEN A VITAL CONCERN to the United States for over 150 years. For much of that time, the difficulty of reconciling the state of affairs on the island, the wishes of the Cuban people, and the strategic interests of the United States has baffled American statesmen.

From the earliest days of the Republic, American statesmen considered Cuba an essential part of the American system. Its links with Europe were regarded as artificial—the result of mere historical accident rather than the expression of genuine political bonds. Thus John Quincy Adams, looking forward to the "probable course of events" in 1823, found it "scarcely possible to resist the conviction that the annexation of Cuba . . . will be indispensable to the continuance and integrity of the Union itself";[1] a quarter of a century later President James Buchanan proposed to purchase Cuba from Spain; Cuba, like Louisiana, could be safely absorbed, the President believed, for Cuba contained a large "white population" which would in the course of time be "Americanized." American opinion was nevertheless divided as to the wisdom of annexing Cuba,

1. John Quincy Adams to Hugh Nelson, April 28, 1823, in Ruhl J. Bartlett, *The Record of American Diplomacy* (New York, Knopf, 1959), pp. 231–34.

and Spain would not relinquish its sovereignty freely.[2] The right of the Cubans to control their own affairs does not seem to have been seriously considered by American statesmen.

The Cuban people came to demand a voice in their future when, in 1868, they began to fight the Ten Years War for independence. Spain eventually gained the upper hand but only over an exhausted and devastated island. The years between 1878 and the next eruption were not barren in the history of Cuba, for they produced Cuba's greatest national figure, the writer and patriot, José Julian Martí, a leader of hemispheric importance. Martí had welded the Cuban opposition together and founded the Cuban Revolutionary party in 1892. He did not live to see the attainment of independence, for in 1895 he was killed in a military skirmish on the island.

Exiled Cuban leaders looked to the United States for aid. With the help of skillful propaganda, the Cuban struggle won wide sympathy and could no longer be totally ignored. President Cleveland was faced with a perplexing question: would the security of the United States be more threatened by the continued sovereignty of Spain over the island or by Cuban independence? As we examine his policy, one fact stands out: the complete independence of Cuba was seen to pose dangers more serious than Spanish rule. This provides the key to understanding the American policy before 1897.

The Administration could not openly admit its anti-Cuban bias, which ran counter to the widespread sympathy given any independence movement by broad sections of the American people. The policy contradicted the historic ideals of American liberty; it offended humanitarian sympathies aroused by the barbarism of civil war; it ignored the intense indignation provoked by the (occasional) loss of American lives and (more frequent) damage to property. Whenever some incident

2. James Buchanan to Romulus Saunders, June 17, 1848. Bartlett, *American Diplomacy*, pp. 234–37.

brought the Cuban question to the attention of the American people, the Administration was attacked in Congress for adopting a policy of neutrality and urged to act on behalf of the Cuban people. The resulting schism between executive and the legislative branches severely handicapped the evolution of any effective Cuban policy.

Cleveland and Olney were determined to resist congressional pressure and to keep Cuban policy in their own hands. They were perhaps naively optimistic in believing that they could find a solution. They did not succeed because they failed to gain a sound grasp of the problem. Their faith was pinned on solving the issue by diplomacy in much the same way as they were resolving the Venezuelan boundary conflict. Perhaps Spain might agree to diminish her control over the island; perhaps the Cuban revolutionary leaders would accept something less than complete independence. These were not the ingredients of a lasting solution. The Spaniards were not Britons, nor were the Cubans dependent, as the Venezuelans had been, on the good offices of the United States. Olney's proud boast that the will of the United States "was law upon the subjects to which it confines its interposition" rang hollow in Cuba.

Olney faced the difficult Cuban question with the conviction that American interests were imperiled; he had no mind to help the Cubans toward national independence. The ever-present danger that one of the great European powers might gain control over Cuba appeared to draw near as the strength of Spain declined.

Superficially, the Administration's Cuban policy appears strikingly different from its Venezuelan policy. Many Americans, Theodore Roosevelt included, thought that the President's Venezuelan message (of December 1895) had made it clear that Cleveland would, if necessary, fight in defense of the Monroe Doctrine. "Personally I rather hope the fight will come soon," Roosevelt exuberantly wrote to his friend Lodge, "the clamor of the peace faction has convinced me that this country needs a war." [3] To Olney he expressed himself with more circumspection: "I only wish you would take the same line as regards Cuba." [4] But Cleveland and Olney were not as bellicose as the language of the Venezuelan message implies. They felt little sympathy for corrupt Latin American governments. Indeed Olney repeatedly assured the British Ambassador that he was predisposed to favor the English. We need not expect, then, that the Administration looked on the Cuban troubles any differently. Unhappily, neither the British nor the Spaniards could be persuaded that American intentions were entirely benevolent.

Congress demanded a more active Cuban policy by December 1895, and pressure on the Administration was increasing to help the Cubans rather than the Spaniards. The President had in the previous June proclaimed neutrality.[5] He vigorously enforced the neutrality acts which were designed to prevent any aid from reaching the Cuban insurgents; revenue ships were detailed to patrol the Straits of Florida to ensure their observance. A few months later, in his message to Congress of December 2, 1895, the President reaffirmed the Administration's determination to stand by its policy, and he called upon Americans to remain impartial in the conflict and obey the neutrality legislation.[6]

His exhortation fell on deaf ears. On the very next day a resolution was introduced in Congress demanding that Cleve-

3. Roosevelt to Lodge, Dec. 27, 1895. Morison, ed., *Roosevelt Letters*, 1, 503–04.
4. Roosevelt to Olney, December 20, 1895. Olney MSS, Library of Congress.
5. *Statutes at Large*, 29, 870–71.
6. Richardson, *Messages and Papers*, 9, 636–37.

land take steps to "civilize" the war in Cuba.[7] The excitement caused by the President's Venezuelan message fourteen days later interrupted only momentarily the continuous attention Congress was to pay Cuba for four years. Two further resolutions were soon submitted, proposing—rather haphazardly— the independence of Cuba and the purchase of all the islands in the neighborhood of the United States. The Senate Foreign Relations Committee meanwhile decided to examine the Cuban question exhaustively; the various resolutions were accordingly shelved until the committee could make its report.[8] But even before the appearance of this report, the characteristics which were to mark congressional policy became apparent. Some senators were moved not so much by good will to Cuba as by malice toward Cleveland. They not only utilized public sympthy for the suffering Cubans as a stick with which to beat Cleveland, but—and this was less obvious—they tried to exploit the situation still further by trying to limit the prerogatives of the Executive in foreign affairs.

Olney wisely attempted to cooperate with the Senate Foreign Relations Committee. To counteract the pro-Cuban inclination of the committee, he obtained a statement of the Spanish case from the Spanish Ambassador, Dupuy de Lôme, and called on Senator Sherman, a member of the committee, to ask him to consider it. He also handed Sherman a statement from Tomás Estrada Palma, President of the Cuban Republic in exile, and arranged to be available by telephone to the committee during its meeting on January 11, 1896.[9]

But despite Olney's efforts, the committee's report was hostile to Spain and the President. Congress recognized "the fact

7. *Congressional Record*, 54th Cong., 1st sess. (Dec. 3, 1895), 28, 24.
8. *Congressional Record*, 54th Cong., 1st sess. (Dec. 3, 1895 and Jan. 14, 1896), 28, 25, 607.
9. De Lôme to Olney, Jan. 10, 1896; Sherman to Olney, Jan. 10, 1896; Sherman to Olney, Jan. 11, 1896. Olney MSS.

that the matters herein referred to are properly within the control of the Chief Executive until, within the principles of our Constitution, it becomes the duty of Congress to define the final attitude of the Government of the United States toward Spain." [10] Not satisfied with putting forward this (unconstitutional) claim, the Senate then resolved that belligerent rights be accorded to the Cubans. The resolution in this form was too moderate for senatorial sentiment. By a resolution, adopted in February 1896, the President was requested to employ his good offices to secure independence for the Cubans. In short, the Senate demanded the abandonment of neutrality in favor of support for the Cuban insurgents.[11]

Such a course was unthinkable to Cleveland. It was likely to lead to war and Cuban independence. Cleveland and Olney suspected that the congressmen were just playing politics and that they were, as Olney put it, setting "their sails . . . to catch the popular pro-Cuban breeze." [12] Faced with a hostile and, so they believed, irresponsible legislature, the Administration brought its foreign policy to life when Congress was not in session. A solution would have to be found during the months before congressional activities could frustrate the initiative of the Executive.

During the early weeks of the Cuban revolution, Olney appears to have accepted what de Lôme told him. The Spanish version held that the insurgents belonged to the lowest order of the Cuban people and that they did not represent either the propertied or the literate classes of the island. Their triumph, according to de Lôme, would ruin the island; independence would lead to the end of all law and order in Cuba. Olney

10. 54th Cong., 1st sess., *Senate Report,* no. 141, serial 3362, p. 3.
11. *Congressional Record,* 54th Cong., 1st sess. (Feb. 28, 1896), 28, 2241, 2257.
12. Olney to Cleveland, Sept. 25, 1895. Nevins, *Letters of Cleveland,* p. 140.

conceded that if de Lôme were speaking in truth, then all right-thinking Americans ought to hope for Spain's success. But during the autumn of 1895 Olney was no longer sure that de Lôme was telling the truth.

The man who had first sown the seeds of doubt in Olney's mind was Paul Brooks, a native of Rutland, Vermont, the owner of the large sugar estate at Los Canos, Guantánamo.[13] During September 1895 he had called on Olney who, to use his own words, found himself "listening to statements utterly at variance with those to which the representatives of Spain are in the habit of giving currency." Brooks made a good impression on Olney, who heard him out attentively. He told the Secretary of State that the Cuban insurgents were no rabble; practically every prominent Cuban family was represented in the liberation movement. The propertied classes were disgusted with Spanish misrule, although they dared not support the insurgents openly for fear that their possessions would be confiscated by the Spanish authorities. Brooks claimed that nine tenths of the population favored the revolution. The Spaniards would not succeed in suppressing the uprising by force, and mere promises of reform would not induce the Cubans to lay down their arms. Brooks prophesied that Spain would either drench the island in blood or, more likely, tire of the fruitless struggle and offer Cuba to the highest bidder.

This dismal prospect alarmed Olney. Spain as the guardian of Cuba posed no threat to the security of the United States; a European power such as the Kaiser's restless Germany would be. The Queen Regent of Spain fulfilled the same function, in

13. The role of the sugar planters in the formation of the Administration's Hawaiian and Cuban policies has been thoroughly and convincingly analyzed by Richard D. Weigle, "The Sugar Interests and American Diplomacy in Hawaii and Cuba, 1893–1903" (Ph.D. thesis, Yale University, 1939). Our account of the influence of the plantation is indebted to Weigle's analysis, pp. 204 ff.

the eyes of the American Administration, as did the Sultan of
Turkey in the eyes of England. Everyone looked with horror
at the atrocities committed by the Spaniard and the Turk; but
the possible international dangers of replacing weak Spanish
or Turkish rule with a strong military power in the long run
deterred the American as it did the British government from
allowing humanitarian sentiments to dominate diplomacy.

The paucity of reliable information in the autumn of 1895
hampered Olney's capacity to decide the course of American
policy. While Brooks described the Cuban cause as a just
struggle for independence, another wealthy American sugar
planter, Edwin F. Atkins, sought to persuade Olney that the
revolutionary leaders were ruthless and did not deserve American sympathy. Atkins painted a somber picture of the war in
a score of letters to the Secretary of State. The insurgents, he
wrote, were wantonly destroying everything they could lay
their hands on.

Olney judiciously decided to send an American agent to
Cuba to investigate the situation. He made this proposal in a
long letter he sent to the President in September 1895. At this
time he was evidently more impressed by the arguments of
Brooks than by those put forward by Atkins, and he urged
Cleveland to adopt a more active Cuban policy. He suggested
that the recognition of Cuban belligerency, or even independence, should be considered as soon as the American agent's report had reached Washington.[14] After some hesitation, Cleveland rejected Olney's suggestion;[15] he was anxious to avoid a
serious crisis in foreign affairs and may well have become nervous about the outcome of Olney's Venezuelan policy.

As Olney pondered the Cuban problem, his sympathy with

14. Olney to Cleveland, Sept. 25, 1895. Nevins, *Letters of Cleveland,*
p. 140.
15. Cleveland to Olney, Sept. 29, 1895. Nevins, *Letters of Cleveland,*
pp. 410–11.

the insurgents began to wane. The violent pro-Cuban sentiments of Congress during the winter months of 1895 made him
suspicious of Cuba's cause. He resented the successful propaganda campaign, directed by the Cuban Junta, to inflame public sentiment. Olney's laudable ideal was to frame policy according to reason and remove international problems from the
forum of public debate. Somehow he usually managed to
achieve the reverse. He believed a solution could be reached
by secret conversations with foreign diplomats more readily
than by public altercation. Lacking reliable sources of information, the Secretary of State was inclined to listen to the advice
which Atkins continued to offer in his many letters.

The sugar planter strongly opposed a policy of granting belligerent rights to the Cubans; he feared this would lead to the
recognition of Cuban independence. The American planters
on the island had more to fear from the hostility of the insurgents than from the unjust fines the Spanish colonial administration levied on their estates. American recognition of Cuban
belligerency would completely ruin the planters. The Spanish
administration would certainly retaliate by refusing to protect
American investments.[16]

Atkins reported to Olney that the Cuban Junta was deliberately encouraging the destruction of American property as
a way to bring about American intervention. Estrada Palma,
the leader of the Cuban Junta, unwittingly provided evidence
for this assertion. When two Americans had requested protection from insurgent depredations, Estrada Palma had replied
that he could comply only if the American Administration
were prepared to recognize Cuban belligerency. Armed with
this information, Atkins called on the Secretary of State and
added that the members of the Cuban Junta now residing in
New York were actually naturalized American citizens. The

16. Weigle, "Sugar Interests," pp. 208 ff.

sequel was dramatic. When, some time later, three members of the Cuban Junta secured an interview with Olney, he received them coldly. Olney asked Estrada Palma outright whether he was an American citizen, and Estrada Palma and the two other Cubans proudly admitted the fact. Olney next wanted to know whether the Junta had given orders to the Cubans to destroy American property. Palma evaded the question; he had not sent any such specific order, but he knew of them and approved them as a necessary war measure in the Cuban struggle against Spain. "Well, gentlemen," Olney retorted, "there is but one term for such action. We call it arson." [17] And with that he terminated the interview. Unfortunately, from Olney's point of view, Congress could not be dismissed so contemptuously.

Like Scruggs in the previous year, Atkins had arrived in Washington to lobby in Congress and the Administration, but he achieved precisely the opposite results. Whereas Scruggs had made little headway with the Secretary of State but had scored a great success in Congress, Atkins had persuaded Olney and made no impression on Capitol Hill. The same day that the Senate had adopted a resolution calling on the President to mediate in order to secure independence for the Cubans, the Cabinet had met to decide the Administration's policy. They were at a loss to know what to do, but Olney believed he had found an historical precedent to suit the situation: during the closing months of 1875, Secretary of State Hamilton Fish, faced with a similar threat that Congress would get out of hand, had refused to allow Grant to be stampeded. Indeed President Grant in his annual message to Congress of December 1875 had put forward an exhaustive argument against recognition. Olney now read the relevant passages of Grant's mes-

17. Edwin F. Atkins, *Sixty Years in Cuba* (Cambridge, Mass., Harvard University Press, 1926), pp. 213–14. Quoted in Weigle, "Sugar Interests," p. 210.

sage. If the United States desired to go to war, Grant had declared, she should do so straightforwardly and not on discreditable grounds, for the recognition of Cuban belligerency was both legally and morally indefensible. Grant had expressed his readiness to mediate between Spain and the insurgents to help in the restoration of peace. He had warned Spain that, unless the island were pacified soon, America might be forced to intervene to safeguard her interests. Cleveland and his Cabinet considered the argument "as pertinent to the present situation as it was to that crisis." [18] The Administration, on February 28, 1896, had decided one important aspect of its policy —it would not recognize Cuban belligerency or independence, despite the hostility of Congress. The Cabinet rejected as impractical, however, Olney's suggestion that, in order to head off congressional action, the President announce his intention to send a commission to Cuba to discover the facts. As yet there was no positive policy.

Congress went its own way. On March 2, 1896, the House approved a resolution authorizing the President to accord the insurgents belligerent rights and, if necessary, to protect American interests by forcible intervention. Before a conference committee could reconcile the Senate and House resolutions, Senator Hoar of Massachusetts assumed the leadership of a group of New England Republicans anxious to support the Administration. Hoar offered a resolution giving the President an opportunity to communicate any further information concerning Cuba to Congress, inviting Cleveland to express his views. The President was tempted to draft a sharp reply, but in the end he decided to ignore the Hoar resolution. [19] No

18. Festus P. Summers, ed., *The Cabinet Diary of William L. Wilson, 1896–1897* (Chapel Hill, University of North Carolina Press, 1957), pp. 35–36. Nevins, *Hamilton Fish*, pp. 876–80.

19. Olney to Hoar, March 16, 1896, and Hoar to Olney, March 16, 1896. Olney MSS. *Congressional Record,* 54th Cong., 1st sess. (March 2, 9, April 6, 1896), 28, 2342, 2359, 2585, 3627–28.

executive opinion was communicated to the legislature. Some weeks later, on April 6, 1896, the House accepted the Senate resolution by 287 votes to 27. Congress then adjourned.

The President and the Secretary of State had been waiting for Congress to disperse before taking any diplomatic initiative. They had been at work on a note to Spain to clarify American policy since the Cabinet meeting of February 28. They completed the draft on April 7, 1896, but to avoid the impression that it was being sent in response to the congressional resolution of April 6, they predated the dispatch to April 4.[20]

The dispatch is one of the most interesting documents in the history of American foreign relations. It repudiated America's historic mission of placing herself, at least morally, on the side of colonial people in the Western Hemisphere struggling for independence. It rejected abstract principle. The deciding factor was the good of the United States. To be sure, the Secretary of State enumerated the traditional reasons for American concern over the fate of Cuba. He voiced righteous, humanitarian sentiment that the struggle be brought to a close and described the injury done American sugar planters, the havoc that the struggle brought to the economy of the island, and the consequent injury to American commerce. (Olney did not actually believe that injury to American commerce justified intervention. Americans had of their own free will will invested their capital in Cuba, he had written to the President a few days earlier; the rebellion was their misfortune, and he could not see "how this Government can protect them from the inevitable consequences" of their miscalculation.)[21]

The note's most significant portions betray Olney's partiality

20. Olney to de Lôme, April 4, 1896. James, *Olney*, pp. 290–97.
21. Olney to Cleveland, March 21, 1896. Weigle, "Sugar Interests," pp. 216–17.

for Spain: he spoke about the Cuban revolutionaries with marked hostility and claimed that they did not possess the necessary organization and civilization to warrant recognition as belligerents; he blamed the insurgents for destroying the factories and crops of the island and for driving the unemployed to revolution. Olney did not criticize Spain's military conduct on the island; he condoned it, declaring that the Spanish government "wisely undertook to make its struggle with the present insurrection short, sharp, and decisive." Olney's only complaint was that Spain's armies had failed.

The success of the insurgents in the face of the unprecedented military efforts made by Spain had convinced Olney that Spain could not pacify the island. Sooner or later, Spain would be driven to abandon Cuba "to the heterogeneous combination of elements and of races now in arms against her." In the passage that followed he implicitly compared the probable future of Cuba to the wretched situation caused by the partition of one Caribbean island into the "black and white" states of Haiti and Santo Domingo:

[The defeat of Spain] cannot be viewed even by the most devoted friend of Cuba and the most enthusiastic advocate of popular government except with the gravest apprehension. There are only too strong reasons to fear that, once Spain were withdrawn from the Island, the sole bond of union between the different factions of the insurgents would disappear; that a war of races would be precipitated, all the more sanguinary for the discipline and experience acquired during the insurrection, and that, even if there were to be temporary peace, it could only be through the establishment of a white and a black republic, which, even if agreeing at the outset upon a division of the Island between them, would be enemies from the start, and would never rest until the one had been completely vanquished and subdued by the other.[22]

Olney offered the President's good offices to end the conflict and avoid calamity by conciliation; he also intimated that Spain could count on the support of the United States to achieve the pacification of the island; but time was of the essence. According to Olney's plan, Spain would accept the American offer before exhaustion forced it to withdraw; the longer Spain hesitated, the stronger the insurgents would become. Olney assured the government in Madrid that the United States intended to do nothing to impair Spanish sovereignty. The President's solution was to cooperate with Spain in pacifying the island immediately "on such a plan as, leaving Spain her rights of sovereignty, shall yet secure to the people of the Island all such rights and powers of local self-government *as they can reasonably ask.*" [23] Cleveland would judge what was reasonable; Spain could trust him, knowing that the United States would maintain its sovereignty. As for the insurgents, they too could trust him, since "anything assented to by this Government which did not satisfy the reasonable demands and aspirations of Cuba would arouse the indignation of our whole people." A demand for independence, according to Olney's thinking, was not reasonable. Olney did not spell out exactly how he intended to pacify the island if the insurgents proved recalcitrant. No doubt he thought that the threat of American intervention would suffice to bring the insurgent leaders to their senses.

22. Olney to de Lôme, April 4, 1896, *Spanish Diplomatic Correspondence and Documents, 1896–1900* (Washington, D.C., 1905). It is interesting to note that this well known and important dispatch was not published in *Foreign Relations,* to spare Spanish susceptibilities. De Lôme to Olney, April 10, 1896; Olney to de Lôme, April 10, 1896. Olney MSS.
23. Ibid. Italics added.

The plan was fantastic. Most Americans would not have tolerated intervention on behalf of Spain; certainly Congress would have attempted to block any such attempt. The feelings of Congress and public opinion had extraordinarily little impact on the Administration. It is difficult to understand how Olney and Cleveland could have deluded themselves into believing that the Cuban leaders would accept American mediation on the terms proposed to Spain, but delude themselves they did.

Olney received the Spanish reply two months later, in June 1896. De Lôme tactfully conveyed a message that amounted to rejection of the President's offer. To accept American mediation, wrote de Lôme, would be derogatory to Spain's sovereignty; the insurgents would in any case spurn American mediation, since they suspected America of wishing to annex the island. If the Americans foresaw the disastrous consequences of Spain's defeat, was it not more logical, he asked, for the Administration to help Spain to put down the revolution by curbing the activities of the Cuban exiles residing in the United States? [24]

The Spanish government evidently did not believe that Cleveland and Olney were partial to Spain. They were unable to reconcile Olney's claim that the United States could impose its will on the Cubans with the fact that the Administration was unable to control American agitation in support of Cuba. Olney, for his part, was rather naïve in expecting from the Spanish government any great concern over the fate of Cuba or the security of American interests, should Spain lose the island.

As the war continued on its barbarous course through the summer and autumn of 1896, reliable, official American evidence showing that the Cubans controlled and administered a

24. De Lôme to Olney, June 4, 1896. James, *Olney*, pp. 297–303.

substantial part of the island multiplied.[25] Judson Harmon, the Attorney General, believed that the Cubans merited recognition as belligerents and that the President's refusal to grant this status substantially aided Spain:

> In reading the Spanish Minister's letter and memoranda, I am impressed with the idea that he regards a state of war as actually existing in the Island of Cuba . . . If it be true that the Spanish Government have information sufficient to convince it that a state of war exists, it seems to me that, by failing formally and officially to recognize a state of war, it must be regarded as contributing to the ill success of attempts to prevent filibustering expeditions by means of our penal laws.[26]

But Cleveland showed no sign of changing his attitude toward the Cuban "insurgents." In July 1896 he renewed his neutrality proclamation of the previous year and called attention to the decisions of the Supreme Court on the neutrality laws.[27] That same month he refused to accept the advice of the American Consul General in Havana that a warship with a complement of Marines be sent to Havana as a "precautionary measure." Commented the President: "I do not want now anything of that kind made a convenient excuse for trouble with Spain." [28] Cleveland was determined to avoid war with Spain. He believed that to recognize the Cubans as belliger-

25. W. Hallett Phillips to Olney, April 1896; Lee to Olney, June 24, 1896; Captain J. H. H. Peskine (American military attaché in Madrid), report no. 26, "Cuban Affairs," August 17, 1896; Peskine to War Department, Aug. 17 and Sept. 15, 1896; Consul Barker from Sagua la Grande, Cuba, Sept. 19, 1896. Olney MSS.

26. Harmon to Olney (copy), Sept. 29, 1896. Olney MSS.

27. *Statutes at Large*, 29, 881–82.

28. Olney to Cleveland, July 14, 1896; Olney to Lee, July 15, 1896; Lee to Olney, July 22, 1896. Olney MSS. Cleveland to Olney, July 16, 1896. Nevins, *Letters of Cleveland*, pp. 448–49.

ents would destroy all hope that Spain might eventually accept his offer to mediate the conflict. Cleveland's Cuban policy presents some striking analogies to his Hawaiian diplomacy: he resisted popular pressure, gave the Administration time to decide on its course, and then produced a plan designed to settle all difficulties which was totally unworkable.

Despite Spain's refusal in July 1896 to accept the President's good offices, Olney did not abandon his search for a diplomatic solution. He was encouraged by de Lôme to believe a Spanish–American agreement possible. The Spaniard hoped in this way to delay American intervention. During the autumn months of 1896, the Spanish Ambassador and the Secretary of State discussed a very complicated diplomatic arrangement. They tried to find a way to embody in the form of a treaty a Spanish undertaking to the United States to introduce reforms in Cuba, and they hit upon an ingenious plan to accomplish this diplomatic acrobatic trick: Spain and the United States would sign a commercial treaty whose preamble would enumerate the reforms Spain was ready to introduce. But these negotiations came to nothing.[29] The Spaniards still hoped for victory in Cuba and saw no reason why they should bind their hands by giving such concessions to the United States.

Olney meanwhile made strenuous efforts to discover whether a substantial section of the Cuban population would accept autonomy. The information he received from the American Consul General at Havana was not reassuring. Cleveland had appointed Fitzhugh Lee, a Southern Democrat and former governor of Virginia, to this important post. Lee sought to discourage Olney's belief in the viability of autonomy. There was no longer an autonomist party in Cuba, he wrote Olney in June 1896; the insurgents first wanted their independence from Spain; then they would vote for annexation to the United

29. Olney to Blandford, May 29, 1897. James, *Olney*, pp. 165–66.

States.[30] A month later, the serious news from Havana and the danger to American lives and property, induced Cleveland and Olney to propose the despatch of a cruiser there. The Cabinet met in the morning of December 8 and approved this suggestion; but after lunch, Secretary of the Navy Hilary Herbert, with almost prophetic insight, began to fear that an accident might befall the American warship and so exacerbate America's relations with Spain. He went straightway to see the President and without difficulty persuaded him to reverse the decision.[31] Cleveland did not trust the reliability of the information he received from Lee, the Consul General in Havana. The previous summer the President had observed, "He seems to have fallen into the style of rolling intervention like a sweet morsel under his tongue." [32] Lee's advice was still not welcome. During the month of December 1896, Lee, then on leave in Washington, sought to persuade the Administration to intervene in Cuba and to work for an American protectorate. But Olney would not listen to him. The Secretary of State was searching for a way to end Cuban unrest without impairing Spain's ultimate rights of sovereignty—reform without independence.

Atkins approved; he saw no need to accede to the demands for independence. Cuban autonomy would provide a solution satisfactory to all parties. He claimed that all the most intelligent people he had spoken to in Cuba had "expressed a wish that the United States might use its friendly offices to such an end." [33] This was exactly what Olney wanted to hear. He simply dismissed Lee's advice to the contrary and concluded that he could not rely on him to carry out the Administration's

30. Lee to Olney, June 24, 1896. Weigle, "Sugar Interests," p. 220.
31. Summers, ed., *Wilson Cabinet Diary*, p. 184.
32. Cleveland to Olney, July 16, 1896. May, *Imperial Democracy*, p. 89.
33. Atkins to Olney, May 5, 1896. Weigle, "Sugar Interests," p. 218.

policy. Olney turned to two American planters, Atkins and Oscar B. Stillman, manager of the Trinidad Sugar Estate. With their help, Olney initiated secret negotiations with the leaders of the Cuban revolution in the autumn and early winter of 1896.

Olney received several hopeful messages from Atkins. Many prominent Cubans in New York, Atkins wrote, would accept Cuban autonomy; an emissary Atkins sent to the Cuban leaders on the island reported that a number of insurgent leaders would be satisfied with autonomy. On Olney's instructions, Stillman left for Cuba in December on a secret mission to the Cuban army commanders in the field. He was to explain Olney's policy and to win their approval.[34]

Meantime the Administration remained as anxious as ever to restrain Congress. Congressional resolutions promising support for Cuban independence might easily induce the Cuban leaders to reject the compromise Olney was endeavoring to secure. Cleveland and Olney calculated that Congress would only hold back if the Administration itself appeared ready to take a militant stand on the Cuban issue. That is why Cleveland, in his message to Congress on December 7, 1896, referred to the Cuban problem in such forceful language. The United States could not be expected to remain a spectator of the Cuban war. "[We] may be drawn into such an unusual and unprecedented condition, as will fix a limit to our patient waiting for Spain to end the contest, either alone and in her own way, or with our friendly cooperation." [35] Cleveland was not entirely candid, for he did not mention that the Administration was already attempting to embark on a policy of "friendly cooperation" with Spain. Cleveland's message was mistakenly inter-

34. Weigle, "Sugar Interests," pp. 221–22. Summers, ed., *Wilson Cabinet Diary*, p. 183.
35. Richardson, *Messages and Papers*, 9, 717–21. May, *Imperial Democracy*, p. 93.

preted by many Americans at the time (and by many historians since) as foreshadowing American intervention in Cuba.

The supporters of Cuba in Congress, however, rightly suspected Cleveland's true intentions and were not prepared to leave the initiative with the President. James Donald Cameron of Pennsylvania, Republican member of the Senate Foreign Relations Committee, had introduced a resolution on December 9, 1896, demanding that the United States recognize Cuban independence immediately. Olney at once explained to Chairman Sherman that to recognize Cuban independence would be tantamount to declaring war on Spain. Sherman appeared to agree, but on the very next day he asked Olney to call on him in his committee rooms and there informed him that the committee had decided to adopt the resolution. They would be grateful for the Secretary of State's advice on how to word it.[36] Olney responded forcefully on his own authority on December 19 by issuing a statement to the press saying that the power to recognize the so-called "Republic of Cuba" rested exclusively with the President, and that the resolution passed by Congress could be "regarded only as an expression of opinion by the eminent gentlemen who vote for it." [37] Although Olney's statement aroused a furore in the Senate, the Cameron resolution was shelved. But violent debate continued in Congress during the last few weeks of the lame duck session. Resolutions similar to Cameron's were offered, but none reached a vote.[38]

The months of December 1896 and January 1897 were

36. 54th Cong., 2d sess., *Senate Reports*, nos. 1160 and 1534, serials 3474 and 3476.
37. New York *Times*, Dec. 20, 1896. Summers, ed., *Wilson Cabinet Diary*, pp. 192–93.
38. Chadwick, *The Relations of the United States and Spain*, pp. 486–90.

critical for Cleveland's Cuban policy. The President was still optimistic about the outcome of the secret pourparlers, remarking on Christmas eve, "I want to dispose of as many of these difficulties as I can so as to clear the way for McKinley." [39] The President-elect, waiting in Canton, Ohio, for the inauguration, heartily agreed. During the early weeks of the new year, the majority of the senators reached the conclusion that nothing more could be done before the new Administration assumed office. Olney, on the contrary, hoped to solve the Cuban crisis before leaving the State Department.

Stillman returned to Washington in January 1897. Olney now arranged a conference at which he, Stillman, and the Spanish Ambassador were present. The Ambassador offered no new suggestions. He repeated the promises of his government to introduce reforms; he referred to the possibility of joining with the United States in undertaking to provide them. The Cubans would be granted rights of self-government but not their independence. Stillman returned to Cuba without delay to place these terms before the insurgent leaders. The Cuban commander in the field, General Maximo Gomez, rejected the overture. In February 1897 even Atkins was obliged to admit that the insurgents would not touch the reform project.[40] Olney was forced to bequeath the dilemma of America's Cuban policy to the incoming Administration after all.

Defeated by the Republicans and rejected by the majority of their own supporters, Cleveland and Olney relinquished office under a cloud of disapproval and public contempt. But as the bitterness of the controversies of the mid-nineties faded, their reputations grew. Posterity has stressed their successes and dealt kindly with their failures.

Cleveland cannot altogether escape responsibility for the

39. Summers, ed., *Wilson Cabinet Diary*, p. 193.
40. Weigle, "Sugar Interests," pp. 223–24.

disastrous decline in the fortune of the Democratic party, which, after his retirement from public life, was kept out of power for sixteen years. Admiration for Cleveland's courage must be balanced against the charge that he was obstinate and maladroit in his handling of political issues. Nor should Olney's successful conduct of Anglo–American relations at the time of the Venezuelan dispute hide the fact that he was foolhardy in overestimating the military capacity of the United States; he brought about a crisis in Anglo–American relations that he had sought to avoid, and he settled it in a high-handed manner. It was lucky for Olney that the sudden intensification of rivalry among the European powers came to the rescue of his Venezuelan policy when it seemed most likely to founder. It is difficult to censure the Administration for so persistently seeking to avoid war with Spain. It is, however, equally hard to justify its failure to recognize the belligerency of the Cubans. Cleveland and Olney were committed to an unrealistic policy of mediation.

The most striking aspect of Olney's diplomacy was his naked assertion of American power in the Western Hemisphere. He did not understand the nationalist aspirations of the Cubans, the Venezuelans, and the peoples of Latin America; although in his approach to new problems he tried to be judicious and impartial, he found it difficult to grasp any divergent views once he made up his mind. Had these weaknesses in foreign policy continued, they would have undermined the development of good relations between the United States and its neighbors.

Chapter Eight

The Expansionists:

The Education of Henry Cabot Lodge

THAT THE REPUBLICAN VICTORY and the inauguration of McKinley in 1897 delivered American diplomacy into irresponsible hands is often asserted. A distinguished historian writes that it gave a group of expansionists the chance to apply the principles they espoused: a "few men in powerful positions were able to plunge the nation into an imperialist career that it never explicitly decided to follow." [1] Most of these expansionists are forgotten today. Senators Platt of Connecticut, Dolph of Oregon, Teller of Colorado, Chandler, Morgan, and Frye were among the most prominent. Three men who became close friends and associates, Alfred Thayer Mahan, Theodore Roosevelt, and Henry Cabot Lodge, have gone down in history as apostles of the new imperialism. But perhaps too much has been made of their influence on the course of American foreign policy in the years before the war with Spain.

Lodge has been depicted as one of the leaders of this expansionist clique which pushed America into foreign adventure, imperialism, and war. He has been dubbed a jingo and an anglophobe. Historians have described him as a symbol of imperialism in the 1890s and in the next breath a symbol of isolationism in the 1920s. Labels such as "imperialism" and

1. Howard K. Beale, *Theodore Roosevelt and the Rise of American World Power* (Baltimore, Johns Hopkins University Press, 1956), p. 55.

"isolationism" often lead to confusion; they obscure Lodge's real point of view.

Lodge in fact did not lead public opinion in the early 1890s. He was slow to grasp the importance of America's foreign relations. In his biography of George Washington, published in 1889, the following passage occurs: "Our relations with foreign nations to-day fill but a slight place in American politics, and excite generally only a languid interest. We have separated ourselves so completely from the affairs of other people that it is difficult to realize how large a place they occupied when the government was founded." [2] In 1892 Lodge published an appreciation of Seward's statesmanship without referring to the Secretary of State's grandiose concept of American foreign policy. He did not even consider the purchase of Alaska sufficiently important to mention.[3] Further evidence for Lodge's lack of concern about world affairs comes from his private correspondence. Practically no discussion of foreign policy is to be found there before 1893. Lodge was, in the early '90s, far more moderate than some of his fellow senators who were calling for an aggressive and forceful foreign policy. An account of the education of Henry Cabot Lodge may at least serve as a starting point for the task of disentangling fact and fiction.[4]

2. Henry Cabot Lodge, *George Washington* (2 vols. Boston, Houghton Mifflin, 1889), 2, 129.

3. Lodge, *Historical and Political Essays* (Boston, Houghton Mifflin, 1892), pp. 1–46. Lodge had actually first published this essay in the *Atlantic Monthly* in May 1884, but when he reprinted it in his collected essays he stated that he had not materially changed his views.

4. John A. Garraty, *Henry Cabot Lodge, A Biography* (New York, Knopf, 1953), is the most satisfactory life of the Senator and the first to be based on a scholarly analysis of Lodge's personal papers; the author has also provided an exhaustive bibliography. Our own conclusion of Lodge's outlook and policy during the formative 1890s nevertheless differs at times widely from those of Garraty's. Our researches would suggest that a general reinterpretation of Lodge's ideas might be attempted.

Lodge attained his majority in 1871; he had already graduated from Harvard and married. As a young scion of one of Boston's elite families, he had received the best formal education that money could buy. But his real education had scarcely begun. Little distinguished Lodge from the wealthy, lively young men of his day. After his wedding, he took his bride on a leisurely European tour to refine their tastes, the proper trip for a prominent Bostonian. The Lodges dutifully saw the sights of London, Oberammergau, Paris, Leipzig, Rome, and then Paris again—where in April 1872 Nannie gave birth to a daughter. Their enthusiasm for monuments and museums waned soon enough, and Lodge became increasingly bored. In Rome he had long discussions about philosophy, politics, and life in general with Michael Henry Simpson, a Harvard classmate. In Paris he resolved to find a worthwhile career, though he did not have the slightest idea what to do. Lodge did not need to earn his living. He now turned for advice to Henry Adams, the one teacher at Harvard who had inspired him with enthusiasm during his last year there.[5]

Lodge was fortunate to know Henry Adams in his prime, before a sense of failure had turned Adams into a cynical observer of the political scene. Adams responded warmly to the request of his young pupil. Lodge's senior by twelve years, Adams was just then embarking on his career as an historian. The historians who had brought fame to Boston were growing old. Francis Parkman, the youngest, was 49, John Motley was in his late fifties, and George Bancroft was in his seventies. Who would carry on their tradition twenty years hence? Boston was "running dry," Adams surmised. He now hoped to provide for the future by training a school of younger historians in the

5. For Lodge's relations with Henry Adams see particularly Garraty, *Lodge*, pp. 37 ff.; Ernest Samuels, *Henry Adams, The Middle Years* (Cambridge, Mass., Harvard University Press, 1958); Elizabeth Stevenson, *Henry Adams, A Biography* (New York, Macmillan, 1955).

scientific, German tradition of scholarship founded by Ranke. And so Adams counseled Lodge to make for himself an "historico-literary" career. Thus began an association which for twelve years dominated Lodge's life.

Lodge returned to Boston in August 1872, enrolled in the Harvard Law School, and threw himself heart and soul into the study of early Germanic law, which, not surprisingly, he found a rather depressing business; but Adams, who was spending that year in Europe, kept in touch and encouraged him to persevere. Adams returned to Harvard the following year, and Lodge joined his seminar on medieval institutions. Adams now took Lodge under his wing. Then the editor of the *North American Review*, Adams asked Lodge to act as unpaid assistant. Shortly before Adams left Harvard in 1876, Lodge took over Adams' course on American colonial history. Although these academic pursuits eventually led to a doctoral dissertation on Anglo-Saxon land law and a position on the Harvard faculty, Lodge was neither an inspired teacher nor a dispassionate scholar.

Lodge wrote several biographies during the course of the next ten years. His *Life and Letters of George Cabot Lodge* was followed by biographies of Alexander Hamilton, Daniel Webster, and George Washington. The most that can be said for these books is that they were well written and profitable to the author and publisher. Today they are chiefly of interest as a source for Lodge's own outlook.

Adams introduced Lodge into politics; this proved of more lasting importance than Lodge's historical apprenticeship. The life of a scholar and teacher had not entirely satisfied Adams. Soon after his arrival at Harvard, Adams complained about the tedium of his work and the parochial outlook of Boston and Cambridge. He came to look upon Harvard as a dignified refuge during an era of corrupt politics, and he tired of remaining a passive spectator. In 1874 he began to organize a "party of the center" whose intervention he hoped would rid Washington of the spoilsmen. Henry Adams envisioned a kind of political "armed neutrality." His party would back the party—Republican or Democratic—that was ready, in return for this independent support, to attack graft and political corruption; civil service reform became its most important plank. Adams left much of the practical work of organization to Lodge, who had proved his efficiency as assistant editor of the *North American Review*. With the nomination of Rutherford B. Hayes as Republican presidential candidate, however, the notion of a reform party fell to pieces.

Although deeply disillusioned, Lodge did not lose his taste for politics. For some years he continued to pin his hopes on a reform party, independent of both the Democratic and Republican machines. Lodge's transformation from high-minded idealist to practical politician was gradual. The process had clearly been completed when in 1884 he cast his support for Blaine, the Republican presidential candidate, who stood for everything Lodge had earlier so ardently opposed. Unlike Adams, Lodge came to terms with the less savory aspects of party politics; he recognized that the struggle for reform would be fruitless without the backing of a great political machine. Adams became the detached and cynical observer, Lodge a participant in the shaping of national policy. What use, he asked, was it to be right if one were without the influence to affect the trend of great events? "It is better to agree on some course which may seem to some of us less wise than to disagree upon the wisest course possible," he observed in a letter many years later.[6]

It is not difficult to assess the influence of Henry Adams

6. Lodge to David Hall Rice, Jan. 25, 1893, Lodge MSS (deposited in the Massachusetts Historical Society).

on Lodge's career; far more difficult, however, is the task of assessing how far Lodge's general outlook was influenced by Adams' views. Clearly Lodge's genuine interest in political reform owed much to Adams. He also shared Adams' fierce patriotism and ambivalent attitude to England. Adams, like Lodge, profoundly admired British culture and achievements; both men were deeply conscious of the heritage the two nations shared and wished to win Britain's friendship.

To regard Lodge as an anglophobe is to misunderstand him. He asserted his opposition to the aping of English customs and manners because he felt that Americans had not yet completely lost what he described as the colonial attitude—a point he vividly brought out in his *Early Memories*:

> The society into which I was born and of which I became a part was, aside from politics, in its standards and fashions essentially English. The colonial habits of thought, very natural in their proper time, still held sway . . . the dominance of English habits, fashions, and beliefs may have been more pronounced in Boston and New England than elsewhere in the United States, but I doubt if there was any serious difference . . . Our literary standards, our standards of statesmanship, our modes of thought, apart from politics and diplomacy, where we were really independent, were as English as the trivial customs of the dinner-table and the ballroom.[7]

This passage echoes the views of Adams, who had earlier written, "All through life, one had seen the American on his literary knees to the European, and all through many lives back for some two centuries, one had seen the European snub and patronize the American." [8]

7. *Early Memories* (New York, Scribner's, 1913), pp. 203–04.
8. *The Education of Henry Adams* (Boston, Houghton Mifflin, 1918), p. 319.

Adams and Lodge battled against what they regarded as a false sense of American inferiority. They believed England's contempt of American civilization had succeeded in persuading many Americans that they were nothing but degenerate Englishmen. Adams repudiated this notion. He summoned "the new science of dynamic sociology" and reached the conclusion that the organization of American society had already enabled Americans to outstrip Europe, which, hampered by class divisions and anachronistic political institutions, was sinking into decrepitude. We may safely surmise he discussed these ideas at Harvard with Lodge and the small band of young scholars he had brought together.

Adams' views were not entirely conditioned by theoretical speculation. As a young man he had, in May 1861, accompanied his father, Charles Francis Adams, to the Court of St. James's. Henry Adams had expected the British government to offer them, as representatives of the Union, a friendly and sympathetic reception. He was soon disillusioned. British policy seemed to him to be dictated neither by morality nor by a detestation of slavery, but by economic self-interest. It was a lesson he never forgot. As time passed, he concluded that malevolence had always characterized official British policy towards the United States. In his *Education*, Adams referred to the "two hundred years of stupid and greedy blundering which no argument and no violence affected." [9] Britain, he concluded during his stay in London, respected only power. Anglo–American relations could therefore not be placed on a sound footing until the British government had learned the lesson that America was not to be trifled with.

Lodge later expressed the same point of view. In his life of *George Washington,* he said of the British treatment of Gouverneur Morris: "It was the fit beginning of the conduct by

9. Ibid., p. 362

which England for nearly a century has succeeded in alien-
ating the good-will of the people of the United States. Such a
policy was neither generous nor intelligent, and politically it
was a gross blunder." [10] But Lodge's conclusions, unlike those
of Adams, were not based on first-hand experience. When he
wrote this passage, he still had taken no real interest in foreign
affairs.

Lodge also saw America's economic difficulties in the 1880s
and 1890s through the eyes of Adams and blamed them on
England. "I believe myself that the selfish action of England
in demonetizing silver has been the cause very largely of our
present troubles." [11] Until the eve of the Spanish–American
conflict, Lodge's view of England remained clouded by strong
prejudices which reflect the influence of Henry Adams. Many
years later, Lodge condemned these anti-English feelings
when he wrote: "The colonial attitude of mind was displayed
as clearly by the deep hatred of England which most Americans felt as it could have been by the most servile admiration." [12] Lodge had, by then, outgrown Adams' tutelage.

In 1890 Lodge stood on the threshold of fame. He had already
gained a reputation as a popular historian; he had risen to
prominence in state politics and had served in the House of
Representatives since 1887. He had not yet made his mark on
the national scene. In 1893 he embarked on his senatorial
career, and within three years he won a commanding place
in the Senate as a spokesman on foreign affairs, a position he
was to retain for three decades.

This was an astonishing transformation—the sudden change
historians are apt to mistrust. Lodge's biographers have attempted to show that his passionate concern for America's

10. Lodge, *George Washington*, 2, 135 ff.
11. Lodge to D. A. Gleason, Dec. 15, 1890. Lodge MSS.
12. *Early Memories*, p. 205.

foreign relations developed gradually, even from childhood. The Lodge papers do not confirm such conclusions. The '90s matured men quickly; a new era seemed at hand. The Kaiser, impressionable and sensitive, proclaimed the age of Weltpolitik. Ten years later, on the eve of his retirement, Lord Salisbury darkly prophesied: "We are near some great change in public affairs—in which the forces which contend for the mastery among us will be differently ranged and balanced. . . . The large aggregation of human force which lies around our Empire seems to draw more closely together, and to assume almost unconsciously a more and more aggressive aspect." [13] These two men, so different in temperament and outlook—the German young and aggressive, the Englishman old and cautious—both sensed that world politics were changing. By the end of the century, the United States and Japan had joined England, Germany, and Russia in the ranks of world powers.

Midway through the decade, Lodge responded vigorously to the challenge. Admiral Luce, Theodore Roosevelt, and Alfred Thayer Mahan all contributed to the dramatic change in his outlook. Perhaps Henry Adams was right when he warned Lodge in 1878 of his inclination to fall "under the control of the man or men whose thought in the times you deal with, coincides most nearly with your prejudices." [14] Lodge was deeply indebted to Luce for his views on naval expansion, to Mahan for his concepts of America's strategic needs, and to Roosevelt for his emphasis on force as a determining factor of international relations. But Lodge did not slavishly copy the ideas of others. As he told a Harvard audience, "Thinking for yourself is the only real independence . . . It is, after all, largely a matter of seeing things as they are, and not mistaking

13. Grenville, *Salisbury*, pp. 339–40.
14. Samuels, *Henry Adams*, p. 16.

names for things." [15] Luce, Roosevelt, and Mahan influenced Lodge, but they never dominated him as Henry Adams had once done.

It seems likely that Luce did most to stimulate Lodge's early interest in the Navy. The relationships between the Luces and Lodges was close. Nannie's sister had married Luce's son. Lodge, moreover, took his place on the House Committee on Naval Affairs in 1887, just at the time when Luce was attempting to rally support for the War College. We can be sure that Luce did not neglect to win his relation by marriage to the cause, and he brought about a meeting between Mahan, Roosevelt, and Lodge. In any case, when in April 1890 Lodge supported the appropriation for three battleships in the House, Mahan's book had not been published. Nor did Lodge yet think of American foreign policy in any but the most traditional terms. He was not then an advocate of the large policy. The three battleships projected in 1890 were, after all, only to possess the coal capacity to fight within the radius of a thousand miles from their base. Lodge was therefore able to refute the proposition that the new Navy could be used for offensive purposes—an argument the opponents of naval expansion made much of. As Lodge saw it, the construction of these three battleships did not mark a departure from previous naval policy; on the contrary, he believed they signified a return to traditional policies. After the War of 1812, he explained to his fellow congressmen, "no man argued [any] more against the wisdom of maintaining a small but effective fighting

15. Dr. James E. Hewes, Jr., quotes this interesting statement in an unpublished manuscript, "Henry Cabot Lodge and the League of Nations," which he generously allowed us to read. We should like to acknowledge here our appreciation to Dr. Hewes for placing his time at our disposal and for allowing us to take advantage of his deep understanding of Senator Lodge's life.

navy of the highest type"; this standard had been maintained for the following fifty years, but after the Civil War, "the war of rebellion," as Lodge called it, the Navy had been neglected to the point where the United States possessed "practically no navy whatever." The construction of battleships, he now argued, marked no departure of policy, since no modern Navy could be effective without ships capable of meeting an enemy on the high seas and driving him from our coast. He pointed to America's undefended seaports: one English battleship, he dramatically declared, "could lay the city of New York in ruins or put it to ransom tomorrow." There was not sufficient time to build land fortifications and, in any case, they were too costly.

> The quickest way to defend the coast is by a navy; not by an offensive navy, which is a temptation to war and might bring us into needless conflict with the other nations of the world, but by one which is true to the American policy and the American idea of the Navy . . . ships which can fight at sea and which can be concentrated at any point on the coast in defense of the great cities and the great populations of our Atlantic and Pacific seaboard.[16]

Lodge also asserted that the Navy would serve a second function, namely, to back up American diplomacy. This proved to be an elastic concept in the hands of Lodge and others. But in 1890 he was not looking beyond the immediate vicinity of American territory. He firmly adhered to the policy of holding aloof from complications with other powers, declaring that "the true American policy is that which we have always pursued, of having, not a great offensive navy, but a navy powerful for defense." "Let me tell you, sir," Lodge con-

16. Lodge, *Congressional Record*, 51st Cong., 1st sess. (April 8, 1890), 21, 3169–70.

tinued, "if we had had such a navy as I have described behind us in the negotiations which have dragged on for so many years under every Administration seeking the settlement of the difficulties of our fishermen and of our Behring Sea dispute, those negotiations would have been ended long ago." "By war?", interjected someone from the floor of the House. "No, by diplomacy," Lodge retorted; the lack of adequate defenses tied the hands of American diplomats. Lodge repeated many of the arguments of Luce and other Navy enthusiasts: war could break out suddenly, and so the United States must be prepared; the power to inflict an injury on any enemy is the best guarantee of peace; America's present weakness actually was a temptation to would-be aggressors who, even if they did not attack the United States, might well blackmail it.[17]

None of these arguments was new. The vision of American cities reduced to ruin and rubble by foreign warships had been, as we have seen, the stock-in-trade of the Navy lobby in the '70s and '80s, during which time Lodge had been insensitive to their arguments. His speech in 1890 is therefore important not so much for what he said but because it was Lodge who said it. He had hitherto been absorbed in domestic problems; his support for the new Navy in 1890 marks an important stage in his evolution as an exponent of a new and dynamic foreign policy.

If Luce had opened Lodge's eyes to the need for battleships, Roosevelt was responsible for Lodge's realization that Germany's growing might also posed a threat to the United States. Their celebrated friendship dated from 1884 when, on Henry Adams' advice, Lodge had sought the support of a group of New York reform politicians, Roosevelt among them, to frustrate the nomination of Blaine as the Republican presi-

17. Ibid., 3267–68.

dential candidate. But the immediate campaign of the two young politicians ended in failure. Lodge and Roosevelt decided to support Blaine, the party's choice, while many of their friends and their political allies, the Mugwumps, declared their support for Cleveland and bolted the ticket. They abused Lodge and Roosevelt as timeservers and hypocrites. Exposed to fierce personal attack, Lodge and Roosevelt drew together, their political alignment developing into a close personal friendship.

In some ways, it was an attraction of opposites. Lodge looked frail, reserved, and shy, and he gave the impression of being cold and aloof to all but his intimate friends. Roosevelt, on the other hand, was an elk of a man, gregarious and sociable, at ease alike with cowhand and prince. Lodge stood aside from the crowds; although sensitive to criticism he did not allow it to affect his choice of causes. He suspected the good judgment of the masses. But Roosevelt's faith in the virtues of the American people—when properly led—bordered on mysticism. Roosevelt's image was larger than life; his exploits became legends in his lifetime, and his public presence was electrifying. Lodge was cool and calculating; his speeches were not likely to move crowds, and his admirers called him the scholar in politics. He made more enemies than friends, and historians have generally judged him harshly as a man ruled by malevolence and narrow prejudice.

For all their differences, Lodge and Roosevelt had much in common. Descendants of early settler families, they possessed wealth and social position and had enjoyed a privileged education. They were intensely patriotic and passionately interested in the history of the United States. During the early years of their friendship, Roosevelt also contributed to the biographical studies published in the American Statesmen Series, writing the volumes on Thomas Hart Benton and

Gouverneur Morris. They discussed each other's manuscripts, and in their correspondence they encouraged each other's efforts. Personally incorruptible, they fought against corruption in politics; indeed a strong streak of idealism is evident in both Lodge and Roosevelt at this time.

Roosevelt's senior by eight years, Lodge first as a congressman and then as a senator possessed the necessary influence to further the career of his friend. He persistently praised Roosevelt's qualities and services to the Republican party. He helped to secure an appointment as Civil Service Commissioner for Roosevelt in 1889 and, eight years later, supported his candidacy for the post of Assistant Secretary of the Navy. Until the turn of the century Lodge's importance and contribution to the formation of national policy overshadowed Roosevelt's. Then their roles were dramatically reversed, but their close friendship endured. Roosevelt later described their relationship: "From that time on [1884] he was my closest friend, personally, politically, and in every other way, and occupied toward me a relation that no other man has ever occupied or will ever occupy. We have not always agreed, but our subjects of disagreement have been of little weight compared to the matters upon which we did agree. For the past twenty-four years I have discussed almost every move I have made in politics with him, provided he was at hand." [18] Their partnership did not, however, lead straightway to the pursuit of the large policy.

Until 1893 their correspondence was almost wholly confined to a discussion of party politics and civil service reform, al-

18. The relationship between Roosevelt and the Lodge family can be followed in Elting E. Morison, John M. Blum, and John J. Buckley, eds., *The Letters of Theodore Roosevelt* (8 vols. Cambridge, Mass., Harvard University Press, 1951–54), *1*. See also *Selections from the Correspondence of Theodore Roosevelt and Henry Cabot Lodge: 1884–1918* (2 vols. New York, Scribner's, 1925).

though Roosevelt occasionally referred to questions of naval expansion and foreign policy. But then Roosevelt, as one of his classmates had once said, was always spoiling for a fight. Until the miseries of the battlefield in Cuba and the responsibilities of the presidency sobered him, Roosevelt used to express his conviction that war provided a jolly good training for national character. He greatly admired the spirit of the pioneers who had won the West and glowingly described their exploits. These same virtues, Roosevelt believed, were nurtured by war. Of course, one first had to find an enemy.

From the very outset, Roosevelt's attitude made him responsive to dangers, both real and imagined. In 1889 the behavior of the Germans in Samoa aroused his patriotic fervor. "I don't know that I should be sorry to see a bit of a spar with Germany," Roosevelt confided to his friend Cecil Arthur Spring Rice, adding with characteristic exaggeration, "the burning of New York and a few other seacoast cities would be a good object lesson on the need of an adequate system of coast defenses." [19] Lodge was not impressed by Roosevelt's bravado, but the weakness of America in the face of attack struck him forcibly. In the House debate on the Navy a year later, he expressed his misgivings about the Kaiser's personal policy, now no longer restrained by Bismarck: "What if Germany then [at the time of the Samoan crisis] had been under her present guidance, passion and not reason might easily have ruled, and we might have found ourselves plunged suddenly into a naval war, and have seen our great coast cities laid in ruins before we could gather means to defend them." [20] Yet despite their interest in naval matters, Roosevelt and Lodge paid only

19. Roosevelt to Spring Rice, April 14, 1889. *Letters of Roosevelt, 1,* 156–67.

20. Lodge, *Congressional Record,* 51st Cong., 1st sess. (April 10, 1890), *21,* 3268.

sporadic attention to foreign affairs in 1890. Not so Nannie Lodge, who had become Secretary of State Blaine's confidante.

Anna Lodge was by all accounts a remarkable and unconventional woman. She possessed good looks, charm, intelligence, and a forceful personality. She certainly did not stand in awe of her husband, whom she irreverently nicknamed "Pinkie." Henry was a difficult man to know well, but Anna attracted a devoted band of followers to their homes in Washington, Boston, and Nahant. Contemporaries rhapsodized about the precise color of her violet eyes. She captivated Theodore Roosevelt; to Henry Adams she became "sister Anne," and Secretary Blaine danced attendance on her. In an age when young wives were still regarded at best as mere social assets, intelligent and experienced men sought out her advice and respected her judgment.

The Lodge papers reveal how Anna Lodge, the wife of a young congressman, was made privy to the secrets of the State Department. Blaine pined for her company; he constantly wrote to her, sent her poems and copies of secret State Department correspondence. Blaine called the occasions when she went for a drive with him his "red letter days." And when Mrs. Lodge was away from Washington, Blaine was miserable. "I shall miss your presence here for the next six weeks incalculably—I have no one with whom I can chat over Foreign Affairs—and no one with whom I care to take a drive in the lumbering old carriage of the State Department." In May 1889 he asked her opinion on the instructions he had sent to the Samoan commissioners, adding, "pray keep the document quite out of sight, for if it should be published Count Arco would commit suicide." A few months later he sent her a copy of his speech to the Gentlemen of the International American Conference. In March 1890 Mrs. Lodge was made the recipient of a recent map of Alaska to enable her to "look over it and thus understand the fur seal question when I come to you some of these days to talk over our Behring Sea troubles"; Nannie responded by inviting him over to read to her the dispatches bearing on the dispute. In another letter that same month, Blaine enclosed a cipher telegram from Berlin announcing Bismarck's dismissal. "The most remarkable man that has appeared on the continent of Europe since the first Napoleon—what an insufferable fool that young Emperor must be," was Blaine's sagacious comment.[21] What advice, if any, Mrs. Lodge gave the Secretary of State we do not know. But we can be sure that she tried to further the interests of her friends. When Blaine asked her whether she knew of any suitable candidate for the post of Assistant Secretary of State, she suggested Theodore Roosevelt. For once Blaine resisted, although he declared "it gives me great pain to stand in the way of your slightest wish"; he felt that Roosevelt lacked the necessary "repose" and patient endurance; he suggested to her that although Roosevelt was quick to apprehend he might be "too quick in execution."[22] That December, however, he did favor another of Mrs. Lodge's protégés, adding in mock despair that he fully understood what she meant when she had told him, "I am to call when Charles Campbell is promoted."[23]

Henry Cabot Lodge played no part in these tête-à-têtes. For years he had cordially disliked Blaine and all he stood for. Blaine had written to him a few times but only once with any warmth, when he had sent Lodge a bottle of the "Poland Water" to which he ascribed his freedom from kidney trouble.

21. Blaine to Mrs. Anna Lodge, May 9, 1889; Oct. 1889; March 12 and 25, 1890; Sept. 6, 1890. Lodge MSS.

22. Blaine to Mrs. Anna Lodge, March 19, 1889. also a second letter undated but probably sent in March 1889. Lodge MSS.

23. Blaine to Mrs. Anna Lodge, Sept. 14, 1890. Lodge MSS.

Lodge accepted a pressing invitation to visit the Blaines at their house in Bar Harbor, but he never entirely overcame his antipathy for the "plumed knight." This may well explain why he took so little interest in Blaine's diplomacy. During the winter months of 1891 he nevertheless felt obliged to concede that Blaine's conduct during the Chilean crisis was statesmanlike. Lodge did not share Theodore Roosevelt's bellicose enthusiasm; he thought Blaine's moderate course was right. Quite fortuitously he even played a small part in supporting Blaine against the more belligerent President Harrison.[24] But the three issues that absorbed most of Lodge's attention at that time were the currency question, the tariff, and immigration policy; corrupt government in the cities, he thought, was greatly aided by the votes of recent immigrants for machine politicians. But Lodge for once confused the evil itself with the innocent citizens whose support was being exploited. He failed to grasp the human problems of the immigrant.

Lodge had been studying the six volumes of *Appleton's Encyclopaedia of Biography*. In an article published in 1891, he laboriously classified 14,243 entries by profession, state, and race (by which he meant national origins). Lodge concluded that the British (including the Irish) contribution to the "upbuilding of the United States" had been by far the greatest. All this might be dismissed as rather naïve if Lodge had not drawn morals from his scientific investigation. His conclusion was relatively harmless: those immigrants who assimilated most quickly to the American way of life were the most successful. But when he tried to show, in a second article entitled "The Restriction of Immigration," that the new immigrants—the Jews and other oppressed peoples from eastern Europe—were inferior in "character," his arguments clearly displayed a

24. Garraty, *Lodge*, pp. 148–49.

chauvinistic tendency. To "guard our citizenship against an infusion which seems to threaten deterioration," Lodge claimed, was the most important task for the American people in the coming years. He advocated the application of a literacy test to exclude "undesirable elements," a scheme that eventually won the approval of Congress and only failed to become law when Cleveland properly vetoed the measure shortly before leaving office.[25]

During the autumn of 1891 Lodge contributed an article to the magazine *Forum,* entitled "Political Issues of 1892." He listed the issues of the presidential election in order of significance: free coinage of silver he regarded as the most important; the future tariff came second; civil service reform and immigration were lesser questions likely to be debated; but, as Lodge put it, the importance of an immigration policy "cannot be overestimated, for it touches directly the quality of American citizenship and the wages of American workmen"; unhappily, he noted, the American public was not yet sufficiently alive to this issue. Those, he concluded, were "the only questions." America's role as an emergent world power and her foreign policy were problems notably absent from Lodge's enumeration.[26]

The Influence of Sea Power upon History had been published eighteen months before Lodge's essay. Mahan had sent a complimentary copy of his work to Lodge in May 1890; Lodge read it and praised it. But to suggest that Lodge "was a quick convert to his [Mahan's] point of view"[27] seems doubtful, for Lodge did not grasp at first the full significance or application of Mahan's doctrine of sea power. His support

25. Lodge, "Distribution of Ability in the United States," *Historical and Political Essays,* pp. 138–68; "The Restriction of Immigration," *North American Review, 153* (1891), 27–36.

26. Lodge, "Political Issues of 1892," *Forum, 12* (1891), 100–15.

27. Garraty, *Lodge,* p. 147.

for naval expansion had predated the book. Lodge subsequently made use of Mahan's ideas to justify his own advocacy of the Navy. During the naval appropriations debate in 1891, Lodge referred to the need that might arise to enforce the Monroe Doctrine once the isthmian canal, "that great artery of commerce," was built.[28] A year later he sought more general support for a policy of naval expansion by utilizing Mahan's theory of the interdependence of commercial development and sea power, maintaining that without a Navy commerce "retreats and disappears." Nevertheless Lodge's concept of the role of the United States Navy remained traditional. He continued to stress that the construction of modern and powerful vessels implied no departure from previous policy: "We are not a nation devoted to conquest and annexation." [28a]

The contrast at this time between the views of Lodge and Mahan is most striking. Mahan's study of sea power had led him to the conclusion that the United States must look outward; he forecast that with proper military preparation, its preponderance in the Caribbean would follow "from her geographical position and her power, with mathematical certainty." In the Pacific, the United States could not permit the Hawaiian islands, situated as they were on the great trade route to Australia and China, to pass into the hands of a foreign nation. Mahan especially stressed that once the isthmian canal had been constructed, the days of America's isolation would be over; the United States would then be exposed to great danger unless it were prepared. America's destiny lay in securing its share of commerce in the Atlantic and Pacific; to safeguard it the nation would need not only a merchant fleet, but a modern Navy and the necessary bases, which alone would assure supremacy in the Caribbean and the eastern

28. Lodge, *Congressional Record,* 51st Cong., 2d sess. (Jan. 23, 1891), 22, 1804.
28a. Ibid.

Pacific. He profoundly admired England, however, and from the first advocated Anglo–American cooperation to curb the aggressive policies of other nations.

In 1892 Mahan looked outward, Lodge still inward. The hostile intentions of England had, however, become an idée fixe with Lodge. He tried to arouse the American people to the need for a Navy able to defend our great cities from a British attack. Force must be met with force; otherwise England would move forward with its imperial policy, not content until it had crippled American power. The "attitude of the present Tory government . . . indicates a readiness to have a conflict precipitated with the United States." "England has drawn about us, from Halifax to the West Indies, a line of strong fortifications and of naval stations." [29]

Lodge's attitude was never rigid; he was a man of strong, but not blind, prejudices. Eventually he became a good friend of England and handsomely acknowledged the error of his ways. He was continually adjusting to the changing conditions of the 1890s. In the process he drew closer to Mahan and became more ready to follow Mahan's advice. In 1898 the two men began to work closely together. Historians have been right to stress Mahan's profound influence on Lodge, but they have ascribed to it too early a date.

It was not Mahan who first opened Lodge's eyes to the importance of Hawaii and the Pacific. The question had been discussed for years in the press. Many months before Lodge expressed his own opinions, a number of newspapers had agitated for the annexation of Hawaii. As early as December 1891, the New York *Tribune*, for example, had favored this policy, reasoning that "the growth of our Pacific States, the fact that

29. Ibid. and *Congressional Record*, 52nd Cong., 1st Sess. (Apr. 16, 1892), 23, 3362.

90% of Hawaii's trade comes into and goes out from their ports, the enormous investments of American capital in Hawaiian enterprises, the position of the islands in the path of our Chinese and Australian commerce, their strategic importance and their political and commercial relation to the Nicaraguan Canal combine to render it absolutely necessary for us to take such steps as will insure us against their absorption into a foreign colonial system." [30] Other newspapers kept the issue of Hawaii before the American public throughout the spring and summer of 1892. During the autumn and winter of that year a campaign in favor of annexation was intensified. It may well have been stimulated by Lorrin A. Thurston, a leader of the annexationist party in Hawaii, who had visited the United States during the spring. In any case the press seemed to be preparing its readers for an imminent political crisis in Hawaii —and for annexation. The danger that Britain might forestall America in the islands was particularly stressed. Yet if we turn to the Lodge papers, we find that the Senator did not write one line on the subject throughout these months; nor did he make a single public pronouncement on Hawaii. The conclusion is inescapable: Lodge was not a leading protagonist of the large policy. The newspapers were conditioning his mind along with the minds of his fellow countrymen.

The Hawaiian revolution of January 1893 and Stevens' proclamation of an American protectorate could hardly have taken Lodge or anyone else entirely by surprise. Judging from an interview he gave the Boston *Globe,* it is clear that Lodge endorsed the annexation once it had become a fait accompli.[31] Apart from this, however, he played no prominent part until December 1894, when he participated in the debate over the future of Hawaii. But not until 1895 did Lodge come to per-

30. Sylvester K. Stevens, *American Expansion in Hawaii, 1842–1898* (Harrisburg, Archives Publishing Co. of Pennsylvania, 1945), p. 211.
31. Garraty, *Lodge,* p. 150.

ceive that America's role in the changing conditions of international affairs posed questions for America's future welfare as serious as those of tariff and sound money. He thereupon abandoned his aversion to the annexation of territories lying beyond the continental United States. He now recognized that the United States could not be adequately defended by a small modern Navy with only a limited cruising range, and he appreciated that America's future policy could no longer be entirely derived from the traditions of the past. He never ceased to revere these traditions, but he now sought to meet new conditions with new policies. He also began to perceive that other nations might threaten the United States, and he pointed to the growth of Japan's naval power. Only in one respect did he not change: he continued to be haunted by the belief that England's selfish polices endangered America. By 1895 Lodge had nevertheless evolved a new philosophy. Belatedly, but wholeheartedly, he proceeded to identify himself with Mahan's strategic concepts. In the Senate he now became a powerful advocate of Mahan's doctrines.

For all that, Lodge's outlook remained defensive rather than expansionist. He emphatically rejected a policy of active intervention in Turkey to save the Armenians. "We have no political interests . . . [in Turkey]," he wrote to one correspondent, "and our consistent policy has always been to hold entirely aloof from the affairs of Europe." [32] He insisted that, conversely, Europe must not be allowed to meddle in the Western Hemisphere. To Lodge the maintenance of the Monroe Doctrine was a principle that the United States now, more than ever, could not afford to abandon. If abandon it she did, then the European powers would parcel out Latin America as they were already partitioning Africa.[33]

32. Lodge to H. T. Cheever, Dec. 12, 1895. Lodge MSS.
33. Lodge to Weld, Dec. 20, 1895. Lodge MSS.

Although Lodge pointed out that the Monroe Doctrine did not prevent America from acquiring territory,[34] he did not in fact advocate American expansion southward or the acquisition of colonies. On the other hand, he was ready to see those bases in the Caribbean, vital to the defense of the Western Hemisphere, pass into American hands. Apart from that, Caribbean republics and Latin American states concerned him little. They could safely be left to quarrel among themselves —so long as no European power intervened in their disputes. He was a strong believer in the absorption of Canada. "I am heartily in favor of continental union . . . in my judgement, it is for the best interests of the people of both countries." [35] He looked forward to the day when the European powers no longer possessed any territory in the Western Hemisphere, for then a strong American Navy would be able to ensure the Pax Americana.

If these are views of an imperialist, Lodge was an imperialist in only a very special and limited sense. The nucleus of Lodge's pre-1898 views fit in much better with the definition of an isolationist. He was never persuaded by Mahan's argument that colonies were an essential requisite of sea power. Before 1898 he did not believe that America's industrial progress and prosperity obliged it to seek markets overseas: there was plenty of room for development at home. In economic policy he stood for protection and sound money; thus he once advanced as an argument for the acquisition of Cuba that it would stop the drain of gold. To further his policies, Lodge appealed to all sections of the American public. The stress he placed on "manifest destiny" and "commercial supremacy in the Pacific" is striking. Yet in his private correspondence he scarcely refers to such objectives and he probably put them

34. Lodge to Frewen, March 11, 1896. Lodge MSS.
35. Lodge to F. W. Glen, Dec. 18, 1894. Lodge MSS.

forward, at least in part, out of a sense of political expediency.

Lodge had developed his views on America's new role and policies during 1893 and 1894. These two years were crucial to his political development. The fiasco of the Hawaiian annexation and the temporizing policy of Cleveland had together led him to a fresh appreciation of Mahan. When in December 1894 he became an ardent champion in the Senate of Hawaiian annexation, he justified this course by resorting to arguments first put forward by Mahan four years earlier. The islands, he declared, were an essential bastion of America's defense and necessary for the protection of the future isthmian canal. He claimed, quite erroneously, that Britain was endeavoring to replace American influence by its own. In short, Lodge looked upon Hawai not as a stepping-stone to influence in China, but as the necessary Western frontier. But to his chagrin, the cause of Hawaiian annexation did not triumph until 1898. The debate over the future of Hawaii was soon overshadowed by the Venezuela boundary dispute and by the Cuban crisis.

Lodge's strong stand during the Venezuelan crisis in 1895 has caused historians no surprise. It was to be expected of a man who held the view that British policy was malevolent. But there was outside influence that explains his passionate interest in the dispute, and we have been misled by the picture of Lodge as the proponent of the large policy, endeavoring to persuade Americans to follow the expansionists and jingoes. On the Venezuelan question Lodge once again followed, rather than led, public opinion. He did not make his own views public until June 1895, when he published his well-known article, "England, Venezuela, and the Monroe Doctrine" in the *North American Review*.[36] By that time the American press had already been giving much coverage both to Venezuela and to

36. *North American Review*, 160 (1895), 651–58.

the Monroe Doctrine. Before 1895 Lodge, however, had remained extraordinarily complacent about Latin America. His vision did not at first extend beyond the Caribbean islands close to American shores. Who, then, had brought about a change in his attitude and thus contributed to Lodge's education? The principal credit belongs to William Lindsay Scruggs.

Scruggs first met Lodge in January 1895. Several months later Scruggs recalled, "it was with some difficulty that I induced Mr. Lodge to study this question. He seemed very indifferent January last." [37] But Scruggs persevered. He supplied Lodge with copies of his pamphlet and was delighted to see his efforts bear fruit when, in June, Lodge published his article. Lodge had relied on Scruggs for his facts and they fitted in well with Lodge's preconceived notion of British imperialism. Thus he accepted Scruggs' contention that Britain was guilty of aggression and that it was attempting to secure "control of the Orinoco, the great river system of Northern South America." America, Lodge now warned, must either maintain the Monroe Doctrine or witness the partition of the Caribbean islands and Latin America by England and the European powers—and America's security would vanish. Lodge contended that the American people must face the crisis or give up "their rightful supremacy in the Western Hemisphere." A firm stand, Lodge believed, would lead to a peaceful settlement; but even if it came to war, the issues involved justified the use of force in defense of America's vital interests.

Soon after the appearance of the article, the Lodges, accompanied by Spring Rice and Henry Adams, set sail for Europe. Lodge spent five weeks in London. There he met many prominent political leaders including Joseph Chamberlain, who, as Colonial Secretary, was most intimately concerned with the Venezuelan boundary question. Lodge tried to impress on

37. Note by Scruggs, Dec. 3, 1895. Scruggs MSS I.

Chamberlain that the United States intended to assert her supremacy in the Western Hemisphere and could not allow Europe to meddle. "Oh yes," Chamberlain replied soothingly, "of course everyone recognizes that." [38] But the Colonial Secretary probably did not appreciate what was in his visitor's mind. Venezuela (let alone the colonization of Latin America) was far from his thoughts at a time when he was preoccupied with the problem of South Africa.

Lodge returned to Washington a few days before Congress reconvened on December 3, 1895. He immediately introduced a resolution in the Senate that solemnly reasserted the Monroe Doctrine. A fortnight later, America learned that Britain had rejected the President's demand for arbitration. Lodge wholeheartedly approved of Cleveland's special message and at once gave his support to the Administration. When it came to foreign policy, he declared, differences of party politics were to cease. He had reached that conclusion, he wrote to the historian Rossiter John, while studying the times of his great-grandfather, George Cabot. The weakness of the Administration at that time and the "Federalist opposition which created political division in the face of differences with a foreign power was utterly wrong" [39] and had helped to bring about the War of 1812. The same must not happen again. Lodge explained his point of view in a powerful speech to the Senate on December 30 and in his private letters. He made use of the facts supplied by Scruggs, who bitterly commented, "while Mr. Lodge felt at liberty to make free use of [my] pamphlet and other papers furnished him by me at his request, he did not it seems deem it necessary to say in his speech to whom he was indebted for the material used therein." [40] Scruggs had certainly succeeded in convincing Lodge that the Monroe Doctrine was at stake.

38. Garraty, *Lodge,* pp. 157–58.
39. Lodge to Rossiter John, Jan. 5, 1896. Lodge MSS.
40. Note by Scruggs, Dec. 1895. Scruggs MSS II.

America did not seek war, Lodge wrote to one correspondent, but worse could befall her, and he did not fear it or doubt what the outcome would be: "At the end of the war, Canada would have passed from British control and the British empire on this continent would have ceased to exist." [41]

Once England accepted arbitration, Lodge ceased to care about the territorial outcome of the dispute. The Monroe Doctrine had been upheld. "We have won the Venezuelan case," he wrote in March 1896. The danger of a partition of Latin America, he believed, was over.[42] But as long as Hawaii was not in American hands, the isthmian canal and the Pacific coast lay exposed to enemy attack. Not until every trace of European domination had been removed from the Western Hemisphere could the United States prosper, even if defended by its battleship fleet. This was Lodge's most cherished belief in the years before the war with Spain.

The Venezuelan crisis made a deep impression on him. The United States had stood firm, and mighty England had bowed to the will of the American people. As Lodge saw the situation, the unanimity of the President and Congress and a readiness to fight had upheld American interests without resort to force. That was the lesson Lodge learned from the crisis. He did not want the United States to go to war with England. The risk of serious conflict seemed slight, and he assured his English friends that if the British government would abandon its hostile policy, England could win America's friendship more easily than any other nation, "because we really like each other better than any two other people." [43] But for Lodge the time had come when the United States must assert its supremacy

41. Lodge to F. C. Sanford, Dec. 20, 1895. Lodge MSS, quoted by Garraty, *Lodge*, p. 162. The Director of British Intelligence independently reached the same conclusion; see pp. 172–73.
42. Lodge to Higginson, March 25, 1896. Lodge MSS.
43. Lodge to Frewen, Jan. 17, 1896. Lodge MSS.

in the Western Hemisphere. The annexation of Hawaii and the settlement of the Cuban question were essential prerequisite steps towards the fulfillment of Lodge's vision of a Pax Americana.

More than a year earlier, on June 18, 1894, Lodge had written to a friend: "We intend to take Hawaii . . . we ought to have Cuba also unless I am greatly mistaken." [44] This appears to have been the first time Lodge referred to Cuba. By the following year his views were well known. He vigorously attacked the Administration policies during the early months of 1895. To Lodge's disgust, Cleveland seemed to be blind to the needs of the nation; he would not annex Hawaii, and he would not defend the Monroe Doctrine, imperiled as it was on the frontiers of Venezuela. During the spring of 1895, Lodge delivered impassioned speeches in the Senate and contributed an article to *Forum* entitled "Our Blundering Foreign Policy": "England has studded the West Indies with strong places which are a standing menace to our Atlantic seaboard. We should have among those islands at least one strong naval station, and when the Nicaragua canal is built, the island of Cuba . . . will become to us a necessity." [45]

To conclude from these expressions of his views, as so many historians have done, that during the years before the war with Spain Lodge was a militant jingo and an imperialist who wished to create an American empire overseas is to misunderstand him.[46] Such conclusions have led to the legend that Lodge was working for a war with Spain and that he and Roosevelt conspired to seize the Philippine Islands as a step-

---

44. Lodge to E. F. Atkins, June 18, 1984. Lodge MSS.
45. Lodge, "Our Blundering Foreign Policy," *Forum,* 19 (1895), 8–17.
46. Pratt, *Expansionists of 1898,* p. 232. Although many may hold a different opinion on this and one or two other points, Pratt's study is of course fundamental for an understanding of the period.

ping-stone to influence in Asia.[47] In fact Lodge made no significant reference to the Philippines either publicly or privately before the war. The prospect of retaining the islands did not occur to him at all until *after* news of Dewey's victory had reached the United States.

His views on Cuba, on the other hand, were clearly formulated before 1898. What mattered to him was to bring the conflict on the island to an end. Like Senator Charles Sumner, his distinguished predecessor in the Senate and a fellow Bostonian, Lodge regarded Spanish colonies in the Caribbean as anachronisms. Spain's weakness, he feared, might tempt it to hand Cuba over to another European power. To Lodge, the whole question of Cuba was a part of a larger problem, as he succinctly explained in a letter written at the height of the Venezuelan crisis: "One reason for which we fought our war [of Independence] was that we might not have the countries side by side on this continent armed to the teeth with great armies and navies. If we permit Europe to enter and parcel out South America, if we allow England to take Cuba, we must become a great military nation. Do you think that desirable? I do not." [48] But, provided the danger of European interference in the hemisphere could be exorcised, Lodge had little more interest in extending American sovereignty over Cuba than over Peru. He repeatedly disclaimed any desire to see the United States "enter on an unlimited career of acquisition of colonial possessions . . . We hold the citadel of our greatness here on this continent within the borders of the United States." Lodge went on to warn his fellow senators in March 1895 that the United States could not afford to neglect the necessary outworks of its continental defenses.[49] He was thinking of Hawaii and Cuba.

47. Beale, *Roosevelt and American World Power*, p. 55.
48. Lodge to Henry (Higginson?), Dec. 26, 1895. Lodge MSS.
49. Pratt, *Expansionists of 1898*, p. 206.

His attitude toward Cuba has often been cited as contradicting the contention that he was no imperialist. At first, certainly, he had assumed that Cuba, like Hawaii, would one day be annexed by the United States. Before the outbreak of the Cuban insurrection in February 1895 he simply had not envisaged the possibility of Cuban independence. During the course of that year, however, he began to realize that to help the Cubans gain their own independence would be a preferable solution to a war with Spain for control of the island. Lodge brushed aside the objection that the Cubans would not govern themselves as well as the Americans could. "They are fighting for liberty and I sympathize deeply," Lodge wrote. "It is no answer to say that they will not be able to establish as good a government as ourselves. I do not think they will, but they will establish a government which is much better than that of Spain . . . *Cuba in the hands of the Cubans* would open to us a market of enormous value, add to our commerce, and give a field for profitable enterprise second to none in the world." [50]

Lodge visited Spain in October 1895. He called on the First Minister of the government, Antonio Canovas del Castillo. Canovas made a good impression on Lodge, but Spain evidently did not. Lodge regarded Spanish power as bankrupt and became convinced that however brutally the Spaniards might attempt to quell the rebellion, they would never be able to master the Cuban situation. Soon after his return to the United States, the Venezuelan crisis—not Cuba—absorbed the attention of Congress.[51]

Lodge linked the cause of Cuba with the Venezuelan boundary dispute from the first, for they both involved the Monroe Doctrine. During January and February 1896 he wrote that American foreign policy was faced with issues of no greater

---

50. Lodge to Pickman, March 12, 1896. Lodge MSS. Italics added.
51. Garraty, *Lodge*, pp. 159–60, 180.

importance than that of the construction of the Nicaraguan Canal and Cuba. They were not partisan questions, and Lodge enthusiastically supported Cleveland's Venezuela policy.[52] Might not the President and Congress also work together to help the Cubans gain their freedom? Lodge supported a Senate resolution to grant belligerent rights to the Cubans; but to his chagrin Cleveland refused to move resolutely on the question.

Lodge attacked the Administration once more. In an article he contributed to *Forum*, "Our Duty to Cuba," he called for the immediate recognition of Cuban belligerency; any other course, he declared, unjustly favored Spain to the detriment of both Cuban and American interests. Lodge maintained with some justice, as we have seen, that the Administration had not only been indifferent to Cubans struggling to be free, but also "had thus far ranged themselves upon the side of Spain." He pointed to the achievements of the Cuban insurgents, who had fought for more than a year: "They have established a government, fought many battles, and have overrun the island." America must meet her national responsibilities; Lodge believed that the outcome of the struggle would inevitably be Cuban independence.[53] He supported Senator Cameron's resolution of December 1896 that Cuban independence be recognized. But when the Administration refused to follow the lead of Congress, Lodge ceased to agitate further on behalf of the Cubans. Cleveland's term had only a few more weeks to run, and Lodge believed that the President would hardly reverse his earlier policy during the closing days of his stay in the White House.[54]

52. Lodge to Elias Cheney, Jan. 16, 1896, and to Henry D. Blackwell, Feb. 7, 1896. Lodge MSS.
53. *Forum*, 21 (1896), 278–87.
54. It is generally believed that Lodge was playing at sordid politics in allowing himself to be influenced by McKinley's wishes to bring the

Lodge and the Cuban Crisis

Before the presidential elections of 1896, Lodge had at times made a party issue of the Administration's foreign policy. But he had only done this when Cleveland chose to adopt a stance toward Hawaii and Cuba that was weaker than his Venezuela policy. Lodge was doing what he sincerely believed to be right; he was not pandering to party advantage, for he genuinely despaired of Cleveland's response to the larger needs of the Western Hemisphere. Lodge hoped for better things from the McKinley Administration. But his reluctance to press the Cuban question in the Senate before the outbreak of war in 1898 strikingly contrasts with his behavior during Cleveland's period of office. His attitude once again has been ascribed solely to party political motives.

There can be no doubt that Lodge thought a Democratic victory in 1900 would be a disaster entailing Bryanism, silver, and national bankruptcy at home and continued neglect of the requirements of hemispheric security abroad. It is therefore not to be wondered at that he refused to attack and discredit McKinley, although he was at first disappointed with the President's Cuban policy. But Lodge's attitude was dictated by another equally cogent motive: America's success during the Venezuelan crisis, he believed, was due to the unanimity of the President and Congress; the same conditions would have to prevail if the Cuban policy were to be brought to a successful consummation, for "It is not possible for this government to carry out any foreign policy effectively unless Congress and

---

crisis to a head before his inauguration. See, for example, Garraty, *Lodge*, p. 183. This appears to do an injustice both to McKinley and to Lodge. On Dec. 22, 1896, Lodge wrote to William Bigelow, "Mr. Cleveland will retire to private life in two months. He represents no party and he is of no political consequence. No one would think of trying to put him in a hole for the simple reason that there is no possible object to be gained by doing so." Lodge wished to place the support of Congress for Cuban independence on record for the future; no doubt it would impress McKinley.

the Executive are united. In the case of Venezuela there was perfect harmony between the administration and Congress and the policy then adopted proved absolutely successful and enabled us to establish a principle of great importance to the welfare and rights of the United States. This is not the case in regard to Cuba. Under these circumstances it is not possible that anything effective should be done." [55]

The pro-Cuban feelings of Congress had been clearly demonstrated by 1898. In these circumstances, Lodge believed that the rest was up to the Administration. As late as April 4, 1898, Lodge adhered to this line of conduct, writing that he had been doing everything he could to preserve unity and "prevent Congress from breaking away." He doubted that McKinley would give the necessary leadership and privately expressed his conviction that if McKinley failed, both the Republican party and the country would be ruined.[56] A week before the outbreak of the war, the strain began to tell on him. He wrote excitedly of the "very rich Jews in Europe and the Roman Catholic Church" as the party of "peace at any price," whose influence could lead to a dishonorable settlement.[57] If the country believed its honor had been sold through the machinations of Wall Street, Lodge warned a friend, the Republican party would be swept out of existence. "In 1900 we should have free silver, Bryan, and probably a Spanish war." [58] Although he began to doubt the President's resolution, he would not join those senators who attempted to force McKinley's hand in Congress. Instead he sent his advice to the White House privately. He had told the President some weeks earlier that public opinion was excited and would hold Spain respon-

55. Lodge to C. S. Crouch, Jan. 13, 1897. Lodge MSS.
56. Lodge to George (Lyman?), April 4, 1898; Lodge to Henry (Higginson?), April 4, 1898. Lodge MSS.
57. Lodge to John (?), April 15, 1898. Lodge MSS.
58. Ibid.

sible if it turned out that the *Maine* had in fact been blown up by a mine—even though no one really believed that Madrid ordered the destruction. War could still be avoided by a show of firmness. McKinley should recognize Cuban independence and demand reparations. The recognition of Cuba, argued Lodge, did not constitute a casus belli, but if Spain chose to interpret it as such, then the country would unite "as one man," and public opinion all over the world "will be with us." [59] Far from being a jingo, Lodge continued to err on the side of caution. This could not be said of Roosevelt. Although Lodge and Roosevelt agreed on the need to build up America's naval power—they both accepted Mahan's strategic conception of hemispheric defense and believed in the necessity for national preparedness—their views at this time were not identical; they differed profoundly. Whereas Roosevelt was emotional, impulsive, and belligerent, Lodge never thought of war as anything but a disaster: "I am as adverse to getting this country into war as any man could possibly be and I think I feel the responssibility involved in any question of foreign relations, as much at least as those who are not called upon officially to deal with it." [60] "I do not want war. I do not want to annex the island, but I do want to see the conditions now existing in Cuba, which are a disgrace to civilization, to be brought to an end." [61] He repeatedly stressed that war was only the outcome of the faulty policies previously adopted. Thus a week after the *Maine* disaster Lodge wrote that, although the American people were now almost unanimously demanding that an end be brought to the fighting in Cuba, "I hope it will be possible to do it without war; if the administration stands perfectly firm I believe it can be." [62] In March 1898 he lamented that if only

59. Lodge to McKinley, March 21, 1898. Garraty, *Lodge*, pp. 187–88.
60. Lodge to William (Bigelow?), Dec. 31, 1896. Lodge MSS.
61. Lodge to Weld, Dec. 19, 1896. Lodge MSS.
62. Lodge to Hayes, Feb. 23, 1898. Lodge MSS.

Cleveland had recognized Cuban belligerency and McKinley had recognized Cuban independence, the insurgents might have won on their own.[63] A month later Lodge regarded war as inevitable. Since the resources of diplomacy had failed, he accepted a war with Spain as the lesser of the two evils, for he believed that if the United States shirked the task at hand, it would have to face in the Western Hemisphere a few years later not Spain but a combination of European powers.

Lodge's speeches were bellicose at times precisely because he was convinced that in this way peace might be preserved. With the opening of the British and German archives, we may today conclude that Lodge's fears were exaggerated. The British government was not following the aggressive policies in the Americas and in the Pacific that Lodge thought. The Germans did not possess the means to sustain such policy, although the Kaiser may have wished to do so. Geographical isolation still conferred safety on the United States. The decade of the 1890s did however witness an astonishing change in international relations. The rise of modern Japan and the aggressive spirit of Germany heralded grave changes for the United States, not in the immediate future, as Lodge and Mahan foretold, but three decades later.

Lodge endorsed some of the precepts of Realpolitik. He was, for instance, ready to accept the notion that national interest overrode the abstract principles of international morality. He was also convinced that in international affairs force counted far more than sentiment and good will.

As a young man, Lodge had been highly susceptible to the influence of others. Henry Adams, Roosevelt, and Mahan had all in their turn contributed to his education. By 1897, however, Lodge accepted or rejected the advice of his friends as he thought fit. He followed to its conclusion the course he set for

63. Lodge to William (Bigelow?), March 25, 1898. Lodge MSS.

himself, without caring for public approval. Lodge tended to see problems in their most extreme terms. By nature he found it difficult to compromise or to ascribe to his opponents any but villainous motives. He was not always consistent, but this is to his credit in changing times. During the course of the war with Spain he suffered from a temporary aberration, as will be seen in a later chapter.

The role Lodge and Roosevelt played in the shaping of American foreign policy before the war with Spain is not as striking as many historians have supposed. Yet these years of Lodge's education reveal how an intelligent American who in 1890 paid little attention to world affairs came to perceive the importance and relevance to the United States of the global changes that were then taking place. Lodge did not lead a clique of rabid nationalists. Many Americans shared his views.

Lodge took a middle course in the great debate on America's role in world affairs. He rejected alike the historical prophecies of men like John Fiske, who saw the United States as destined to win global predominance, and the rosy visions of those senators who argued that the United States needed no military defenses or military bases beyond the continental United States. He was called by his political opponents a jingo and an imperialist, and the epithets have stuck. But Lodge's approach was pragmatic. He recognized that the United States was not immune to the great international changes taking place, but he did not wish to see America dragged into rivalry for empire or forced to rely either on a great standing Army or on alliance. He believed that the American people could ensure their prosperity by holding aloof from this struggle, by dominating the Western Hemisphere, and by removing from it the last European footholds—and so the danger of any American involvement with the European powers. Then with a mighty Navy to protect the Western Hemisphere and those outlying bases essential to her defense, the United States might look on the struggles of the other powers with comparative equanimity.

As the years passed and Lodge witnessed the tremendous growth of Germany's military strength, he was ready to discard outworn policies. The titanic European struggle of World War I finally convinced him that America could not isolate itself from the rest of the world. For many years he had looked upon England as a friend, and when the Allies were facing defeat, he sought to use the power of the New World to redress the balance of the Old. The wheel had come full circle. Washington's admonition against nonentangling alliances now no longer held much validity for him. But an analysis of his changing attitudes in maturity will not be treated in this study. On the eve of the war with Spain, Lodge could still believe in the golden future of American progress, unhampered by the follies of Europe.

Chapter Nine
The Breakdown of Neutrality:
McKinley Goes to War with Spain

WILLIAM MCKINLEY IS CONSIDERED to be something less than a great president. "There are traces of virtue, but few of character," is one recent verdict.[1] Theodore Roosevelt thought: "The President only loves one thing in the whole world and that is his wife. He treats everyone with equal fa-

1. Ernest R. May, *Imperial Democracy, The Emergence of America as a Great Power* (New York, Harcourt, Brace and World, 1961), p. 114. The three most important books on the McKinley period to have appeared in recent years are May, *Imperial Democracy*, Margaret Leech, *In the Days of McKinley* (New York, Harper, 1959), and H. Wayne Morgan, *William McKinley and His America* (Syracuse, Syracuse University Press, 1963). The three books supplement one another. May's work is especially strong on Spanish policy and on the general international setting of American diplomacy. He has made a contribution of great importance in stressing the need to view American policy through other than American eyes. Miss Leech's book abounds in graphic detail and brings together much important material. Morgan's study presents a convincing picture of McKinley's political career; he also provides the first impressive corrective to the generally held dismissal of McKinley as an insignificant and weak president. The three authors, however, broadly agree with the questionable thesis that in April 1898 McKinley capitulated to the pressure of jingoistic politicians. One other recent study, Walter Lafeber's *The New Empire* deserves particular attention. Lafeber stresses the economic influences on the shaping of policy. Some older studies have not been altogether superseded by more recent research. Of particular value are Pratt, *Expansionists of 1898*, J. E. Wisan, *The Cuban Crisis as Reflected in the New York Press* (*1895–1898*) (New York, Columbia University Press, 1934), and Walter Millis, *The Martial Spirit* (New York, Houghton Mifflin, 1931).

vor; their worth to him is solely dependent on the advantages he could derive from them . . . he keeps his ear to the ground, listens and then follows public opinion." [2] McKinley baffled him. The President was not a leader of men in the sense Roosevelt aspired to be. His conduct on the eve of the war with Spain was pusillanimous—so runs the general consensus of opinion. He allowed the jingoes to drive him into war; he lacked the strength and courage Cleveland had shown in a similar situation when he paid public pressure no heed. But these are not altogether sound judgments.

The price of dynamic presidential leadership too often proves to be a barren legislative record; Congress is suspicious of executive power. McKinley did not complain of the conduct of Congress; he was after all an adroit politician who had seen long service in the Capitol. He accepted the right of Congress to a voice in foreign affairs philosophically; the reaction of Congress was an important consideration in the formation of his policy. "We cannot always do what is best," he remarked to one congressman, "but we can do what is practical at the time." In deciding policy the President is not a free agent. Some Presidents have bypassed Congress and appealed to the people for support; they have more often than not seen their policies fail. McKinley chose the opposite course of attempting to manage Congress by skillful maneuvering.

Although it seems curious that historians should have perpetuated a picture of McKinley as a man lacking backbone and political courage, there is perhaps one explanation. Much of the historical discussion of this period reflects a feeling of guilt about America's imperialist role in 1898, an assumption that Cleveland represented what was good and resisted what was

2. Holleben to Hohenlohe, August 25, 1900. *German Foreign Ministry Archives,* microfilm G.F.M. 10/124, Public Record Office, London. Translated from the German by the authors.

bad, and that in the days of McKinley the chauvinistic elements of American society gained the upper hand. This anti-imperialist outlook has led to the search for scapegoats who could be held responsible for the war. Some have blamed Mahan, Roosevelt, Lodge, and the "expansionists"; others have singled out the Hearst and Pulitzer newspapers, crusading Protestantism, and the changing mood of the American people. All have necessarily presupposed that McKinley was driven into the war by forces he found too strong to resist.[3]

The assumption that the United States had no good case for going to war with Spain is at least open to question, whether regarded from considerations of morality or the national interest. But the assumptions that McKinley had no policy of his own or that domestic politics influenced his actions more than his assessment of America's international interests do not seem justified by the evidence.

No penetrating contemporary assessment of McKinley's character has survived. He rarely revealed his innermost thoughts, though his manner was friendly and easy. Few people talked to him without feeling the better for it. He listened

3. See for example, Beale, *Roosevelt and American World Power,* pp. 55–64. Beale ascribes an exaggerated influence to Roosevelt, Lodge, Dewey, and Mahan during the years 1897 and 1898. Lafeber (*The New Empire,* p. 400), stresses that McKinley wished to end the uncertainty in American political and economic life so as to provide "a solid basis from which to resume the building of the new American commercial empire." May (*Imperial Democracy,* p. 159) agrees with many other historians that McKinley had "capitulated to the jingoes" and emphasizes that McKinley was caught between the pressures of public hysteria and the wishes of his principal supporters in the Republican party during the weeks preceding the war; this leads to the conclusion that the authors do not share that McKinley unwillingly led the country to war for a cause in which he did not believe. Morgan (*McKinley,* p. 375) also concludes that McKinley was "swept forward with the tide" in March and April 1898; on the other hand Morgan depicts McKinley as a skillful and resolute commander-in-chief during the course of the war.

courteously to many and diverse opinions and gave the impression of agreeing with everyone. He was "a bit of a jollier," [4] as Roosevelt was quick to observe. There is no denying that on occasion he rather overstepped the mark. When, for example, in the autumn of 1898 he assured a group of visiting clergymen that the decision to retain the Philippines had come to him one night in answer to his prayers, his visitors no doubt accepted the tale at its face value. In fact the President's attitude on the Philippine question had been evolving for months without celestial assistance.[5] McKinley simply could not resist presenting his policy in a light calculated to charm his audience.

A year earlier, in speaking to Theodore Roosevelt, McKinley adopted a very different tone. Roosevelt had just delivered a bellicose speech to the Naval War College proclaiming, "no triumph of peace is quite so great as the supreme triumph of war." Secretary of the Navy John D. Long was shocked, but the President complimented Roosevelt and assured him "that he had read every word of [the speech] and heartily endorsed it." [6] McKinley made everyone who came to see him feel that his views were of particular interest; he gave the impression of being easily influenced by others; yet, in fact, he considered advice critically. McKinley had discovered that flattery usually worked where outspoken opposition served no useful purpose. He was as straightforward as an adroit president could afford to be.

McKinley was very much a product of the Victorian age. He never doubted that the path of righteousness would be revealed to those who sought it; he did not hesitate to form his

4. Roosevelt to Lodge, September 15, 1897. Morison, ed., *Letters of Roosevelt*, 1, 676.

5. The well-known episode is graphically described in Leech, *In the Days of McKinley*, pp. 344–45.

6. Roosevelt to Goodrich, June 8, 1987. Assistant Secretary's File, Navy Department, National Archives, Washington, D.C.

own judgments, and he clung to his decisions with obduracy. He was extraordinarily self-reliant, and this was the source both of his strength and weakness. In ordering his personal life and in framing his policies, he followed simple moral precepts that may strike the modern ear as banal; the most important of the self-imposed rules was the need to do one's duty. He would share with no one the responsibility of making decisions.

The charge of McKinley's weakness is justified on the ground that he failed to take a more decided public stand on the Cuban issue in the face of the uncompromising attitude of Congress and of the majority of the American people. The President, "who is now in the rear, will go to the front. He shivers a little, but he will go," wrote the fiery Senator Chandler on the eve of the war.[7] But McKinley was perfectly aware that his popularity was on the decline. As the excitement in February and March 1898 reached fever pitch, he even feared that his efforts to reach a peaceful solution would expose him to personal danger. His drives in Washington became infrequent, and he confided to Long his foreboding of assassination.[8] But this did not deter the President from following the path of duty as he conceived it. We may reach the conclusion that, since his policy failed, the President was mistaken: that he would have done better to take the people more into his confidence, that his methods were faulty, and that his sense of right and wrong did not necessarily settle the ethical issues involved for all time. Even so, it is difficult to justify the assertion that McKinley's diplomacy lacked political or personal courage.

7. Chandler to Dana, March 29, 1898. May, *Imperial Democracy*, p. 262.

8. An interesting entry to this effect is to be found in Long's journal, January 26, 1898. Long MSS.

McKinley kept his own counsel and, with the help of the Assistant Secretary of State, Judge William Rufus Day, retained control of the conduct of foreign relations. He surrounded himself with a rather second-rate Cabinet. One member, Secretary of State John Sherman, was rapidly declining in senility, while Long, Secretary of the Navy, suffered from nervous troubles. Such an Administration suited the President; he rarely consulted his colleagues on questions of importance. His Cabinet councils were little more than jolly social gatherings. "Cabinet meeting this morning," Secretary Long noted in his journal on February 4, 1898, "like most of our cabinet meetings, it amounts to little: most of the time devoted to chatting about personal matters." [9] But political necessity obliged McKinley to take into his confidence a group of congressional leaders, the caucus of senators and congressmen who supported him on Capitol Hill.

During the periods when Congress was in session, there was always the danger that precipitate action might impede the President's diplomacy. McKinley was convinced that time was of the essence if the Spanish government were to be encouraged to settle the Cuban question. He recognized that to expect the proud Spaniard to capitulate within the space of a few weeks was asking for the impossible. The difficulty was to win the necessary breathing space when the Cuban crisis had already dragged on for two years.

In his inaugural address, McKinley appealed to the country for calm. He declared his intention to settle the tragic and complicated Cuban problem by diplomacy.

It will be our aim to pursue a firm and dignified foreign policy, which shall be just, impartial, ever watchful of our national honor, and always insisting upon the enforcement of

9. Long Journal, February 4, 1898. Long MSS.

the lawful rights of American citizens everywhere. Our diplomacy should seek nothing more and nothing less than is due us. We want no wars of conquest; we must avoid the temptation of territorial aggression. Wars should never be entered upon until every agency of peace has failed; peace is preferable to war in almost every contingency." [10]

These words may have a platitudinous ring, but McKinley was in fact defining what he regarded as his path of duty. If the war in Cuba could be brought to an end without the armed intervention of the United States—and so without the loss of American lives—then it was the duty of the President to make every effort to strive for peace.

McKinley could count on receiving some support in Congress, although he could never rely on it. The House was dominated by Republicans, but in the Senate the Republicans enjoyed only a slender majority. The natural inclination of the majority of Republicans to support a Republican Administration worked in McKinley's favor. Promises of patronage, allotments of postmasterships and other minor offices would keep some senators in line. Tact and courtesy would impress others. But there were members of Congress who could neither be influenced by promises nor deterred by appeals to trust the President. In the management of the Senate, McKinley relied on men such as Mark Hanna, William Boyd Allison, Nelson Aldrich, Eugene Hale, and Orville Platt. Henry Cabot Lodge, too, is to be found among this group, along with John Coit Spooner. In the House, the Speaker, Thomas Brackett Reed, exercised his great power on behalf of the Administration. The doors of the White House were always open to these men, and at times of crisis McKinley encouraged them to call. It is in fact remarkable how much trust McKinley inspired and how

10. Morgan, *McKinley*, p. 301.

well the liaison between the President and these legislators functioned, at least until April 1898. The Republican leaders who supported the Administration nevertheless had to use all their guile, influence, and powers of persuasion to keep Congress in line.

The mood of Congress at the time of McKinley's inauguration left little room for optimistic illusions. Despite Senator Lodge's plea that the Administration should be given the "opportunity to inform itself with the utmost thoroughness as to the conditions" [11] existing in Cuba before being asked to act, a resolution to recognize Cuban belligerency, introduced by Senator Morgan of Pennsylvania, passed the Senate in May 1897. It was rejected by the House. McKinley now anxiously waited for Congress to adjourn before he embarked on an active Cuban policy. He hoped to present the nation with the fruits of his diplomacy in the interval before Congress met again in December. He would have liked to convince all but the irreconcilable minority that the Cuban conflict could be resolved without resort to war.

We have no means of knowing with what degree of confidence the President counted upon such an outcome; the making of policy becomes, after all, a tidy, logical, and seemingly inevitable process only in retrospect. At any one moment, the President is faced with making piecemeal decisions on the frequently incomplete facts presented to him. McKinley's love of peace was genuine, but he did not deny the possibility of war while he did his best to avoid it.

The President received little encouragement from the American representatives abroad. Consul General Lee's dispatches from Havana were gloomy. The war in Cuba, he advised, was a stalemate; neither side had the strength to defeat the other;

11. *Congressional Record,* 55th Cong., 1st sess. (May 11, 1897), 30, 998.

the whole island would be devastated until an exhausted Spain withdrew or another country intervened; as for the Spanish reforms, they were not worth the paper they were written on.[12] From Madrid, Hannis Taylor had reported that nothing was to be hoped for from the Conservative ministry of Canovas: "The one iron hand that governs Spain is that of Señor Canovas who has no sympathy whatever . . . with local self-government as an instrument of colonial rule . . . When the final moment comes his tactics will be to grant the shadow and withhold the substance." [13] More, perhaps, was to be expected from the liberal opposition in Spain if it ever came to power. But when, after a short constitutional crisis, the Queen Regent reinstated the Canovas ministry in June 1897, Taylor declared that he was profoundly discouraged." [14] It seems hardly likely that McKinley could have altogether discounted these opinions when, during the summer months of 1897, he framed his Cuban policy. More likely he was determined to act upon the intentions he had expressed at his inauguration and to exhaust every effort of diplomacy; war was justifiable, he implied, but only when all else had failed.

The outlines of McKinley's policy can be followed from the documents preserved in the State Department archives, many of which have been published. To give the negotiations every chance of success, McKinley conducted them in great secrecy and even under the cover of private letters. No indiscretions

12. Analyzed by Morgan, *McKinley*, pp. 340–41.

13. Taylor to Olney, January 7, 1897. U.S. Department of State, *Spain*, National Archives, Washington, D.C. There is preserved in the McKinley Papers a cutting from *Le Temps* of Paris (November 9, 1897), which reports the views of a "distinguished statesman" in Madrid: "If we must lose the island of Cuba, we would rather, believe me, lose it with honor, after a disastrous war, than through a cowardly abdication." McKinley MSS.

14. Taylor to Sherman, telegram, June 6, 1897. State Department, *Spain*.

could be allowed to reach a press ready to seize every chance to inflame public opinion.

It is often, but erroneously, asserted that Cleveland's and Olney's attitude to Cuba toward the close of their Administration foreshadowed McKinley's own policies. A comparison of Olney's and McKinley's Cuban policies does indeed reveal certain similarities, but also crucial differences. Like Olney, McKinley in his first important note to the Spanish Minister on the problem of Cuba (June 26, 1897) reserved the ultimate right of the United States to intervene; McKinley, as Olney had done, promised that Spain would be granted reasonable time to pacify the island and intimated that America would not be able to stand by for very long.[15] The President also sought to spare Spain unnecessary humiliation by refusing to engage in public polemics. But here end the similarities.

McKinley's policy differed from that of the previous Administration in two major respects: McKinley not only demanded that Spain pacify Cuba but expressly insisted that the campaign on the island must be conducted "according to the military codes of civilization"; he protested in the name of the American people against Weyler's measures of driving the Cuban people from the countryside into the towns, and "against the cruel employment of fire and famine to accomplish by uncertain indirection what the military arm seems powerless to directly accomplish." [16] How very differently Olney had spoken of Spain's "justified" campaign. Olney would not permit the Cubans to stand in the way of a satisfactory American–Spanish agreement. But McKinley from the first refused to impose any solution that would be repugnant to the Cubans, even if the Spanish government were to accept the President's offer of

15. Sherman to de Lôme, June 26, 1897. U.S. Department of State, *Spain;* Morgan, *McKinley,* p. 342.
16. Sherman to de Lôme, June 26, 1897. U.S. Department of State, *Spain;* Morgan, *McKinley,* p. 342.

mediation. This latter point is of the utmost importance to understanding McKinley's policy. It made a settlement of the Cuban policy dependent not only on Spanish concessions but also on their acceptance by the Cuban leaders. As it turned out, the Cubans would not lay down their arms until independence had been achieved; and no Spanish government was ready to grant this. McKinley's efforts were thus doomed from the start.

The President's proposals to Spain were embodied in the Secret Instruction Number 4 Secretary Sherman sent on July 16, 1897, to Stewart Lyndon Woodford, Ambassador to Spain.[17] It opened with a brief account of the history of the Cuban revolution and dwelt on the injuries sustained by the United States. The Administration was obliged to decide on its course, for a "policy of mere inaction" could not be safely prolonged. Spain could not defeat the Cubans by the present methods. The Spanish government was faced with the alternative of introducing measures in Cuba to ensure peace or of accepting the "good offices of the United States" to help bring the conflict to an end. For fear of wounding Spanish susceptibilities, McKinley did not at once specify the assurances he required from Spain. Neither did he attempt to define how American good offices might be exercised, but he emphasized that his suggestion was "altogether friendly."

The President made secret inquiries at the same time as to the likely attitude of the European powers if it came to a war between the United States and Spain. McKinley's anxiety on this score is shown by the fact that he repeated these inquiries five months later.[18] Although the replies he received were en-

17. Woodford refers to their content in Woodford to Sherman, telegram, Sept. 23, 1897. U.S. Department of State, *Spain; Foreign Relations, 1898,* pp. 558–61.

18. In Aug. 1897 Woodford reported to Sherman: "I believe that most Englishmen, Frenchmen and Germans regard Cuba as within the legiti-

tirely satisfactory, the President felt—with justifiable caution —that some element of risk remained.

McKinley did not lay down the precise terms Spain should offer the insurgents before March 1898. He did not feel called upon to do so as long as Spain rejected American mediation. If the Spanish government should entrust mediation to McKinley, he could give two assurances: the United States would not seek to acquire Cuba for itself; the President personally favored Cuban autonomy and would allow Spain such rights of suzerainty over the island as proved acceptable to the Cubans. He would give Spain no guarantee that Spanish sovereignty could be maintained if the Cubans were to reject it.[19]

When Woodford formally presented McKinley's note of July 16, 1897, to the Spanish Foreign Minister that September, the Conservative ministry was still in power. Woodford suggested to the Spanish Foreign Minister that a reply should reach him before November 1, so that McKinley could present Congress, which would reconvene in December, with the assurance that the Cuban crisis was being satisfactorily settled: "It is sincerely hoped that during the coming month of October the Government of Spain may *either* be able to formulate some proposal under which this tender of good offices may become effective, *or* may give satisfactory assurance that peace in Cuba will, by the efforts of Spain, be most promptly secured." The Ambassador was not very hopeful of success and privately confided to the President: "The chances are against

----

mate zone of American influence." Woodford to Sherman, Aug. 30, 1897. U.S. Department of State, *Spain*. McKinley repeated the inquiries at the major European capitals on Dec. 8, 1897. U.S. Department of State, *Spain*.

19. McKinley's ideas are probably accurately reflected in the explanations of American policy which Woodford gave to Sir Henry Drummond Wolff, the British Ambassador in Madrid. They are reported in Woodford to Sherman, Sept. 13, 1897. U.S. Department of State, *Spain; Foreign Relations, 1898*, pp. 562–65.

my getting peaceful settlement. My only chance is to be as I have said kind, just, persistent and unyielding." [20] The possibility of securing genuine concessions appeared to brighten when a Liberal ministry under Praxedes Sagasta assumed office early in October 1897. Woodford did not have much confidence in Sagasta, but he soon became convinced that a group of Cabinet ministers led by the Minister of the Colonies, Segismundo Moret, was genuinely anxious to reform Cuba. On October 9, McKinley learned from the Spanish Minister in Washington that the hated Governor General Weyler was to be recalled. Two weeks later Woodford received a conciliatory Spanish reply to the President's July proposal. While the Spanish government declined the President's mediation and expressed its determination to pursue the war against the insurgents, it did pledge itself to grant some form of autonomy to the Cubans; most important of all, Spain promised to conduct the war humanely and as proof cited its intention to recall Weyler. "You have won a great victory," Woodford wrote to McKinley, "by your firmness and courage you have compelled the recall of Weyler and have made Spain promise better behavior in the future." [21] On November 25, the Queen Regent announced her government's long-awaited plan of autonomy; by December 1897 not a single American citizen languished any longer in Cuban prisons.

As the year 1897 drew to a close, McKinley had already achieved much. A number of senators were in sympathy with Lodge's plea that the President should be left more time to work out his own policy. But the majority of Democrats opposed him, as did some bellicose Republicans. The President

20. Woodford to Sherman, telegram, Sept. 23, 1897. *Foreign Relations, 1898*, p. 568. Italics added. Woodford to McKinley, Sept. 24, 1897. U.S. Department of State, *Spain*.

21. Woodford to Sherman, Oct. 26, 1897. *Foreign Relations, 1898*, pp. 581–89. Woodford to McKinley, Nov. 7, 1897. U.S. Department of State, *Spain*.

could nevertheless be satisfied that he had so far kept the legislature in check and was handling the situation well. In his annual message to Congress that December he outlined the Administration's policy. He avoided detailed proposals; he asserted Spain must be left more time to work out the reforms on which it had now irrevocably embarked; but should the strife be prolonged, the Administration would decide on its course in accordance with "its own high sense of right and in consonance with the dearest interests and convictions of our own people." [22] It all seemed vague, a mere repetition of what had already been said many times and for several years. If, however, McKinley's public statements are read along with his secret diplomatic communications to Woodford, there is no mistaking the President's determination to make it clear to the Spaniards that they could no longer evade the real issue: to establish without delay conditions of lasting peace in Cuba. In a long note on December 20, 1897, McKinley encouraged the Liberal government to persevere on the part of reform in Cuba: "Spain has entered upon a pathway from which no backward step is possible." He bluntly asserted that the previous Conservative policy of attempting to crush the Cubans by force was doomed to failure. He attempted to dissociate the Spanish government from the actions of its predecessor in office. Since the Spanish preferred to give assurances that peace would be brought to Cuba by Spain's own efforts, the United States for its part was ready to wait in "kindly expectancy . . . so long as the event shall invite and justify that course." [23] Despite the friendly tone, the Spanish ministers were painfully aware that McKinley had not departed from his original demands.

22. Richardson, *Messages and Papers*, 10, 127–36.
23. Woodford to Sherman, Dec. 23, 1897, enclosing Woodford's note to the Spanish Foreign Minister of December 20, 1897. U.S. Department of State, *Spain; Foreign Relations, 1898*, pp. 646–54.

Meantime Moret, the Minister of the Colonies, had persuaded Woodford that the conclusion of a commercial treaty between the United States on the one hand and the autonomous Cuban government and Spain on the other would be a practical way of showing that Spain was ready to allow the Cubans control of domestic affairs. The negotiations as far as Cuba was concerned, so Moret suggested, should be conducted by a Cuban delegate. But when these private discussions were followed up officially, Woodford discovered that the Spanish Foreign Minister was not so accommodating. No Cuban delegate would be allowed to participate in the negotiations, though at a later stage a Cuban might be asked to assist the Spanish representative.[24] Moret had aroused expectations that his fellow ministers were not prepared to fulfill. This much was clear in Washington during the first week of February. The prospects of conducting long and tortuous negotiations with Spain for a commercial treaty, as such, held no attractions for McKinley. That these negotiations had not even been taken seriously in Madrid was suggested a few days later when the New York *Journal* printed de Lôme's celebrated letter.

The *Journal* headlined it the "Worst Insult to the United States in Its History." The Spanish Minister (never imagining that his private letter would be intercepted) had called the President "weak," "a bidder for the admiration of the crowd," and "a would-be politician." [25] He had also referred to the negotiations for a commercial treaty as a blind; negotiations should be conducted in Washington, he advised, by a high-ranking Spanish delegate "even if only for effect"; they would, he hoped, impress congressional leaders, win over the Cuban

24. Woodford to Sherman, Jan. 24, Feb. 3 and 4, 1898. U.S. Department of State, *Spain*.

25. For a good discussion of the de Lôme letter, Morgan, *McKinley*, pp. 356–59.

refugees, and discredit the Junta. ·The letter was painful for McKinley, not merely because of the disparaging personal remarks it contained, but also as evidence of Spanish insincerity.[26] It made him more hesitant about engaging in further negotiations; the President now sought absolute guarantees of Spanish conduct that would assure peace for Cuba.

The day after the publication of de Lôme's letter, the Spanish reply to the President's proposals of the previous December reached Washington. The tone of the Spanish note was stiff, even threatening. The royal government berated McKinley for criticizing the colonial policy of the previous, Conservative ministry, defended the honor of the Spanish Army, and denied the United States a voice in the Cuban question: "The idea which has slipped into the American note that Spain can reasonably count upon the United States maintaining [its] present attitude only until an undetermined future shall prove whether indispensable conditions of peace have been realized is . . . [not] justifiable . . . [or] explicable. Spanish government does not admit the right of neighboring country to limit duration of struggle. Aspirations for peace and friendly observations are justified. Foreign intrusion and interferences are never and in no way justified. These might lead to the intervention which every country that respects itself must repel with force. Peace . . . can be found only in the formula of colonial self-government and Spanish sovereignty." [27] It was for the Spanish government alone to determine how Cuba should be governed. If McKinley nevertheless

26. Day to Woodford, Feb. 23, 1898. U.S. Department of State, *Spain.*

27. This important note, the Spanish reply to Woodford's note of Dec. 20, 1897, has, curiously enough, been generally overlooked. Woodford to Sherman, Feb. 9, 1898 (a telegraphic summary of the Spanish note of Feb. 1, 1898). U.S. Department of State, *Spain; Foreign Relations, 1898,* pp. 657–64.

attempted to impose a solution he would find Spain ready to fight.

Five days later the *Maine* exploded in Havana harbor. It was an extraordinary coincidence that de Lôme's letter, the Spanish reply, and the sinking of the *Maine* should all occur within one week. Public hysteria was mounting, but the President did not lose sight of the main objective of his diplomatic efforts. The de Lôme incident was not worth a war. "If a rupture between the countries must come, it should not be upon such personal and comparatively unimportant matter," Day telegraphed to Woodford.[28] A settlement of the *Maine* disaster could also be reached. The fundamental issue remained the problem of peace for Cuba. But in the public mind and on Capitol Hill the loss of the *Maine* transformed the Cuban question: patriotic fervor now demanded vengeance for the *Maine*—not just independence for Cuba.

The President had been personally responsible for sending the *Maine* to Havana. During the previous December his advisers had discussed the possibility of riots in Havana. It was decided to hold the *Maine* in readiness at Key West, and Consul General Lee was secretly empowered to call the warship to Havana in case of sudden emergency. In allowing Lee such discretion, the President wrote that he had "full confidence in [his] judgment . . . to use it wisely."[29]

When riots actually broke out in Havana on January 12, 1898, Lee kept his head and did not send the secret message to Key West.[30] To serve the double purpose of protecting Americans and lending more weight to his diplomacy, the

28. Day to Woodford, private, March 31, 1898. U.S. Department of State, *Spain.*

29. Department of State to Lee, Dec. 2, 1897. Navy Department, R.G. 45, area 8, National Archives, Washington, D.C.

30. Department of State to Lee, Dec. 2, 1897; Secretary of the Navy to Sigsbee, Dec. 7, 1897. Navy Department, R.G. 45, area 8.

President now ordered the battleship to Havana on a supposedly friendly call. In his journal, Secretary Long noted with premonition: "There is of course the danger that the arrival of the ship may precipitate some crisis or riot . . . I hope with all my heart that everything will turn out all right." [31] Unhappily, Long did not voice his misgiving to the President.

During the six weeks that elapsed between the loss of the *Maine* and the publication of the report of the American naval experts, McKinley made every effort to secure from Spain the promise of reforms that, in his judgment, would assure peace for Cuba.

Early in March the President sent fresh instructions to Woodford. He stressed that his requirements for a settlement of the Cuban question had not changed since the previous December. He also observed that the Spanish attempt to make autonomy workable on the island had failed, that the distress on the island continued unabated, and that the Spanish Army had won no successes.[32] Three weeks later the President, through Woodford, warned the royal government that unless he could assure Congress that peace would be established on the island, he would have to lay the whole question before Congress.[33] The legislature would very likely pass resolutions recognizing Cuban independence.[34]

Throughout that month McKinley attempted to reassure the European ambassadors in Washington that his intentions were pacific, to convince the government in Madrid that a Cuban settlement could no longer be delayed, and to restrain Con-

31. Long Journal, Jan. 24, 1898. Long MSS.
32. Day to Woodford, telegrams, March 1 and 3, 1898. U.S. Department of State, *Spain; Foreign Relations, 1898*, pp. 666–69, 680–81.
33. Day to Woodford, telegram, March 20, 1898. U.S. Department of State, *Spain; Foreign Relations, 1898*, pp. 692–93.
34. Day to Woodford, telegram, March 30, 1898. U.S. Department of State, *Spain; Foreign Relations, 1898*, p. 721.

gress from taking precipitous action. His message early in March requesting $50 million for the national defense calmed senatorial fears that the President might act less vigorously than they hoped. Then on March 27, McKinley transmitted the report on the *Maine* to Congress, accompanied by a mild message. The loyal and hardworking senators who supported the Administration now warned McKinley that they could not control Congress much longer.

The time for decision had come. McKinley enumerated his conditions for peace with Spain after consulting a number of leading Republican senators. He made two distinct proposals on two successive days. The first he sent on March 26.[35] It was based on the assumption that the Spanish government was willing to open direct negotiations with the insurgent leaders. If the Spanish ministers preferred to negotiate with the Cubans, then only a Spanish offer of "full self-government" (which meant independence, Day telegraphed two days later) would, in the President's opinion, afford a reasonable guarantee of peace. He added that he would be willing to aid in the restoration of peace on this basis. McKinley's alternative proposal (it will be recalled that the President had left to Spain a choice of two different ways of settling the Cuban question since the previous summer) was sent to Madrid on March 27.[36] It was based on the assumption that the Spanish government was not prepared to offer the insurgents independence straightway. Since, if that were the case, any Spanish attempt to initiate negotiations with the Cuban leaders would be abortive, McKinley insisted that he would be able to persuade the Cubans to lay down their arms only if Spain were ready to accept his mediation and grant an armistice until October

35. Day to Woodford, telegram, March 26, 1898. U.S. Department of State, *Spain; Foreign Relations, 1898*, p. 704.
36. Day to Woodford, telegram, March 27, 1898. U.S. Department of State, *Spain; Foreign Relations, 1898*, pp. 711–12.

1. McKinley hoped that, if the terms of peace had not been agreed upon before the expiration of the armistice, Spain would also agree to his acting as final arbiter. He did not make this condition a sine qua non. McKinley made it clear that he expected the Spanish to take immediate steps to relieve the distress of the Cuban people, whichever alternative Spain decided to accept—direct negotiations on the basis of independence or American mediation and an armistice.

There was not the slightest chance that Spain would accept either proposition. Immediate independence was out of the question; to invite the mediation of the American President was unthinkable. The Spanish ministers did eventually grant an armistice, but its duration was conditional; an armistice by itself, even if unconditional, did not in any case meet the President's requirements. In Madrid, Ambassador Woodford was rapidly getting out of his depth.

In February Woodford had been in despair; he had reported to McKinley and Day that no further concessions were to be expected from Spain.[37] The Queen would rather fight the United States over Cuba than endanger the dynasty by handing Cuba to the Cubans, thereby exposing her son, the King, and herself, as Regent, to the wrath of the people. But during March Woodford believed that a settlement could be reached; Moret had evidently convinced him of Spain's sincerity. Woodford met the leading members of the Spanish government and began to sympathize with them in their dilemma. They would, he thought, move forward as fast as their sense of pride could permit them.[38] He therefore did not give up his hope of peace

37. Woodford to McKinley, Feb. 19 and 23, 1898. U.S. Department of State, *Spain.* Woodford to McKinley, Feb. 26, 1898. *Foreign Relations, 1898*, pp. 664–65.
38. Woodford to Day, telegrams, March 25 and 27, April 4 and 6, 1898; Woodford to McKinley, telegrams, March 17, 25 and 26, 1898. U.S. Department of State, *Spain; Foreign Relations, 1898*, pp. 710–11.

even when, on March 31, the Spanish insisted that an armistice could be granted only if the insurgents asked for it. The Spanish ministers, he surmised correctly, had not yet said the last word. Woodford believed that the obstacles to peace were more matters of form than of substance. "It has turned, as I feared, on a question of punctilio. Spanish pride will not permit the Ministry to propose and offer an armistice," Woodford wrote to the President on the last day of March.[39] If he could secure an armistice, he assured McKinley and Day, then the fighting on the island would end permanently and Cuba would become the property of the United States.[40] Woodford's optimism and desire to reduce the President's alternatives to a single condition, a Spanish proclamation of an armistice, aroused misgivings in Washington. Did Woodford really grasp his instructions precisely? On April 3, Day reminded the Ambassador in Madrid that the President could make no new suggestions. He also explained that a Spanish proclamation of armistice would not suffice: "An armistice involves an agreement between Spain and insurgents which must be voluntary on the part of each, and if accepted by them would make for peace . . . An armistice to be effective, must be immediately proffered and accepted by insurgents." [41] As for the peace Woodford had written he was confident of being able to secure, was Spain ready to give Cuba her independence?

Day's warnings had no effect; Woodford's desire for peace was so ardent that he began to believe what he wanted to believe: time and patience would lead all sides to an accept-

39. Woodford to McKinley, telegram, March 31, 1898, U.S. Department of State, *Spain.*
40. Woodford to McKinley, telegrams, April 3 and 5, 1898. U.S. Department of State, *Spain; Foreign Relations, 1898,* pp. 732–35.
41. Day to Woodford, telegram, April 3, 1898. U.S. Department of State, *Spain; Foreign Relations, 1898,* p. 733.

able solution; the Spanish government might be induced to proclaim an armistice. No more than that—but Woodford thought that if Spain took this step, peace for Cuba would be secure. In Washington, McKinley took a more realistic view, although the President did not give up hope that Spain would meet all his essential conditions. On April 5, Woodford telegraphed that the Queen, at the behest of the Pope, was considering the proclamation of an armistice to last until October.[42] Four days later he was able to report triumphantly that an armistice had actually been granted at the request of the Pope and the great powers. Now Spain should not be humiliated: "You will win the fight on your own lines," Woodford advised the President.[43]

McKinley continued to hope that good sense would prevail in Madrid; if this were not possible, at least that the European powers and the Vatican would find a way of persuading the Spanish ministers to accept the demands of the United States. McKinley probably knew that not one of the European ambassadors in Washington believed the United States justified in going to war. Foreign diplomats had come to the White House on April 6 to express their collective wish for peace. Far more significant than this demarche itself, however, was the fact that the British Ambassador had been instructed to inquire in advance whether such representation would be welcome to the President, who had accordingly consulted Day beforehand.[44] With all sincerity, McKinley could reply to these distinguished diplomats gathered in the Blue Room that

42. Woodford to McKinley, telegram, April 5, 1898. U.S. Department of State, *Spain; Foreign Relations, 1898*, p. 734–35.
43. Woodford to McKinley, telegram, April 10, 1898. U.S. Department of State, *Spain; Foreign Relations, 1898*, p. 747.
44. Grenville, *Salisbury,* pp. 201 ff. May, *Imperial Democracy,* pp. 196–219.

his sentiments corresponded exactly to their own. The behavior of the British had given McKinley whatever final proof he may have been seeking that no European intervention on behalf of Spain was possible. Germany, France, and Russia could exercise no pressure on the United States without the help of the British Navy. In fact they had no such designs. The credit given England for having blocked a hostile coalition was thus undeserved.

It was on the day of the visit that McKinley intended to send his message on the Cuban question to Congress. But he won a few more days from the impatient legislature by convincing congressional leaders of the need for time to evacuate American citizens from Cuba. The supporters of the Administration had already warned the President that they would not be able to hold Congress in check much longer. Senator Lodge, as well as a number of other senators, was supporting the President "with all his might," to prevent Congress from "breaking away." Any other course, he feared, would discredit the Republicans at home, humiliate the country abroad, and lead to the election of Bryan and silver.[45]

Senator Spooner, who complained "the world does not know what war is today, with the modern arms, projectiles and death-dealing instrumentalities," described the Senate proceedings during the last days of peace. "Apparently Congress cannot keep its head. It looks at this time of writing as if a majority had their watches out, waiting for the arrival of a particular hour on Monday, to force the hand of the President, and let loose the dogs of war. I have with others, done all in my power thus far to give the President time to work out the delicate and difficult negotiations which he has in hand. I have believed that he, if let alone, could pull through . . .

45. Lodge to Higginson, April 4, 1898. Lodge MSS.

The situation is calculated to make a man distrust our system a little bit." [46]

The Spanish reply reached Washington on April 10.[47] The European ambassadors in Washington then believed—and the same view has frequently, but erroneously, been expressed since—that Spain had capitulated to McKinley at the eleventh hour. In fact the Spanish government rejected the President's terms. An armistice was proclaimed, but only "for such length of time" as the Spanish commander-in-chief "may think prudent to prepare and facilitate the peace earnestly desired by all." It was not a just armistice. The Cubans were asked to stop fighting for as long as the Spanish commander-in-chief thought it convenient and were offered autonomy. When Day asked the Spanish Minister whether Spain was ready to grant Cuba independence if the President considered it necessary, the Minister said "No." [48] In short, the armistice was of no practical value; the Cuban leaders were certain to reject the demand to cease their struggle on Spain's terms just at the time when they believed they were winning their fight for independence. Peace on the island had not been brought one step closer. The Spanish ministers also remained adamant in refusing the President's mediation.

On April 11, McKinley sent his message to Congress. It did not close the door to a negotiated settlement and was so worded, Day cabled Woodford, as to ensure some days of congressional debate. It may be well asked why the President hesitated even in mid-April 1898 to lead the nation boldly to war. He evidently thought there was a chance that, faced with an ultimatum—for that was what he had delivered by

46. Spooner to Frank Bigelow, March 9, 1898; Spooner to Turner, April 2, 1898. Spooner MSS, Library of Congress, Washington, D.C.
47. Woodford to Day, telegram, April 9, 1898. U.S. Department of State, *Spain; Foreign Relations, 1898*, p. 746.
48. May, *Imperial Democracy*, p. 157.

leaving the decision of war to a bellicose Congress—Spain might still yield. He could, after all, look back on six months of negotiations during which Spain had, in the face of unremitting pressure (and frequently at the last moment), made concessions such as few sovereign states have ever made in times of peace. It seemed as if Spain had to take only one more step to settle the crisis. But in Madrid, this one step— willingness to grant Cuba its independence if no other solution could be found—no Spanish minister was ready to take. Recognition of Cuban independence was not regarded as just one more concession: the maintenance of Spanish sovereignty over Cuba was the one condition which the Spanish ministry would not yield, whatever other concessions might be wrung from its government. This was the final obstacle to peace. McKinley's message to Congress had gained eight more days for the Spanish government, but all to no avail, and when war came McKinley was prepared.

The President would have been ready to see Cuba pass into the hands of a government chosen by the Cubans if thereby a war could have been avoided. But once he had gone to war, McKinley would cause the Cuban settlement to coincide with the long-term interests of the United States. Many knowledgeable Americans doubted whether the Cubans were really ready for self-government and feared that immediate independence would create fresh problems for the United States. McKinley shared these fears and inclined to the view that the Cubans would first have to pass through a period of American tutelage before they could be trusted to make wise use of a representative government. It had never been part of McKinley's policy to recognize the Junta leaders as the lawful government of Cuba. No more was it part of his policy to do so in the early days of April. His message of April 11 advised Congress not to recognize the insurgent regime and merely expressed his eventual intention to recognize an independent Cuban government.

While a large majority of the House was ready to grant the President the power and discretion he was asking for, the Senate was less docile. A group of idealistic Democrats, who looked upon war with Spain as a holy crusade for the sake of the Cubans, combined with a group of Republicans, led by Foraker of Ohio, who suspected that McKinley would even now wriggle out of a declaration of war. They added to the resolutions reported by the Senate Foreign Relations Committee a clause recognizing "the Republic of Cuba as the true and lawful government of that island." The Senate also adopted the now famous Teller amendment, disclaiming any intention on the part of the United States to exercise any control over the island. Once Cuba was pacified, the government of the island was to be left to the people of Cuba. Although the House–Senate conference committee subsequently struck out the provision requiring the immediate recognition of the insurgent government, a compromise was reached only at the price of leaving the Teller amendment untouched. To this extent, McKinley's hands were tied, and the Administration did not enter the war entirely free from commitment. The amendment thus represented a defeat of Administration policies, but it is doubtful whether in fact the will of Congress very much affected McKinley's subsequent Cuban policy.[49] Nor had congressional pressure before the war influenced the President's policy as much as has been supposed. He had been following a purposeful Cuban policy since July 1897.

We now know there was only one possible end—war. Short of Cuban independence, there could have been no Spanish–

49. For a discussion of the origins of the Teller amendment, two useful sources are Nathanial Wright Stephenson, *Nelson W. Aldrich* (New York, Scribner's, 1930), pp. 156 ff., and Leon Burr Richardson, *William E. Chandler, Republican* (New York, Dodd, Mead, 1940), pp. 575–82.

Cuban settlement, and the Spanish government was not ready to grant independence. McKinley was searching for an alternative where there was none.

For nine months McKinley steadily increased the pressure in Madrid. His notes to Spain were clear and unequivocal. If Spain could not bring peace to Cuba then the United States would do so—if possible by diplomacy, if necessary by war. He had threatened to leave the Cuban decision to Congress, in this way hoping to induce the Spanish government to accept his terms. As long as McKinley believed that his policies might succeed, he skillfully held Congress back—even after the disaster to the *Maine*. No President before had been faced with such a weight of public opinion in favor of war, encouraged as it was by a sensational press, making use of the added effectiveness of mass circulation. The President's messages to Congress were designed to calm the rising hysteria; his notes to Spain were meant to convince the royal government that the time for words and promises had passed and that only the restoration of peace in Cuba could stop American intervention. Evidence suggests that McKinley's policy was steadily moving to the point where he would have presented an ultimatum to Spain quite independently of the *Maine* disaster. The jingoes believed that they had driven McKinley into war, de Lôme thought the President was weak and easily influenced by public opinion, and Roosevelt felt that he had no more backbone than a chocolate eclair. While the roles these men played in the crisis of 1898 have generally been condemned, their judgment of McKinley has not been questioned. McKinley had to make clear his Cuban policies in the instructions he sent to Madrid, and the reconstructed story shows neither weakness nor indecision.

For more than two nerve-racking months, McKinley had strained party loyalty to the limit, courted widespread unpopularity, allowed the impression to prevail that he was indecisive, unable to lead the nation, and abdicating leadership to Congress. The methods of his diplomacy required this sacrifice. The risk of unpopularity did not deflect the President from doing his duty as he conceived it. These are not the actions of a man lacking character or political courage. The inflexibility of both McKinley and the Spanish was the ultimate cause of war. The President would not deviate from his duty to the Cubans. He profoundly believed that the United States could no longer avoid war; the dictates of civilization and humanity impelled her to act. The Spanish ministers denied the United States any voice in the settlement of Spain's internal problems. They based their contention on the accepted standards of international conduct. Both sides believed that they had shown great patience and forbearance. And so President McKinley and the Queen Regent of Spain went to war in 1898, each firmly convinced of the righteousness of the cause.

Chapter Ten
The Influence of Strategy upon History:
The Acquisition of the Philippines

MAHAN STUDIED HISTORY to distill from it the general principles of strategy. The influence of strategy on history still remains to be systematically explored. The attack on the Philippines during the Spanish-American War is a fascinating illustration of the impact of strategic decisions on the relations of the great powers. The occupation of the islands has profoundly influenced American diplomacy in the twentieth century. The significance of the event is generally acknowledged, but there is little agreement on why the United States went there in the first place. In a well-known phrase, one distinguished American diplomatic historian has referred to the event as a "great aberation." Others have sought to show that the Philippine adventure was the logical outcome of earlier American policies. To support their argument they have pointed to America's growing concern in the Far East, stimulated as it was by missionaries and merchants. But by the turn of the century optimism gave way to a more sober appreciation of the obstacles to American influence. When the Kaiser seized Kiaochow in November 1897 and Russia sent a fleet to Port Arthur, it appeared plain to everyone, and to none more so than Minister Denby in Peking, that the partition of China was at hand, and with it the possible ruin of America's future commerce. The merchants reacted strongly to this threat to their future prospects. The breach of the principle of the open door in Asia, one historian has recently concluded, "constrained the administration to make thorough preparations for offensive operations in the Pacific." [1]

Other evidence apparently supports the notion that some Americans had cast covetous eyes on the Philippines before the battle of Manila Bay, on May 1, 1898. "The Philippines are logically our first target," Senator Albert J. Beveridge had declared in Boston on April 27, 1898.[2] A few days later, but before Dewey's victory was officially announced in Washington, Senator Lodge wrote: "If, as now seems almost certain, we have captured Manila, we ought I think, to hold that great strategic point in the East, which would enable us to get our share of the Pacific trade." [3] Such statements have lent support to the "conspiracy theory"—that a few men in important places had been planning for some time to seize the Philippines.

Dewey's battle of May 1 captured the imagination of the American people. The business community involved in the China trade, previously fearful that the Administration was not lending sufficient support to American interests in China, now clamored for the Philippines as a valuable market, the gateway to the Orient. We have ample reason for believing that the American interest in the Chinese market was large and vocal. But—and this is really the question—did anyone look upon American possession of the Philippine archipelago as likely to further American commercial or strategic policies

1. Lafeber, *The New Empire*, p. 362. Richard Warner Van Alstyne, in his perceptive book *The Rising American Empire* (Oxford, Blackwell, 1960), stresses the continuity of policy. Samuel Flagg Bemis, in his *A Diplomatic History of the United States* (New York, Holt, 1936), refers to the acquisition of the Philippines as "The Great Aberation of 1898."
2. Quoted and discussed in Pratt, *Expansionists*, p. 228.
3. Lodge to L. S. Amonson, May 3, 1898. Lodge MSS.

in China before rumors of Dewey's impending attack on the Philippines reached the United States from Europe? There appears to be no trace of such sentiment earlier than March 1898.

Before March, the attention of the business community had been focused on China and not on the Philippines. That was also true of the State Department. When, in December 1897 and January 1898, the pressure on the Administration for a more active China policy had dramatically increased, Dewey was instructed to reconnoiter and advise on the acquisition of a Chinese, not a Philippine, base.[4] Congress and the American public meanwhile were prepared to fight for Cuba. They did not foresee that a war with Spain would change America's role in the Far East.

The dramatic story of how Roosevelt, during Secretary Long's temporary absence from the Navy Department, sent his famous telegram to Commodore Dewey on February 25, 1898, to prepare for the attack on Manila, is a commonplace of the history books. Roosevelt had not acted impulsively. He was carrying out, so we are told, a plot he and Lodge had concocted to seize the Philippines in the event of war with Spain. Commodore Dewey, so the story runs, was made privy to the secret when Lodge and Roosevelt had helped to secure his appointment to the command of the Asiatic Squadron some months earlier.[5]

This tale belongs with the legends of history. The order to attack Manila was finally sanctioned by the President at a con-

4. Memorandum by Long, Feb. 1, 1898. Navy Department, R. G. 45, area 10 file. For the "China lobby" of businessmen, see esp. Charles S. Campbell, Jr., *Special Business Interests and the Open Door Policy* (New Haven, Yale University Press, 1951).
5. For example, A. Whitney Griswold, *The Far Eastern Policy of the United States* (New York, Harcourt, Brace, 1938), pp. 11 ff. Historians have tended to accept the idea of Roosevelt's "plot" rather uncritically.

ference in the White House on Sunday, April 24, 1898.[6] He was acting according to a war plan first worked out before Roosevelt had joined the Navy Department. This secret war plan was known to President McKinley, Secretary of the Navy Long, and the chiefs of the Navy Department; it was under constant revision during the years before the outbreak of the conflict. Neither Roosevelt nor Lodge played any part in its formulation. It was not the politicians but a group of officers in the Navy Department and at the Naval War College who had initiated the Philippine attack. Now it might be supposed that these strategists in planning an attack on the Philippines had from the outset intended to strengthen the United States' position in the Far East. But this was not their objective, although the importance of the Far East to the United States had not been overlooked by naval officers.

American naval officers had for some years been concerned about the growing hostility of Japan toward the United States. In March 1893, soon after his retirement from the command of the Asiatic Squadron, Rear Admiral Belknap warned Secretary of the Navy Herbert that the Japanese were pursuing a plan of colonization not only in Korea and Hawaii but in Mexico and Central America as well. Japan's victory over China and her unfriendly response to the projected Hawaiian annexation sharpened these fears. In September 1897, Captain Barker,

6. Long to Agnes Long, Oct. 9, 1898. Long MSS. This describes the immediate origins of the dispatch: "The war was declared Thursday, April 21st. I immediately went to the President and told him that it was the judgment of the Department and the leading officers there that he should order Dewey immediately to Manila to attack the Spanish forces. He preferred to consider the matter a little longer. On the following Sunday morning I went over again and took with me the despatch, as it was afterwards signed and sent. Even I did not write the despatch. It was written in the Bureau of Navigation, as a matter of routine work. The President did not dictate a word of it. No Cabinet officer was consulted about it. No one would have objected to it if he had been. The President ordered it sent, and it went that afternoon."

Commanding Officer of the battleship *Oregon,* warned the Navy Department that he regarded the danger from Japan as more serious than the threat of Spain. The Japanese, he claimed, had designs on the Nicaraguan Canal, Mexico, and Central and South America. He hoped his warnings would induce the Administration to send more warships to the Pacific while there was still time; the United States would have to provide adequately for the defense of Hawaii and the Pacific shore.[7] But it occurred to no naval officer to advocate the seizure of a base in the Philippines in order to defend Hawaii or the Pacific coast. Nor did American naval officers suggest that the Philippines should be annexed to strengthen American claims in China; neither missionaries nor merchants had taken an interest in the islands. In short, the attack on the islands was not influenced by any of the pressures that were increasing the American involvement in the Far East.

When Admiral McNair handed over the command of the Asiatic Squadron to Dewey in December 1897, he commented on the conditions of the ships, their disposition, and the American interests he had been charged to protect. He discussed China, Korea, and Japanese designs on Hawaii. But his reference to the Philippines was brief. "The newspapers have contained accounts, for some time past, of the rebellion in progress in the Philippine Islands. No official information has been received in relation thereto, and no information of any sort that shows American interests to be affected." [8]

The arguments employed later to persuade the Administration to retain the islands did not occur before the battle of Manila Bay. One conclusion appears to be inescapable: but

7. Belknap to Herbert, March 17, 1893. Navy Department, R. G. 45, area 10 file. Barker to Navy Department, Sept. 15, 1897; Aug. 30, 1897. Navy Department, *Miscellaneous letters.*

8. McNair to Dewey, Dec. 31, 1897. Navy Department, R. G. 45, area 10 file.

for two war plans, the first of which bears the signature of Lieutenant William Wirt Kimball, the United States would not have extended her sovereignty over the Philippine Islands.

It is one of the ironies of history that the projected attack on the Philippines was no more than a secondary consideration in the general strategy of Kimball's war plan. The main purpose of the descent on Manila was not to strengthen America's commerce in the Far East but to weaken Spain by depriving it of the revenues it derived from the islands. The Asiatic Squadron was assigned the tasks first of destroying the inferior Spanish warships in Philippine waters and then of capturing Manila, and at the same time blockading all the principal ports of the islands so that, as Kimball put it, "the release of our hold on them may be used as an inducement to Spain to make peace after the liberation of Cuba." [9]

The plan was evidently not the work of Kimball alone. On Admiral Luce's suggestion, the Naval War College had in the summer of 1895 begun to study the strategic implications of a war with Spain. Replying to one of Luce's letters, Captain Taylor, President of the War College, cannily prophesied: "What you say about Cuba and Spain interests me very much and will . . . produce greater results than you fancy." [10] The plan was worked out in collaboration with the Office of Naval Intelligence; it was named after Kimball, the officer who prepared the final draft. Kimball undertook the task at the request of his immediate superior, Lieutenant Commander Richard Wainwright, Chief Intelligence Officer. [11] By a curious chance,

9. "War with Spain, 1896, General Considerations of the War, the Results desired, and the Consequent Kind of Operations To Be Undertaken." Plan by W. W. Kimball, Lt. U.S. Navy, Staff Intelligence Officer, June 1, 1896, R. G. 313, Naval Operating Forces, North Atlantic Station, Entry 43, Box 11. Navy Department, National Archives, Washington, D.C.

10. Taylor to Luce, Aug. 5, 1895. Luce MSS.

11. Richard Wainwright three years later, the Executive Officer of the *Maine*, was one of the few survivors of the disaster.

the Office of Naval Intelligence was presided over in 1896 by the Assistant Secretary of the Navy, William McAdoo, the very man who eight years earlier had ridiculed the notion of a War College. Once in office, however, McAdoo became an enthusiastic convert to strategic planning. When handing his post over to Theodore Roosevelt in March 1897, he pointed with pride to the work done by the Naval War College and the Office of Naval Intelligence, advising Roosevelt that "in case of war or any foreign trouble it [the Office of Naval Intelligence] is the first place to go to get accurate information. The War College problems are deposited there. It is a good office, well kept up, and possibly the best anywhere . . . We are abreast, if not ahead, of some of the other countries in these matters." [12] Roosevelt took over an efficient working organization; he also inherited the war plan against Spain. The search for the "culprits" of the attack on the Philippines thus leads to the planners—Taylor, Wainwright, Kimball, and McAdoo—and not to the agents—Roosevelt and Dewey.

Lacking executive guidance about the objectives of American policy in the event of war, the officers who drew up the war plan made their own political assumptions. In 1896 they simply took for granted that the United States did not desire any of Spain's possessions for itself. Thus the war plan begins with a discussion of "the object of the war" and of "the results desired":

It is apparent that the real cause of the war will be friction between the United States and Spain upon the Cuban question . . . Whatever may be the especial act which leads to the rupture of peaceful relations, it would seem to be a foregone conclusion that the object of the war to be waged

12. McAdoo to Roosevelt, "Memorandum Regarding Naval Attachés Abroad," and "Memorandum Regarding the War College," April 15, 1897, R. G. 80, Entry 124, Records of the Assistant Secretary of the Navy, Letterpress, 5, National Archives, Washington, D.C.

by the United States would be to liberate Cuba from Spanish rule, to exact from Spain a fair war indemnity for the cost of the war, and to force a settlement of the particular question which was the direct cause of the outbreak of hostilities.

Kimball explicitly explained that he meant by the "liberation of Cuba": the establishment of a Cuban Republic. These suppositions about Cuba and the Philippines, although they did not harmonize with Olney's and McKinley's policies, influenced the basic strategy of the war. The fighting role was primarily assigned to the Navy, and not to the Army.

[A naval campaign] would be attractive from a diplomatic or sentimental rather than a purely strategic point of view, because it would contemplate the establishment of a Cuban Republic through the efforts of its own citizens within its own borders, aided only by the extraterritorially applied sea power of the United States, instead of a conquest and occupation of Spanish territory by an organized army of invasion from this country . . . a resort to invasion would be necessary only in case naval operations alone were not effective, or required a longer time to be made so than the policy of the United States government in regard to the duration of the war could allow.[13]

Though the revised war plan against Spain of 30 June 1897 envisaged military operations, and McKinley sanctioned an invasion of Cuba, the Army command proved unequal to the task of organizing a landing efficiently.

In 1896, a year earlier, a purely naval war held out attractions. It was likely to involve the fewest American casualties and would cost less than a large-scale military operation. It was a cheap war; the successful naval campaign would cripple Spanish

13. Kimball, "War with Spain, 1896."

trade and humble Spanish pride. In any case, no other way of injuring Spain would be open to the United States should the war break out in the rainy season—so argued the naval officers.

The essence of the naval plan of operations was to make America's sea power felt wherever Spanish ships could be engaged by an equal or superior United States naval force. The immediate role of one part of the fleet was to blockade Cuba at the outset of the war. It was anticipated that the main naval battle of the war would occur when Spain sent its battlefleet to the relief of Cuba. The North Atlantic Squadron was thus assigned the task of gaining command of the Florida Strait, so that the Spanish fleet might be intercepted and destroyed before it could reach the shelter of the fortress guns in Havana harbor.

American naval superiority, the strategists believed, would also permit the United States to engage in offensive operations beyond the Caribbean theater. The Mediterranean coast of Spain was ill defended, and the seaports of Barcelona and Malaga were open to attack. In the Far East, Spanish ships guarding Manila were no match for the Asiatic Squadron. But without bases in the Far East and Europe, the difficulty of securing adequate and reliable coaling facilities presented the principal obstacle to striking at Spain and her colonies. The strategists hoped to solve the problem in Europe by chartering British colliers to meet the United States warships. But in the Far East "the difficulty of arranging a flying coaling base for such a squadron, and the strategic importance of Manila would seem to point to the latter place as a military objective to be reached even at the expense of sending an armored ship or two for its attainment." Thus injury to Spain by a strike at the Philippines involved the seizure of Manila. Kimball and his colleagues could not have thought this difficult, since they calculated that the American cruisers would only need to be reinforced by "an armored ship or two." They never dreamed that the American Army would be sent to capture and hold the principal islands. The plan merely envisaged the occupation of Manila as a hostage of war. And so it came about that a war plan helped to change the course of American history.

Kimball's war plan was first revised in December 1896 by a board headed by Rear Admiral Ramsay—an old opponent of the Naval War College—whose report disparaged earlier War College studies and recommended an attack on the Canary Islands in place of the attack on Manila. Another War Board, headed by Rear Admiral Montgomery Sicard, reporting on 30 June 1897, reverted in essentials to the Kimball plan; the attack on Manila was restored but military operations were recommended in addition to naval action. Sicard's report also outlined the first war plan against Japan "in case the United States has to face a war with Spain and Japan, at the same time." [14]

But two interesting questions still remain to be answered. How was it that Roosevelt secured the credit? Why did he send the famous telegram of February 25 to Dewey on that day? Roosevelt owed this good fortune to his friend Senator Lodge, who in his book *The War with Spain* first revealed how Roosevelt—with commendable foresight—had instructed Dewey to make preparations to attack Manila in good time. But it had not been Lodge's first intention to dramatize the episode. When collecting material for his book in the autumn of 1898, Lodge wrote to the Navy Department for help. He already knew the substance of the famous telegram; he had fortuitously been present in Roosevelt's office on the day it was sent. The more he studied the war preparations of the Navy Department, the more he was impressed by the Department's efficiency.

14. "Plan of Operation Against Spain," December 17, 1896 and "Plans of Campaign Against Spain and Japan," June 30, 1897, in J. A. S. Grenville, "American Naval Preparations for War with Spain, 1896-1898," *Journal of American Studies*, 2 (1968) 33-47.

He found that the Navy Department had begun to provide for the possibility of conflict with Spain in January 1898 and placed the United States fleet in readiness. The commander-in-chief of the European station was instructed on January 11 to retain men whose enlistments were about to expire. By the third week of February the commanders of the various squadrons of the Navy had all received preliminary instructions to prepare their vessels for conflict. This fact has a bearing on the controversial instruction sent to Dewey on February 25, 1898; it should be considered in its true relation to the overall policy which the Navy Department had been following for six weeks.[15] The telegram marked a more advanced stage of war preparation, but it followed logically from the decision made earlier within the Department. Nor was the order to Dewey in any sense extraordinary. He was instructed to assemble his squadron in Hong Kong and to hold it in readiness to carry out the war plan against Spain. Similar orders were issued to the commander-in-chief of the European station on the same and following days. Secretary Long was again in active charge on February 26, and—certainly with his approval—all the United States squadrons were ordered to keep their vessels coaled and ready for instant action. It is of course true that Roosevelt had been urging the need for these preparations for several months. But he was not actually personally responsible for their adoption. The real work was done by the bureau chiefs of the Navy Department, and especially by Captain Arent Schuyler Crowninshield, Chief of the Bureau of Navigation.

Lodge wanted to give the bureau chiefs the full credit, but they were reluctant to assume public responsibility for preparing for war at a time when the President was still striving to maintain the peace. "You will probably see yourself," the Chief

15. The chronological sequence of orders sent by the Navy Department is shown in a memorandum preserved in the papers of Senator Lodge. Lodge MSS.

of the Bureau of Navigation wrote to Lodge in September 1898, that to hand over the text of the telegram of February 25 for publication "might appear to put us in a light of being almost over-prepared—in other words it might seem that the Department had as early as February 25 . . . made up its mind and that there was to be a war anyway." [16] Lodge considered the Department's caution foolish. He replied that he would have thought that the Department deserved no blame, but only unstinted praise: "My intention was simply to refer to [the telegram] as an order of the Department, but if the Secretary has the slightest objection to my doing so I will say that the order was sent by Mr. Roosevelt as Acting Secretary, and I have no doubt the Colonel of the Rough Riders will accept the responsibility of being overprepared with perfect equanimity." [17] When Lodge explained the whole story, Roosevelt was amused. He assured Lodge that he was "naturally delighted to shoulder the responsibility." [18] Lodge's popular account no doubt enhanced Roosevelt's reputation, and his standing will not suffer now. After all, his achievements rest on more solid foundations than his allegedly decisive influence on the war with Spain.

The Navy Department, as has been seen, had prepared for the war more carefully than has been supposed. Secretary Long knew nothing of tactics and strategy, but he was intelligent enough to admit to the fact and to leave such practical questions to his bureau chiefs. During the weeks immediately preceding the war, Long suffered from a recurrence of his nervous troubles; he noted in his journal that he was sleeping badly. He did not concern himself overmuch with grand

16. Crowninshield to Lodge, Sept. 19, 1898. Lodge MSS.
17. Lodge to Crowninshield, Sept. 12, 21, and 26, 1898. Lodge MSS.
18. Lodge to Roosevelt, Sept. 21, 1898. Lodge MSS. Roosevelt to Lodge, Sept. 26, 1898. Morison, ed., *Letters of Roosevelt*, 2, 880.

strategy. Roosevelt tried to rouse him, but without success. Long recorded one of their discussions in his journal:

> Mr. Roosevelt came in, shut the door, and began in his usual emphatic and dead-in-earnest manner . . . in case of war with Spain, he intends to abandon everything and go to the front . . . He has gone so far daft in the matter that he evidently regards it as a sacred duty . . . I called him a crank, and ridiculed him to the best of my ability, but all in vain. The funny part of it all is, that he actually takes the thing seriously. Just as if there were anything in the whole business, even if it came to a scrap, that is worth serious thought. He bores me with plans of naval and military movement, and the necessity of having some scheme of attack arranged for instant execution in case of an emergency.[19]

Long paid more attention to unimportant details. On January 15 he confided to his diary that he was "disgusted with the office boy, who prevaricates and shows the poor fiber of which he is made." Early in February he accused Roosevelt of extravagance in having spent $31 on stamps; Roosevelt responded by sending an indignant five-page reply. Later that month the *Maine* disaster badly affected Long's nerves. He now left the business of the Department entirely in the hands of his naval advisers. On February 21 he noted: "My sleep utterly broken and much nervous trouble." Four days later he felt so ill and tired he took the afternoon off.[20] Long habitually left his office punctually at 4 P.M.; he resented having to waste time talking with senators about this "carrion of patronage." He disliked the social round of Washington society; the "lengthening chain of dinners and receptions," he complained, were tiring him to death. On the eve of the war with Spain, the Navy Department

19. Long Journal, Jan. 13, 1898. Long MSS.
20. Long Journal, Jan. 15, Feb. 13, 21, 1898. Long MSS.

was presided over by a weak man. Fortunately the bureau chiefs at this time were exceptionally able. Even so, their final and detailed strategic decisions left much to be desired.

The coordination of war planning had been placed in the hands of the Office of the Naval War Board. The War Board consisted of Assistant Secretary Roosevelt, Captain Crowninshield, and two other officers whose places were taken soon after the outbreak of hostilities by Rear Admiral Montgomery Sicard and Mahan. The Board apparently met for the first time on March 23, 1898, in an office of the Navy Department.[21] Blankets were placed over the doors to ensure the secrecy of the proceedings. The Board advised Secretary Long to divide the warships available in the Caribbean into two squadrons. One squadron was to be assembled at Key West under the command of Rear Admiral William Sampson; at the outbreak of war it was to blockade Cuba. The second squadron, the so-called Flying Squadron, was to be placed under the com-

21. The origins of this board are somewhat obscure. As has been already noted, Kimball's war plan had been studied during the previous year and had been adopted by a board of officers who coordinated their work with the Office of Naval Intelligence. It seems to have been an ad hoc arrangement; judging by Theodore Roosevelt's contemporary letters, no permanent strategy board was in existence early in March 1898. When Mahan that month offered his services as strategic adviser to the Department and asked Roosevelt for advice on whether in the present crisis he ought not to cancel his trip to Europe, Roosevelt told him not to alter his plans, adding that he did not believe the Cuban crisis would end in war. Nevertheless, and in the circumstances it appears rather odd, on the very next day after writing to Mahan, Roosevelt sent a note to Captain Richardson Clover informing him that he had been appointed by the Secretary as "a member of the Board to formulate a plan of campaign." Perhaps the decision to constitute the War Board had been reached that very day; all the same Mahan was not recalled from Europe until April 25. Possibly Long had been averse to employing Mahan, for he noted on May 9, the day Mahan joined the Board, "I doubt very much whether he will be of much value practically." Long Journal, May 9, 1898. Long MSS. One thing is certain: Mahan, a strong advocate of treating all units of the fleet as one great battle squadron, would not have approved the division of the United States fleet as decided upon by the War Board on the eve of the war.

mand of Commodore Winfield Schley, and, with its base at Hampton Roads, was ordered to defend the eastern seaboard against the eventuality of a Spanish attack.

Little did Admiral Pascual Cervera, who was waiting off the Cape Verde islands with a ramshackle squadron of four armored cruisers and three destroyers, realize that his striking force was arousing such apprehensions in the United States that it was immobilizing two American battleships, the *Massachusetts* and *Texas,* and the cruiser *Brooklyn* with their attendant light vessels at Hampton Roads.[22] The division of the American command, moreover, was to lead a few weeks later to the unfortunate misunderstanding between Schley and Sampson at the battle of Santiago. When the Board sent its battle orders to Sampson on April 6, there was still argument about strategic objectives; Sampson balked at his defensive role of blockading Cuba and wrote to Secretary Long that he wished to attack Havana.[23] Meanwhile Dewey was waiting in Hong Kong for his battle orders. But the Board appears to have given Dewey no further thought until the British governor requested him to leave Hong Kong at the outbreak of war. Then, after a White House conference on Sunday, April 24, McKinley hastily endorsed the recommendation of the bureau chiefs that Dewey should attack the Philippines.[24] The disposition of the American fleet on the eve of the war was, despite Kimball's war plan, rather haphazard.

The United States entered the war with Spain in considerable confusion. But the failings of the detailed naval plans

22. For an interesting comment on the strategic decisions taken by the Naval War Board, see Mahan's report of Oct. 29, 1906, "A History of the Naval War Board of 1898," General Board Study, 401–02, *General Board Records,* Navy Department. He regarded the retention of the Flying Squadron off Hampton Roads as the only possible error.

23. Sampson to Secretary of the Navy, April 9, 1898. Navy Department, R. G. 45, area 8 file.

24. See p. 270, n.

were as nothing compared to the chaos that reigned in the Army command. Any plans the Army might have drawn up for the invasion of Cuba did not survive among the records of the Military Information Division; probably no detailed plans existed. In any case the Secretary of War, Russell Alger, still convalescing from typhoid, and Major General Nelson A. Miles, who commanded the Army, were on the worst possible terms. It turned out that Secretary Alger could not, as he had frequently promised, put an army of 40,000 in the field on ten days' notice. General Miles was opposed to landing the Army in Cuba until the Spanish Navy had been destroyed. At a White House Conference on April 20 he insisted on at least two months to drill and prepare the Army for the invasion, and Long noted in his journal, "at present it seems as if the army were ready for nothing at all." [25] Fortunately for the United States, Spain was in worse military shape. For the United States it turned out to be, in John Hay's well-known words, a "splendid little war."

The American attack on the Spanish squadron in Manila must be rated among the worst-kept military secrets of all time. On March 2, 1898, after the Navy Department had cabled Dewey (over Roosevelt's signature), the secret instructions were known in Madrid; on March 6 the New York *Sun* was able to inform its readers of the impending attack. Was it then so obvious that the United States would strike at the Philippines at the outbreak of war? Perhaps the Spanish Government and the editor of the *Sun* had merely made a shrewd guess. The fact that Spanish ministers had received definite information

25. Long Journal, April 20, 1898. Long MSS. For a good discussion of the inadequacy of the Army plans, see Leech, *In the Days of Mc-Kinley*, pp. 201 ff.

is revealed by unpublished documents in the German Foreign Ministry archives. On March 2, the German consul in Hong Kong sent a sensational telegram to the Wilhelmstrasse in which he informed his superiors that according to the "strictly confidential" statement of the American consul general, "the American warships in Hong Kong harbor had received the order to prepare for an attack on Manila." Commented the Kaiser in the margin of the telegram: "At once to be passed on to Madrid where Her Majesty the Queen is to be told verbally in the form of a personal warning from me . . . the scoundrels the Yankees want war!" [26]

The Queen Regent thanked the Kaiser warmly for his message; she suggested that he could best prove his friendship by sending German warships on a friendly visit to Manila immediately. This turn of events, however, alarmed Foreign Minister Bülow, who was not averse to undermining the United States secretly but was determined to steer clear of possibly dangerous involvements. In a memorandum to the Kaiser, he suggested that Spain should ask the French for support and added, somewhat tartly, that the Kaiser's warning had been prompted by feelings of personal friendship for the Queen Regent and not by intentions to help her anti-German government.[27] During the course of the following three months, Bülow held to a cautious policy. In his attitude both to the question of possible European intervention before the war broke out and in his formulation of Germany's policy toward the Philippines, he

26. Bülow to the Kaiser, telegram, March 2, 1898; German consul in Hong Kong to German Foreign Ministry, telegram, March 3, 1898. Microfilms of German Foreign Ministry Archives, Public Record Office, London, G.F.M. 13/141.

27. Radowitz to German Foreign Ministry, telegram, March 4, 1898; memorandum by Bülow, March 5, 1898. German Foreign Ministry Archives, G.F.M. 13/141.

refused to allow Germany to take the lead.[28] When in mid-May Admiral Diederichs was sent with a squadron to Manila, he was instructed merely to secure information on the situation there. Bülow firmly rejected the requests of a number of Filipino leaders for German support. They had suggested to the German consul in Manila that their independence could best be secured by the establishment of a monarchy ruled by a German prince; they had not thrown off the yoke of Spain in order to fall under American domination. But Bülow in another long memorandum to the Kaiser—who he rightly feared might be tempted—argued that the overwhelming sea power of England and the United States dominated the situation; Bülow accordingly concluded that it would be possible for Germany to reconsider its policy only if neither England nor America desired the islands.[29] Spanish hopes to secure German support were thus in vain. None of the great powers of Europe in fact was ready to antagonize the United States for the sake of Spain, with the possible exception of Austria-Hungary. Sir Julian Pauncefote, the British Ambassador, would have liked to register the moral disapprobation of Europe, but even this innocuous step was not sanctioned by Arthur Balfour, the acting British Foreign Secretary, or by the ministers in Berlin and Paris. The result of the war was never in doubt. Even the revelation of Dewey's secret plans did the Spanish government no good. American ships enjoyed an overwhelming superiority

28. For the attitude of the European powers in general, see May, *Imperial Democracy*, pp. 196–239. This may be supplemented as far as the British attitude is concerned by Grenville's *Salisbury*, chap. 9. See also R. G. Neale, *Britain and American Imperialism* (Brisbane, University of Queensland Press, 1965).

29. German consul in Manila to German Foreign Ministry, telegram, received in Berlin, May 12, 1898; memorandum by Bülow, various drafts, May 14, 1898; Bülow to Admiral Tirpitz, May 18, 1898. German Foreign Ministry Archives, G.F.M. 13/123.

over the old, decrepit Spanish vessels anchored in Manila Bay. During the ensuing months, vital decisions were reached not on the far-flung battlefields but in the White House, the Navy Department, and on Capitol Hill.

McKinley's policy is generally depicted as being without adequate guidance and at the mercy of public opinion. His attitude to the question of taking the Philippines is used as a classical illustration of the influence of politics and public opinion on the formation of American policy.

Politics did play a large role in deciding the manner, but not the ultimate objectives, of McKinley's policy. We possess at least one vivid account of the President's outlook during the summer of 1898. William M. Laffan, who spoke to the President in July, recorded that he found him not in the least burdened by his responsibilities; on the contrary McKinley appeared confident, clearheaded, and "cheerful as a sandboy." The President declared:

> We will first take the Philippines, the Ladrones, the Carolines and Porto Rico. Then when we have possession, undisputed, we will look them all over at our leisure and do what seems to be wisest. Personally I am in favor now of keeping Luzon and fortifying Manila. We know very little about the group, but that which we do know makes it very doubtful if there would be any advantage to be derived from holding it all. I think the United States possessed of all Spain's colonies would do well to act with great magnanimity and show European governments that a lofty spirit guides us. Apart from that idea I favor the general principle of holding on to what we get. The more you look into the matter of the Philippines . . . the more doubtful you will be about keep-

ing the whole group. If, however, as we go on it is made to appear desirable that we should retain all, then we will certainly do it.[30]

It is possible, but not likely, that a few weeks before the war with Spain McKinley may have considered retaining some portion of the Philippines if Dewey succeeded in defeating the Spanish squadron. He has left no evidence of such a view. His approach to the making of policy was pragmatic, and he took things one at a time. Until the actual outbreak of hostilities, McKinley would have preferred to preserve peace on the condition that Spain allow the Cubans to decide upon their own destiny. He certainly never would have consented to a war with the purpose of annexing either the Philippines or Cuba. It is questionable whether the United States would have interfered in Cuba if the Spanish government had accepted his terms; the Administration would certainly have taken no steps to acquire the Philippines. But the United States at war created an entirely new situation, leaving McKinley free to act entirely for the benefit of American interests.

The President's actions after April 1898 fit into a single pattern: the United States would first secure absolute control of both the Philippines and Cuba before deciding how American interests might be reconciled with the needs and wishes of the Cubans and Filipinos. What had once been the responsibility of Spain he now assumed to be the responsibility of the United States.

At a White House conference on May 8, 1898, McKinley reached the decision to dispatch an Army of Occupation both to Cuba and the Philippines. The President's instructions to the commander-in-chief of the Philippine expedition were perfectly clear: American rule was not to be severe, and local customs were to be respected; America had not come to the is-

30. William M. Laffan to Lodge, July 14, 1898. Lodge MSS.

lands to make war on any of the natives. But the Filipinos were to understand that ultimate authority lay in the hands of the American commander acting on behalf of his President. No conflicting authority would be tolerated, for "the powers of the military occupant are absolute and supreme, and immediately operate upon the political condition of the inhabitants." If the Filipinos did not accept the fact that "the first effect of the military occupation of the enemy's territory is the severance of the former political relations of the inhabitants, and the establishment of a new political power," then the United States commander might not be able to maintain his beneficent attitude and would have to adopt "measures of a different kind" if they should prove indispensable "to the maintenance of law and order." [31] In the face of such instructions, McKinley's Philippine policy cannot be regarded as weak and indecisive. It is true that the American commander-in-chief in the Philippines received no further instructions during the difficulties that soon developed, but he had been given full authority to act on his own discretion; when it came to that point, he did so.

In Washington meantime, until the treaty of peace had been safely steered through the Senate, McKinley gave the misleading impression that he had not made up his mind about the disposition of Spain's colonies. He waited for the annexationist sentiment to win overwhelming support in the country so that the American people and the Senate might support his own firm policy.[32] To the critics who accuse him of indecision and lack of leadership, McKinley might well have replied that only a handful of senators could have wrecked his policy. Idealism

31. McKinley to Secretary of War, May 19, 1898. Copy in Navy Department, R.G. 45, area 10 file.

32. On this important point the authors have independently reached the same conclusion as Wayne Morgan, *William McKinley and His America,* esp. pp. 379–99.

was a powerful force in American life; combined with politics in this case it could have checkmated McKinley's actions. He made it appear that he had only gradually and reluctantly been driven to the conclusion that his duty to God, national honor, the Filipinos, and the Cubans demanded that the United States assume the burden of governing the Spanish colonies. The supposed "foreign designs" on the Philippines enabled the President to win congressional support. The Teller amendment, however, would have prevented McKinley from proclaiming the annexation of Cuba even if he wished to do so; as for the Philippines, he was careful to leave their future settlement open until after the Senate had sanctioned the peace treaty. Even so he won only by a narrow margin. Twenty years later President Wilson was to adopt the tactics so many critics blame McKinley for not following in 1898. McKinley's success is the best justification for the course he pursued.

The astonishing clamor for the retention of the Philippines that developed so swiftly after May 1898 has fascinated historians for several decades. Julius Pratt, Richard Hofstadter, and other scholars have already graphically described the changing mood of the American people during the 1890s.[33] The consequences of the war with Spain raise other questions of great interest.

It was an historical accident, a mere coincidence, that the Spanish-American War coincided in time with the international crisis that developed in China after the Kaiser's seizure of Kiaochow. At least three countries—England, Russia, and Japan—regarded the future of China as a matter of great concern. "It is impossible to overrate the gravity of the issue,"

---

33. See Pratt, *Expansionists,* for a brilliant analysis, and also Richard Hofstadter, "Manifest Destiny and the Philippines," in Daniel Aaron, ed., *America in Crisis* (New York, Harcourt, Brace, 1952), which however repeats the legend of Roosevelt's responsibility for the seizure of the Philippines.

Chamberlain, the British Colonial Secretary, declared in the town hall of Birmingham. "Our interests in China are so great, our proportion of the trade is so enormous, and the potentialities of that trade are so gigantic that I feel that no more vital question has ever been presented for the decision of the Government and the decision of the nation." [34] Many Americans shared these feelings. They wanted to secure a share of the trade in the Pacific. The United States already enjoyed overwhelming influence in the Hawaiian Republic, and during the summer of 1898 America annexed the islands. But in the western Pacific it was militarily powerless. If it came to the partition of China, the United States would have found itself excluded unless it could secure the aid of Japan, Russia, or England.

Mahan and Lodge speedily recognized the new realities of international politics. Lodge wrote to John Hay on April 21, 1898: "To me this drawing together of the English speaking people all over the world and of the two great nations seems far more momentous, more fraught with meaning to the future of mankind than the freeing of Cuba or the expulsion of Spain from this hemisphere." [35] But Lodge's conversion to an anglophile point of view was not solely due to England's friendly attitude during the crisis with Spain. Already on January 31, 1898, impressed with the importance of the Far Eastern crisis, Lodge had written to Henry White: "If I had my way I should be glad to have the United States say to England that we would stand by her in her declaration that the ports of China must be opened to all nations equally or to none." [36] By the summer, Lodge was ready to align the United States even more closely to England in the Far East.

But Americans on the whole had little interest in the military

34. Grenville, *Salisbury*, p. 169.
35. Lodge to Hay, April 21, 1898. Lodge MSS.
36. Lodge to Henry White, Jan. 31, 1898. Lodge MSS.

realities of foreign policy. Their education had been attempted by Mahan and a small group of politicians and naval officers, but the persuasive power of these propagandists should not be exaggerated. Dewey's victory proved to be worth more than all Mahan's books put together. It dramatically changed the nervousness that Spain might attack the eastern seaboard and the disappointment at the lack of military development in the Caribbean into a national outburst of elation and confidence. One editor even likened Dewey's victory to "the stories of the ancient battles of the Lord in the times of Joshua, David, and Jehoshaphat." [37] Overnight Dewey became the hero of the nation. The very unexpectedness of victory in the Orient added to the thrill of the occasion, and many Americans began to pore over maps to discover exactly where Manila might be. Only now, rather belatedly, businessmen started to consider the potentialities of the Philippines as a commercial outlet for their goods and as an entrepôt for the trade of eastern Asia. But few of them could have been quite as sanguine as Senator Beveridge who, on the authority of having seen things for himself in the Philippines, described the fabulous natural resources of the islands to his fellow senators in January 1900: "the wood of the Philippines can supply the furniture for a century to come"; forty miles of Cebu's mountain chain were "practically mountains of coal." He even claimed to have picked up "a nugget of pure gold" on the banks of a Philippine creek—though he did not say exactly where.[38]

Dewey's victory transformed the narrow, intellectual movement—expansionism—into a broad and popular crusade—imperialism. The strategic implications were little understood by proponents and opponents. Carl Schurz and likeminded anti-imperialists girded themselves for battle to keep the great re-

37. Pratt, *Expansionists,* pp. 289 ff.
38. Claude G. Bowers, *Beveridge and the Progressive Era* (New York, The Literary Guild, 1952), p. 120.

public on the path of righteousness as they saw it and to a policy true to its traditions. Few anti-imperialists were as vehement as Andrew Carnegie. Secretary of State Hay in November 1898 concluded that Carnegie "really seems to be off his head." He wrote frantic letters to the Secretary of State which he signed "Your Bitterest Opponent." He threatened the President "not only with the vengeance of the voters, but with practical punishment at the hands of the mob," and he promised that he would cause the entire labor vote to be cast against the Administration.[39] But for all the high standing of the anti-imperialist leaders, for all their energy and organizational skill, and for all Carnegie's gold, the movement failed to carry with it the necessary one third of the senators on whom the fate of the peace treaty depended.

But what of the strategists? What advice did they tender to the President? The naval officers who had first formulated the war plan of 1896 evidently did not rate Manila's strategic value to the United States highly, for in 1896 they had suggested that Manila be returned to Spain. How far did the Far Eastern crisis and the war with Spain modify these opinions? During the greater part of the war, three officers, Admiral Sicard, Commodore Crowninshield, and Captain Mahan, as members of the Naval War Board, advised the Secretary of the Navy on questions of strategy. Mahan appears to have dominated the deliberations. He had no good opinion of his colleagues and advised Secretary Long to abolish the Board and to replace it with a single officer who would act as chief of staff. (He hoped, no doubt, that this task would be entrusted to him.) In a letter to Luce, Mahan described Sicard, the President of the Board, as "a clearheaded man for Bureau work but very second or third rate for what we had to do . . . during my whole time on the Board, historical parallels to our positions were contin-

39. Hay to Reid, Nov. 29, 1898. Hay MSS.

ually occurring to me. How many men in the Navy do you suppose know naval history . . . or how many, if they read this, would fail to vote me an egotistic, superannuated ass?" [40] Mahan must have been a difficult colleague to work with. Long noted on May 19 that he had attended a meeting of the Board and that "Captain Mahan is on the rampage again . . . he is very frank and manly [and] blurts out his entire dissatisfaction with the entire war board." [41] Mahan disapproved of the earlier decision to divide the battleship fleet. Already in mid-March he had advised Roosevelt (who read his letter to the President) to concentrate the fleet, "to disregard minor punishment, and devote our attention to smashing Spain in Cuba." [42] We may safely surmise that he would not have approved of Kimball's war plan and probably did not know of its existence.

His misgivings about the consequences of the Philippine adventure were not unfounded. After the battle of Manila, once the President had decided on the expedition to the Philippines, the Board was haunted by the fear that a superior force of Spanish warships might be sent to Manila and force Dewey to retire; if that happened, the American expeditionary force would be cut off. The Board recommended accordingly that the Army be supplied with modern guns to fortify the harbor. [43] In this way, no long-term strategic plan but rather the exigencies of war and faulty appraisal of Spain's naval strength led the United States into deep involvement in the Philippines.

Mahan, in fact, never wholeheartedly believed in the policy of annexing the Philippines. Writing to Lodge on July 27, 1898,

40. Mahan to Luce, n.d., Mahan MSS; the first page of this interesting letter is unfortunately missing.
41. Long's journal, May 19, 1898. Long MSS.
42. Mahan to Roosevelt, March 14, 1898. Mahan MSS.
43. Sicard to the Secretary of the Navy, May 30, 1898. R.G. 45, Entry 371, Naval War Board Letterpress, pp. 145–47.

he expressed his misgivings that the President might give way
to public pressure to retain the islands when the war was won.
The feeling about the Philippines, he wrote, "is much more
doubtful . . . I myself, though rather an expansionist, have
not fully adjusted myself to the idea of taking them, from our
own standpoint of advantage." [44] He was inclined to hold on
to no more than the island of Luzon. While serving on the War
Board, Mahan was a frequent visitor to Lodge's house in Washington. Probably on Mahan's suggestion, Lodge wrote to Acting Secretary of State Day on August 11 that he was reluctant
to see the United States assume the burden of holding more
than the island of Luzon with Manila. The only practical solution, Lodge wrote, was to take the whole group of islands and
then to cede them all, except for Luzon, to England in exchange
for the Bahamas, Jamaica, and the Danish West Indies. Lodge
pointed out the advantages of adopting such a course: it would
free the Administration from the charge of handing back the
Filipinos to Spanish oppression, relieve the Administration of
the burden of governing all the islands, and leave the United
States "in the Philippines associated with a friendly power
with whom we should be in entire accord." [45] Lodge's suggestion reflects Mahan's caution as to the strategic difficulty of defending the Philippines, but whereas Mahan desired to see no
entangling alliance, Lodge thought the defense of the Philippines should be shared with England. His proposal foreshad-
ows at least close cooperation with England in the Far East,
if not an alliance. Lodge had reached the conclusion that without England's friendship the position of the United States in
the Far East might become hazardous. "We want to be very
careful how far we draw out in the East," Lodge wrote to

44. Mahan to Lodge, July 27, 1898. Lodge MSS.
45. Lodge to Day, Aug. 11, 1898. Lodge MSS.

Henry White.[46] Mahan had thus, at least for a time, dampened Lodge's enthusiasm for the "foothold" in the Philippines, the archipelago whose acquisition, Lodge had written some weeks earlier, "would be of incalculable value to us." [47]

With the conclusion of the armistice on August 12, 1898, the United States found itself in occupation of Cuba, Puerto Rico, Guam, and the Philippines. But whereas the military situation in the Caribbean reinforced a concept of American policy long cherished, the state of affairs in the Philippines had been brought about largely by the adoption of Kimball's war plan, the strategic advice of the Naval War Board during the course of the conflict, and the policy McKinley followed after the outbreak of the war. No concept of American diplomacy as it had developed before the spring of 1898 lay behind the occupation of the Philippines.[48]

Ten days after the armistice was signed, the Naval War Board advised Secretary Long on the overseas bases the United States should acquire and maintain. But the geographical disposition of naval bases could not be discussed in any meaningful way without reference to the overall objectives of American diplomacy these bases were to support. It is fact that during the years from 1898 to 1917 the strategists were never once informed of the major objectives of the Administration's diplomacy. In the absence of such guidance, the strategists simply had to establish the basic premises of policy for themselves. They usually did so during the period from 1900 to 1917 by applying Mahan's lesson of history that economic rivalry was the basic cause of global conflict. This had one paradoxical result. Mahan was a confirmed anglophile, but the adop-

46. Lodge to Henry White, Aug. 12, 1898. Lodge MSS.
47. Lodge to Charles G. Fall, May 5, 1898. Lodge MSS.
48. On the basis of this new evidence, the authors have thus reached a conclusion similar to that expressed by Samuel Flagg Bemis.

tion of his principles led generations of naval officers to look upon England as a potential enemy. Obliged to work in isolation, the strategists simply imitated Mahan's historical techniques. They formulated war plans that became increasingly unsuited to the actual international conditions as they evolved in the first two decades of the twentieth century.

In August 1898 the Naval War Board postulated the premise that the United States would have to establish its supremacy in the Caribbean and over the isthmus of Central America. With the construction of the isthmian canal, the European powers would be drawn into the Caribbean. This had been one of Mahan's most insistent beliefs, and so the Board now recommended the acquisition of fortified bases commanding both entrances to the future canal. In addition, the Board also urged naval stations in Cuba (Santiago or Guantánamo), Puerto Rico (Culebra), and on St. Thomas. The construction of the canal by the United States had become a national interest, the Board stressed. In view of the defenseless position of the United States in the Pacific during the following two decades, the military policy of the United States might have been better served if the millions of dollars spent on the canal had instead been used to build a large Pacific fleet and the necessary harbor facilities to service it. But Mahan never conceived of such a solution, believing as he did that the first principle of naval strategy must be to keep the fleet undivided, able to pass from one ocean to the other as conditions might demand.

The strategic advice the Board tendered in 1898 about the Pacific Ocean was notably cautious. Here the United States could not establish its supremacy; Pago-Pago, Samoa, Hawaii, Guam, Manila, and one of the Chusan Islands were the only bases the Board felt the United States should hold.[49] But it is

49. Sicard, Crowninshield, and Mahan to Long, August 1898. R.G. 45, Entry 371, Naval War Board Letterpress, pp. 335–54.

difficult to see how the War Board envisaged the defense of these islands without a powerful Pacific fleet. In fact the War Board bequeathed a problem that strategists were unable to solve for half a century.

Chapter Eleven
The Quest for Security:
Admiral Dewey and the General Board, 1900-1917

THE FIRST CONSIDERATION of a rationally conducted foreign policy is to provide for national security. The objectives of diplomacy must be brought into harmony with sound strategic concepts. Some of the failures of American foreign policy during the years from 1900 to 1917 were due to the lack of such harmony. The fault did not always lie with the strategists. The part they played, and more especially Admiral George Dewey's influence on policy, are the subjects of this study. Despite its significance, the strategic aspect of American diplomacy has hitherto not received much attention. One consequence of this neglect has been that the reputation of Dewey remains to be fully recognized.[1]

1. An adequate study of Admiral George Dewey's life has not yet been written. Dewey's own *Autobiography of George Dewey, Admiral of the Navy* (New York, Scribner's, 1913) throws no light on the most important part of his career as President of the General Board from 1900 to 1915. The Dewey Papers in the Library of Congress are not of much value in this respect either. The essential source for American strategic policy during the period are the records of the General Board, preserved in the Navy Department, Washington. They have been progressively declassified since 1959, and were first utilized by J. A. S. Grenville in his "Diplomacy and War Plans in the United States, 1890–1917," *Transactions of the Royal Historical Society*, 11 (1961). The Navy Department records housed in the National Archives, Washington, are incomplete, as the General Board records were not transferred to the National Archives, but careful use is made of the material available in the National Archives by William R. Braisted in his excellent, scholarly

Dewey stood in the limelight of public adulation for only a short time. Unknown to the general public before Manila Bay, he became a national hero overnight. But "being flesh and blood and not a superman," ruefully reflected the Admiral some years later, "it seemed impossible to live up to all that was expected of me." The people of New York outdid themselves to pay him homage when he returned to America in 1899. Dewey flags, Dewey arches, processions, the legend "Welcome Dewey" emblazoned in electric lights across the span of the Brooklyn Bridge—all this greeted the conquering hero. On the steps of the White House, Dewey received a costly ceremonial sword, fashioned at Tiffany's, from the hands of the President. But within a few months the mention of his name aroused derision. His ill-advised bid for the presidential nomination was responsible for this decline in his standing. As if symbolically, the prototype of the triumphal Dewey arch, which was to be constructed by a grateful nation in Madison Square, was carted away by the New York Sanitation Department. It says much for the soundness of Dewey's mental balance that, plunged from the sublime to the ridiculous, he served the nation for the next fifteen years with distinction and success as President of the General Board.

---

study, *The United States Navy in the Pacific, 1897–1909* (Austin, University of Texas Press, 1958). For Army strategy and the relationship of the Army and Navy, the following articles by Louis Morton are important: "Army and Marines on the China Station: A Study in Military and Political Rivalry," *Pacific Historical Review,* 29 (1960), 51–73; "Germany First: The Basic Concept of Allied Strategy in World War II," *Command Decisions* (Washington, D.C., Department of the Army, 1960). Useful too are W. Schilling's "Admirals and Foreign Policy, 1913–1919" (unpublished Ph.D. thesis, Yale University, 1956); Seward W. Livermore, "American Naval-Base Policy in the Far East, 1850–1914," *Pacific Historical Review,* 13 (1944). These accounts supplement and on some points supersede the great pioneer study of the Navy and naval strategy by Harold and Margaret Sprout, *The Rise of American Naval Power, 1776–1918* (Princeton, Princeton University Press, 1946).

Dewey made himself responsible for coordinating the work of the naval and military strategists during these crucial years. The war with Spain had underlined the need for adequate staff work, and the success of the War Board of 1898 pointed the way for the future. Among the most persistent advocates of a general staff for the Navy was Captain Henry Clay Taylor. He had suggested the necessity of creating a general staff to Assistant Secretary Theodore Roosevelt in May 1897; in 1900 he brought the idea once more to the attention of Secretary Long. But Long was reluctant to risk conflict with the well-entrenched bureau chiefs; he was hesitant about allowing the professional officers wide powers beyond civilian control; and he rightly doubted that Congress could be brought to approve such a scheme. Consequently he compromised and in March 1900 created the General Board, which possessed no executive functions and was to serve in a purely advisory capacity to ensure the efficient preparation of the fleet for war and for the naval defense of the coast. Long intended to confine its functions to the considerations of such problems as the Secretary of the Navy might refer to it.[2] The Board was composed of a President, the President of the Naval War College, his principal assistant, the Chief of the Bureau of Navigation, the Chief Intelligence Officer, his principal assistant, and three other line officers. Under Dewey's dynamic presidency the Board did not limit itself to problems referred to it by the Secretary of the Navy but sent advice, often unsolicited, on any question it deemed important. It became the senior military council of the nation. The Board advised the Administration each year on the construction needs of the fleet. It prepared specific strategic studies and war plans. In this way some vital aspects of American defense policy came to be influenced by a group of officers

2. Sprout, *Rise of American Naval Power*, p. 247.

who carefully recorded their decisions. Despite the jealousy of several bureau chiefs in the Navy Department and the active opposition of at least one Secretary of the Navy, Josephus Daniels, the General Board grew in strength and stature. Admiral Dewey found support among officers trained by Luce and Mahan in the traditions of the Naval War College. To Dewey nevertheless belongs the chief credit for the successes (and failures) of the new General Board.

Until after the outbreak of World War I, the Army was very much the weak sister of the services. The defense of the United States was regarded as primarily a naval problem, and yet the garrisoning of the outlying American possessions involved the Army in fresh responsibilities as well. It had hitherto coped successfully with Mexicans and Indians but was caught woefully unprepared by the war with Spain. With no strategy board to coordinate efforts with the other branches of the Army, the chiefs of the bureaus at the War Department had proved unequal to the crisis.

Just as in the case of the Navy, however, a few able young Army officers were aware of the need to reorganize the War Department. Fortunately in Elihu Root McKinley had appointed an outstanding Secretary of War. To still the complaints of the young officers and to meet the criticisms of Congress investigating the mismanagement of 1898, Root was finally responsible in 1903 for the creation of a General Staff. His staff borrowed the prestige of the Prussian name without enjoying any of its power. The influence of the Army General Staff on American strategic and foreign policy before World War I was slight. Yet it became obvious that some degree of Army cooperation would be necessary if the Navy were to play its role, since the defense of naval bases required soldiers. This need was also met in 1903 with the creation of the Joint Army and

Navy Board, presided over by Dewey. But the first years of interservice cooperation proved a lamentable failure.[3]

The three staff organizations, the General Board, General Staff, and Joint Army and Navy Board, were charged with the responsibility of formulating America's strategic policy in the new era of twentieth-century power politics. Their success would depend largely on their accuracy in assessing the development of international relations. Unfortunately they failed to recognize that the growing rivalries of Europe were to aid the United States in pursuing a policy of dominance in the Caribbean, while they would undermine United States security in the Pacific. The doctrine laid down by the strategists from first to last, however, declared that until the United States possessed a fleet powerful enough to be divided between the two oceans, the battlefleet would have to be stationed on the Atlantic seaboard ready to enforce the Monroe Doctrine and to meet any conceivable threat of European invasion.

This problem of national security preoccupied the General Board during the early years of its existence. At the first full meeting of the Board, on April 17, 1900, it designated Guantánamo as the most important base in Cuba.[4] Eighteen months later the Board urged that the United States not leave Cuba until it had obtained leases of land to secure American bases at Guantánamo, Cienfuegos, Havana, and Nipe.[5]

The Board also emphasized the necessity of a strongly fortified base at Culebra, Puerto Rico. And still there remained a grave weakness in the chain of American bases. Dewey repeatedly warned the Secretary of the Navy of the danger posed by

3. P. C. Jessup, *Elihu Root* (New York, Dodd, Mead, 1938), pp. 240–64.

4. General Board Minutes, April 17, 1900. *General Board Records,* Navy Department, Washington, D.C.

5. General Board Minutes, Oct. 30, 1901. *General Board Records.*

the independence of the republics of Santo Domingo and Haiti. "The feeble and chaotic conditions of the Governments in that island make it easy for any country to obtain concessions without a great expense, which may be valuable in a military and naval point of view," runs the General Board memorandum of December 10, 1900.[6] Since the war with Spain, the island—lying between Cuba and Puerto Rico—had become vital to the United States. It was, the strategists thought, likely to be the first objective of an enemy attack on the United States. They believed that if Haiti or Santo Domingo fell to an enemy, American control of the Caribbean would be threatened with collapse. The strategic value of the two republics would become even more important with the construction of the isthmian canal. To meet this danger, a war plan was drawn up in conjunction with the United States Army to seize both Samana Bay and Port Dauphin as the termini of a line of defense that was to be established by an Army expeditionary force occupying the valley between these two points.[7] In the spring of 1901 the General Board also looked beyond the Caribbean and beyond the immediate problem of defending the continental United States. Rear Admiral Taylor, Chief of the Bureau of Navigation (and a former President of the Naval War College), read a disturbing paper on the Monroe Doctrine to the other members of the Board.

The maintenance of the Monroe Doctrine had been for so long one of the high objectives of American foreign policy that its abandonment would have been regarded by politicians and public alike as a national disaster. But few Americans stopped

6. General Board Letter #87, Dec. 10, 1900. *General Board Records.*
7. General Board Minutes, May 21, 1900, April 23 and May 21, 1901; Dewey to Secretary of the Navy, General Board Letter #91, April 24, 1901; Assistant Secretary of the Navy to Secretary of War, General Board Letter #88, April 24, 1901; Dewey to Secretary of the Navy, General Board Letter #198, June 25, 1901. War Portfolios, Folder 138, *General Board Records.*

to think whether the United States possessed the military means to uphold the Doctrine. Basing their conclusions on Taylor's report, the General Board enlightened the Administration on the strategic realities involved; the situation in the seas and islands south of the United States was studied, so that in case of war "we may correctly measure the actual value of our power and influence in the Caribbean Sea and upon the coasts of South America." The Board authoritatively laid down "definite geographical limits within which the Navy may sustain [control] in case of war, and beyond which the Navy cannot, under present or probably future conditions, maintain successfully in war any such control." [8] If bases were retained in Cuba and a strongly fortified base was built in Puerto Rico, the Navy was ready to assert United States mastery of the Caribbean and predominance on the Atlantic coast of South America as far as the mouth of the Orinoco; control of the stretch of coast lying between the Orinoco and the Amazon they believed was doubtful; beyond the Amazon, the Board warned, "we cannot control the naval situation in war against any probable European enemy or coalition . . . Whether the principle of the Monroe Doctrine, so far as it is the policy of the Government, covers all South America, including Patagonia and the Argentine is not for the consideration of the General Board, but only the fact that the principles of strategy and defects in our geographical position make it impracticable to maintain naval control by armed force beyond the Amazon, unless present conditions are radically changed." [9] The memorandum was submitted to the President, who laid it before his Cabinet.

8. General Board Minutes, April 24, 1901; Dewey to Secretary of the Navy, General Board Letter #171, June 25, 1901. *General Board Records.*

9. General Board Study #433; General Board Letter #171, June 25, 1901; Long to Dewey, July 8, 1901; General Board Minutes, Aug. 21, 1901. *General Board Records.*

The General Board memorandum of June 25, 1901, is a notable document in the history of the Monroe Doctrine; it also marks a fresh approach to the problems of bringing American diplomacy into harmony with sound strategy. Dewey and his colleagues on the Board recognized that their conclusions might shock the President and his Administration; they would certainly have shocked Congress and the American people. This did not deter the General Board. "[If] we discover any reason to doubt our ability so to maintain [the fixed principles of the government and the nation] with the fleet, then it is our further duty to place the matter clearly before the Secretary of the Navy, for his information and that of the Administration." [10]

By 1903 the General Board had worked out a long-term building program which would give the United States a fleet capable of meeting its likely responsibilities. The Board particularly stressed the need for a balanced fleet. Battleships required auxiliary warships, tankers, supply ships, and destroyers, without which they could not be effectively employed. Its sage advice that sea power could not simply be equated with battleship strength was generally ignored by Congress, which was ready to authorize the construction of battleships but not of the other vessels necessary for the fleet. The General Board repeatedly referred to the lacks this policy created but with little success. In collaboration with the Office of Naval Intelligence the General Board also drew up a number of war studies in different theaters of operation. In the Far East these included plans for the defense of the Philippines, the seizure of a base in China, an attack on Kiaochow, and an attack on French possessions in Indochina. But in the opinion of the Board the vital need was to provide for the defense of the Gulf

10. General Board Memorandum, June 25, 1901. *General Board Records.*

of Mexico and the Atlantic coast. As the Board concluded in 1903, the "most important war problem to be studied is based on the supposition that Germany is the enemy." [11] In such a war, or indeed in any conflict with a European power, the Board considered that sound strategy required the theater of war to be the West Indies and not the Atlantic coast. Its detailed plans were based on this assumption. The Board accordingly recommended that a proper military policy in principle required the concentration of all battleships in the Atlantic although special situations such as the then impending war between Russia and Japan might require the temporary detachment of some battleships for service in the Far East.[12]

We may well wonder whether the apprehension of the strategists that the Western Hemisphere was threatened by invasion from Europe was well founded. It certainly appears to be confirmed by the discovery in the German archives of military studies for the invasion of the United States.

In December 1899 the Kaiser personally instructed Admiral Otto von Diederichs, Chief of Staff of the Navy, and the now legendary Count Alfred von Schlieffen, Chief of Staff of the Army, to prepare a war plan against the United States. The Kaiser favored an invasion of Cuba as the first stage of an attack on America. He reasoned that the invasion would force the United States to commit its battlefleet. After a decisive and victorious naval battle the mainland could then be invaded. The Army General Staff, on the other hand, at first preferred a direct attack on Cape Cod, making Provincetown their base of operations. Accordingly in March 1901 the German naval attaché in Washington was instructed to reconnoiter Massachusetts and especially Cape Cod. His report did not favor

11. War portfolios, General Board Minutes, July 29, 1903. *General Board Records.*
12. General Board Letter #28, Aug. 21, 1901; General Board Minutes, December 4, 1903. *General Board Records.*

the enterprise. He pointed out that the fortifications and defense of the area from Peaked Cliff to Buzzards Bay would make it difficult for German troops to break out of the Cape Cod peninsula. Schlieffen accepted this appraisal and Schlieffen and Diederichs, in their joint memorandum of January 12, 1902, abandoned the project of a landing on the American mainland. The advantage of the German over the United States fleet was too slight, they argued, and would be lost altogether if the German fleet operated close to the American coast. Instead they designated the island of Puerto Rico as the first objective and suggested that if the German fleet were victorious, the Gulf and Atlantic ports could then be blockaded and Brooklyn, New York, attacked. A year later the Kaiser confirmed these general conclusions. He decided that in the event of war occurring in 1903, the German fleet would attack Culebra, Puerto Rico; further landings should be considered later. Germany must assure victory speedily by offensive operations. He even sketched out the terms of a peace treaty with the United States. The Kaiser wanted to "secure on a sound footing our trade with the West Indies, Central and South America." He would insist on "a firm base (*eine feste Position*) in the West Indies and a free hand in South America, which entails a breach of the Monroe Doctrine." [13] But the hardheaded Ger-

---

13. The possibility of a war with the United States appears to have been considered for the first time in 1889; but in a memorandum by General Goltz, March 13, 1889, the conclusion had been reached that due to the geographical position of the United States such a war was "unthinkable" (*undenkbar*); a reconsideration in March 1899 led the German strategists to a similar conclusion. Germany, so they reasoned, "lacked sufficient military means to defeat the United States decisively." But on Dec. 10, 1899, Diederichs and Schlieffen were summoned to the Kaiser, who personally instructed them to draw up plans for transporting German troops to the American continent. The Kaiser continued to take an active interest in these plans at least until March 1903. See esp. Diederichs to Schlieffen, Feb. 23, 1901; Schlieffen to Diederichs, *Ganz Geheim,* March 13, 1901; joint Army and Navy memoranda on war plans, Jan. 15, 1902, and March 21, 1903. Archives of the German

man strategists recognized that these were pipe dreams. They saw the flaw of their own war plan: the European situation was never likely to permit Germany to send both its whole fleet and large army to the Western Hemisphere.

The British Cabinet, unlike the Kaiser, was content with the status quo in the Western Hemisphere. No British government had expansionist designs in this part of the world although the strategists continued for some years to examine plans for the defense of Canada. At the time of the Venezuelan crisis of 1896 the possibility of an American attack had been taken seriously in London and had stimulated an energetic exploration of the military problem.[14] But the Anglo–American rapprochement made war appear less likely year by year. British interests during the early years of the twentieth century were more imperiled in Europe, the Mediterranean, and the East than in the Western Hemisphere, where the defense of British bases was eventually left in American hands.

While the strategists made their plans and counterplans, the Administration during the five years from 1899 to 1903 endeavored to adjust American policy to the entirely new state of affairs the Spanish–American War had brought about. An army was dispatched to suppress the Philippine rising and a base was retained in Cuba. Secretary of State John Hay adroitly sought to strengthen America's position by diplomacy. The only European power with possessions and naval forces in the Caribbean was Great Britain. Fortunately for Anglo–American relations the British Cabinet was engaged in an agonized reappraisal of foreign policy at the turn of the century. Foreign Secretary Lansdowne led a group of ministers who were dissatisfied with Salisbury's traditional outlook. Lansdowne ar-

---

Admiralty, *Acta Betreffend Vorarbeiten zu den Operationsplan gegen die Vereinigten Staaten von Nordamerika*, Public Record Office, London, GFM. 26/47 (microfilm).

14. See p. 173.

gued that Britain's strength did not suffice to defend all the areas of the world where its interests were imperiled; he persuaded the Cabinet to concentrate Britain's resources where its most vital interests were at stake, that is, in the home waters and the Mediterranean. To meet the specific Russian threat in China the government concluded an alliance with Japan (1902); the Cabinet also decided to abandon all pretense of attempting to match the growth of American power in the Western Hemisphere. The British Admiralty was in agreement with these steps. Diplomatically one important outcome of this change of British policy was the conclusion of the Hay-Pauncefote Treaty of January 1902, whereby Hay not only secured British assent to exclusive American control over the projected isthmian canal but also tacit British recognition of American predominance in the Caribbean.[15]

The problems confronting Hay in the Pacific and in China were infinitely more grave. In this vast region the United States faced not only Britain but also great European powers and Japan, each powerful enough to defeat America's weak military forces. Hay's well-known Open Door Notes of 1899 and 1900 were intended to preserve America's interests in China by purely diplomatic means. By designating the support of equal commercial opportunity and the maintenance of the integrity of China as the two principles of United States policy, and by seeking to give these principles some international sanctions, Hay had announced to the world the United States' intentions. Like President Monroe, Hay spoke knowing the United States did not possess the necessary military force to implement his

15. These negotiations have now been exhaustively studied by Grenville, "Great Britain and the Isthmian Canal, 1898–1901," *American Historical Review, 61* (1955); Charles S. Campbell, Jr., *Anglo-American Understanding, 1898–1903* (Baltimore, Johns Hopkins Press, 1957); and A. E. Campbell, *Great Britain and the United States, 1895–1903* (London, Longmans, 1960).

words. But whereas America's military strength caught up with President Monroe's doctrine in time, this was not true of the Hay doctrine. The acquisition of the Philippines and Hay's notes in effect led the United States into a Far Eastern quandary. There seemed no escape from the situation and four decades later America's China policy lay in ruins.

The urgent need to build up America's military might in this new era was not lost on the more perspicacious men of McKinley's generation, but only when a President entered the White House who was acutely conscious of the realities of force that underlie diplomacy did the Executive provide real leadership in this area. That moment came when Roosevelt succeeded to the Presidency in 1901. Roosevelt preached to Congress and the nation that the defense of America's interests required a large fighting fleet; that both the determination and the ability to go to war were the best guarantees of peace.

Roosevelt was an outstanding Realpolitiker, regarding as worthless a policy that was not backed by the strength to maintain it. He supported with vigor the call of the General Board for a battleship fleet. His estimate of the Kaiser's ambitions made it appear likely Germany would attempt to colonize portions of South America. That day seemed to draw near when British and German warships blockaded the ports of Venezuela in December 1902. Roosevelt evolved his well-known corollary to the Monroe Doctrine to forestall a repetition of European intervention in the Western Hemisphere and approved the policy of retaining the undivided battlefleet in the Atlantic Ocean. His diplomacy also sought more forcefully than Hay's to secure for the United States every strategic advantage in the Caribbean. He capitalized on the Panamanian revolution in November 1903. He hastily recognized the new Republic of Panama and twelve days later secured a favorable canal treaty and the cession of land through which the canal was destined to run; in return the United States promised to defend the independence of Panama. For Roosevelt the revolution had come as a heaven-sent opportunity to ensure American control over the isthmian canal on terms Colombia had not been ready to ratify. The President should not, however, be credited with the degree of foresight he later claimed for himself when he boasted, "I took the Panama Canal."

He was furious with the Colombians for rejecting the canal treaty and would have liked to teach them a lesson. There is some evidence that points to his contemplating a punitive stroke against Colombia proper rather than resorting to direct action on the isthmus. The Navy Department instructed the commander of the Caribbean Squadron to be prepared for an attack on Cartagena, Colombia, and sent him a plan on October 26, 1903, originally intended to defend that port from European attack. The Department thought that "the information it contains and the strategy involved may be readily applied to the present situation . . ." [16] Meanwhile definite news of the impending Panamanian revolution had reached Roosevelt in mid-October. Possibly the Cartagena operation was designed to dissuade the Colombians from sending reinforcements to Panama. The project was, in any case, not handled with any sense of urgency. Rather more warships than usual were ordered to the isthmus to preserve order there but only one of them, the *Nashville*, arrived in Colón on time (November 2). Even so the commander of the *Nashville* did not receive orders

16. Secretary of the Navy to Commander of the Caribbean Squadron, Oct. 26, 1903. *General Board Records.* For the best general account of Roosevelt's diplomacy see Howard K. Beale, *Theodore Roosevelt and the Rise of America to World Power* (Baltimore, Johns Hopkins Press, 1956), but a definitive study remains to be written. The State Department and principal foreign archives for the period of Roosevelt's presidency have not yet been exhaustively examined. An undue reliance on Roosevelt's private correspondence can be misleading—his policies were frequently more sober than his own letters suggest.

to prevent the disembarkation of Colombian troops until after they had landed. What is more, a plan for the occupation of the isthmus, forwarded to the commander-in-chief of the North Atlantic Fleet the previous June, was evidently not suited to the new situation created by the revolution. A revised scheme was not ready in Washington until November 4, one day after the revolution had broken out. It was forwarded in dramatic fashion. A naval lieutenant, Edward Walter Eberle (later to serve as Chief of Naval Operations from 1923–27), was ordered to take the package of war plans on board a steamer of the Panama Railroad Company especially detained in New York on Pier 51. The package was delivered to the commander-in-chief of the North Atlantic Fleet on January 6, 1904, but he, by mistake, returned the Panama plan to the Naval War College. It finally reached the commander of the Caribbean Squadron some three months later. By then the danger of a Colombian attack on Panama had passed. This evidence of hasty improvisation and muddle suggests that American policy owed more to sheer opportunism than to any carefully thought-out scheme.[17]

Preoccupied with Caribbean questions and the menace of Germany, Roosevelt paid scant attention to the Far East during his first three years of office. He was content to leave the Philippine difficulties to Taft, his Secretary of War, and the Chinese question to Hay. Russia, rather than Japan, appeared to be menacing the Open Door in China, and the conclusion of the Anglo–Japanese alliance in 1902—an alliance that ultimately proved disastrous to Anglo–American interests in the Far East—was welcomed in Washington as tending to uphold the integrity of the Manchu Empire. The strategists took an

17. General Board Study #425–1, Chief, Bureau of Navigation, to Commander-in-Chief, North Atlantic Fleet, June 15, 1903; Darling to Barker, Nov. 4, 1903; Secretary of the Navy to Commander, Caribbean Squadron, Oct. 26, 1903, and Oct. 24, 1904. *General Board Records.*

unrealistically rosy view of America's Far Eastern position. The early war plans of 1903 and 1904, providing for the defense of the Philippines, were intended to meet a European foe—not Japan. The General Board decided to establish a first-class naval base in the Philippines; it selected Olongapo in Subic Bay as the most suitable site, and the Joint Board added its agreement.[18] The fact that Olongapo could not be defended from the land did not disturb the strategists: Germany, the probable enemy, could only operate with naval forces. The General Board also looked forward to the establishment of a naval base on the coast of China, so that America would be able to secure its share in the event of the partition of China.

The policy of the strategists ran counter to Hay's diplomatic efforts. Although Hay had, in the winter of 1900, inquired about the possibilities of leasing Samsa Bay on the Chinese littoral, he had been happy enough to allow the matter to drop on learning of Japanese objections. But American Marines were nevertheless stationed in the Philippines until 1906, in readiness for the seizure of a Chinese base. Hypnotized by the prospects of America's future needs in China, the General Board was still pressing for an American coaling station on the Chinese coast as late as November 1905.[19]

While the strategists advocated a policy in the Far East outdated by rapidly changing events, Roosevelt quickly recognized the effect of the outbreak of the Russo–Japanese War on American interests in China. Just as in the Caribbean the threat of European interference was lessened by the preoccupation of the European powers with conflicts nearer home, so in the Pacific American security had in reality been founded on the balance of power provided by the rivalry between Japan and Rus-

18. Dec. 9 and 19, 1903. *Records of the Joint Army and Navy Board,* National Archives, Washington, D.C.

19. General Board Study #408–2, Dewey to Secretary of the Navy, Aug. 13, 1906. *General Board Records.*

sia. During the early stages of the war Roosevelt favored and admired Japanese prowess—a David fighting a Goliath. Japan's naval victories and the efficiency of its Army soon led Roosevelt to view the situation differently. His decision to accept the role of mediator and peacemaker was certainly founded on his desire to help preserve the balance of power in the Far East. His diplomatic success was limited; military realities and the growing antagonisms of the European powers permitted Japan to gain predominance. Britain, hoping to save its Yangtze interests by placing them under Japanese protection, renewed the Anglo–Japanese Alliance in 1905 and again in 1911. Russia, turning its attention once more to the Balkans, was content to sign secret treaties with Japan at China's expense, allowing Japan the lion's share. The United States was powerless to alter the course of events on the Asiatic mainland, yet Hay's notes had identified the United States with the objective of maintaining Chinese integrity. The discrepancy between the proclaimed objective of American policy and the nation's military capabilities created a dilemma that no amount of diplomatic skill could solve. Any insistence on the part of the United States that Japan desist from spreading its sphere, it was feared, might lead to a Japanese attack on America's Pacific possessions.

Soon after the conclusion of the Russo–Japanese War, the strategists took a hard new look at the problems of the Pacific. Their deliberations brought no encouraging news. Gone were the days when America might have shared in the partition of China. Indeed, now it appeared that the Philippines could hardly be held in the face of a Japanese attack. Yet it took another four years before strategic policy was adjusted to new military realities. From 1905 until 1909, it was Roosevelt who led the strategists.

The General Board, as has been seen, had selected Olongapo

in the Philippines as the site for a naval base, but the Army declared that it could not be defended. The reduction of Port Arthur had finally convinced the strategists that a naval base was useless without adequate land defense. The Army therefore suggested Manila and its bay with Corregidor Island as the most suitable site for a naval base. Dewey stubbornly rejected Manila Bay as impractical from a naval point of view. Not even Roosevelt's personal intervention ended the interservice bickering. In the end, in 1909 the General Board declared that no suitable site for a first-class naval base could be found in the Philippines and that accordingly Pearl Harbor should be developed. Clearly the strategists had come to the conclusion that the Philippines were virtually impossible to defend.[20]

Roosevelt, however, had already anticipated this result of the discussion two years earlier, when he referred to the Philippines as America's Achilles' heel. While the sailors despaired, the diplomats were left with the thankless task of trying to appease Japan without sacrificing China.

From 1905 to 1917 they negotiated a number of agreements with Japan. The Taft–Katsura conversation of 1905 was the first of these and was followed by the Root–Takahira understanding of 1908 and the controversial Lansing–Ishii agreement of 1917.[21] The objective of American policy was to provide for

20. See esp. Nov. 6, 1907, Jan. 29 and 31, 1908, Feb. 19, 1908. *Records of the Joint Army and Navy Board.*

21. For a useful summary of the texts of these argeements and notes, see Ruhl J. Bartlett, *The Record of American Diplomacy* (New York, Knopf, 1959), pp. 414–23. A detailed account of the Wilson Administration's Far Eastern policy in 1915 is to be found in Arthur S. Link, *Wilson: The Struggle for Neutrality, 1914–1915* (Princeton, Princeton University Press, 1960), pp. 267–308. Professor Link's conclusion, however, that Wilson "set the American government implacably against any further Japanese expansion in China" does not appear to be supported by the evidence he has skillfully marshaled. Secretary Bryan's second "statement" of May 11, 1915, formulated the "non-recognition doctrine,"

the safety of the Philippines, equal commercial opportunity, and the political integrity of China—a cynic would add, "in that order of preference." Nevertheless, it is not the case that successive American Administrations sold China down the river for the sake of preserving America's own interests. Such concessions as the United States made to Japan were intended to limit, rather than to extend, Japan's control over large portions of China. The nearest approach to an unworthy bargain is possibly to be found in the agreed text of the Taft–Katsura conversation (July 29, 1905), when Taft informed Count Katsura that in his personal opinion the establishment by Japanese troops of suzerainty over Korea was "the logical result of the present war and would directly contribute to permanent peace in the East." Korea, after all, was not Taft's to dispose of. And where was the line to be drawn? The Japanese were later on to apply the argument with equal force to Manchuria.

In due course American statesmen came near accepting Japanese contentions. Secretary Bryan's admission in his statement to the Japanese ambassador in Washington (March 13, 1915) that "the United States frankly recognizes that territorial contiguity creates special relations between Japan" with regard to Shantung, South Manchuria, and East Mongolia—an admission Lansing repeated in the third paragraph of the agreement that bears his name (November 2, 1917)—was unnecessary and a diplomatic blunder. The meaning of the phrase "special relations" was elastic; it enabled Japan virtually to claim suzerainty and reduced the value of its assurances to respect the territorial integrity of China. But no American Administration could evade the fact that the United States was militarily pow-

---

with which Wilson (as did Stimson seventeen years later) quieted the American conscience. It represented no effective policy in 1915 or in 1932.

erless to defend China against Japan, even if it so desired. As Lansing in November 1914 explained in a letter to Minister Paul Samuel Reinsch at Peking, "It would be quixotic in the extreme to allow the question of China's territorial integrity to entangle the United States in international difficulties." But the last word may fittingly be left to the Chinese government. After having been notified of the Lansing–Ishii agreement, it replied that China intended to respect the treaty rights of all nations but would "not allow herself to be bound by any agreement entered into by other nations." [22] The question whether the intentions of American diplomats were laudable or cynical will continue to be discussed, but the conclusion that American policy in the Far East made very little impression on the larger international developments there in the years from 1906 to 1917 appears inescapable.

What most perturbed Roosevelt and the strategists was the defenseless position of America's possessions in the Pacific Ocean. In such circumstances it seemed the height of folly to injure sensitive pride by humiliating Japanese immigrants on the West Coast. Roosevelt did his best to avoid a crisis in American–Japanese relations over the problem of Oriental immigrants, but he did not succeed before a Japanese war scare swept America.

Theodore Roosevelt, who possessed a sound grasp of the strategic realities underlying diplomacy, believed that only a large Navy could guarantee the safety of America's island possessions in the Far East and gain respect for the country among the great nations of the world (all of which were arming to the teeth). He now redoubled his efforts to win congressional approval for new naval construction. He got two new battleships each year—having asked for four—and in February 1907 secured congressional approval for the construction of the first

22. Bartlett, *American Diplomacy*, pp. 414–23.

American dreadnought. In battleship strength, with sixteen first-class battleships, America had already gained a safe margin of superiority over Japan. Roosevelt sent the fleet around the world to show the American flag in the Pacific (December 1907 to February 1909), and he dealt with the American–Japanese differences in a conciliatory, but firm, way. These were the elements of Roosevelt's Far Eastern policy from 1906 until he left the White House in 1909.

His successor, Taft, sought to meet the problem by the new expedient of substituting dollars for guns in the Far East and law for brute force in the world at large. Wilson was forced during his first five years of office to focus on the European catastrophe.

The two great war plans, worked out by the strategists during these years, were defensive in character. A color represented the possible enemy: orange for Japan, black for Germany. While War Plan Orange is chiefly of academic interest and shows just how defenseless was the United States position in the Pacific, War Plan Black reveals the thinking behind the advice the strategists tendered to the President during the years that preceded the American entry into World War I. Together they represent a tremendous advance in American strategic planning and are in fact the first modern war plans in American history.

War Plan Orange, completed in 1914, showed a realistic grasp of the Pacific situation.[23] Naval strategists saw that logistics dominated the problem. If the means to insure delivery of full naval strength to the decisive battle area were lacking, the national calamity would be as great as if the fighting fleet were actually inferior to the enemy. The naval experts calculated that by way of the Panama Canal, Pearl Harbor, Midway, and

23. "War Plan Orange." War Portfolios, *General Board Records.*

Guam, it would take the first section of the United States fleet 68 days to reach Manila, whereas the Japanese fleet and troop transports would arrive in the Philippines 8 days after leaving Japanese ports. This gave the Japanese full control of the western Pacific for 60 days if the Panama Canal could be utilized by the United States fleet and, if not, full control for 104 days. The defense of the Philippines thus depended on the Army plans for defending Corregidor Island. The Army mission was to hold out for at least 60 days, and the Navy mission was to engage the Japanese Navy in battle on its arrival in the western Pacific in order to relieve Japanese pressure on the Philippines. Guam was held to be the vital strategic point of control, and the Navy strategists believed that the decisive battle would be fought within a 1,200-mile radius of that island.

So much for the plans—now for the realities of the situation: the strategists frankly confessed that the plan was not based on the actual strength and capability of the United States Navy in 1914. It could, indeed, only be carried out if the reforms proposed by the General Board were actually effected before a war with Japan occurred. In 1914 the position was bleak indeed. Congress had approved appropriations for the construction of a battleship fleet superior to the Japanese. But the United States fleet was unbalanced, for Congress had ignored the persistent requests of the General Board, passed on by the Secretary of the Navy, for adequate personnel to man the ships and for the necessary auxiliary ships, cruisers, destroyers, transports, ammunition ships, and above all colliers and oil supply tankers upon which the movement of the fleet depended. In 1914 the battleship fleet could without assistance hardly reach San Francisco, let alone make a voyage of 10,000 miles from the Atlantic base to the Philippines. Moreover the construction of defenses and docks and the establishment of garrisons on the Pacific island holdings had been neglected. The

Army in the Philippines could not hope to resist a Japanese assault for 60 days, while Guam, Midway, and Hawaii were virtually defenseless and Pearl Harbor as yet could not dock a battleship. War Plan Orange thus underlined the fact (true for many years to come) that the United States was incapable of fighting Japan. Presumably American diplomacy during this period had to be, and was, shaped on this assumption, as illustrated by the Lansing–Ishii Agreement. But what of War Plan Black?[24]

Here, as the strategists saw it, the situation was reversed, for Germany rather than the United States would suffer the handicap of long lines of communication. As against this, the strategists had to face their estimate that a large German army of 750,000 men could be transported to the West Indies and the United States. It was thus held that the mission of the United States fleet, based on Guantánamo, Cuba, and its advanced base at Culebra, Puerto Rico, would meet the German fleet in the Atlantic once it passed into the zone of control at a radius of 500 miles from Culebra, and prevent a German landing in the West Indies or on the American mainland. The chances of success were rated rather gloomily at about even. Clearly the strategists failed to recognize the enormous problems involved in endeavoring to send an army with all its supplies across the Atlantic Ocean. As yet geographical isolation and the rivalry of the European powers still provided the North American mainland with a considerable degree of protection.

As war engulfed the continent of Europe in August 1914, President Wilson, absorbed as he had been by domestic and hemispheric problems, was totally unprepared. His personal sympathies were with England, and he looked upon German militarism with loathing. Yet the President never wavered in the high

24. "War Plan Black." War Portfolios, *General Board Records.*

objectives of his diplomacy through all the vicissitudes of the first three years of conflict, the dilemmas occasioned by the war policies of both sides, and the unfortunate but necessary position of compromise.[25]

President Wilson remained an enigma even to the men close to him. Few members of his Cabinet could predict the details of his policy. Colonel House came nearest to being the President's confidant and friend, but even he lost touch with the President after his abortive peace mission to Europe in 1916. Wilson was driven by an exalted sense of his mission to the world, which in the last resort must be adjudged an intense assertion of personal power based on complete confidence in his own judgment. He alone, Wilson believed, was not actuated by material interests but by principles based on Christian beliefs. He alone, by virtue of his office and ideals, should therefore shape the policies of the United States on which the future of the world would depend. Wilson suffered from the loneliness of the messianic position he had imposed on himself.

Until the eve of America's entry into the war, Wilson strove to maintain American neutrality. Though his motives have often been misunderstood, old and new evidence leaves little room for doubt, and to the historian, at least, the enigma vanishes. Wilson was aware that the majority of the American people were in favor of maintaining peace and saw no reason to involve America in the folly of Europe. He shared these feelings; he also looked beyond American interests to the global mission that he believed America was called upon to

25. Wilson's diplomacy during World War I has been ably analyzed by Ernest R. May, *The World War and American Isolation, 1914–1917* (Cambridge, Mass., Harvard University Press, 1959), Link, *Wilson: The Struggle for Neutrality,* and by Link, *Woodrow Wilson and the Progressive Era: 1910–1917* (New York, Harper, 1954), but neither May's nor Link's accounts were able to utilize the essential military and naval records of the Wilson Administration which became available in 1958.

fulfill. His own certainty that no war was a just war—indeed, that America's involvement would prove disastrous to world history—was the mainspring of all his actions. One great nation, the United States, must keep clear of the general madness and reconstruct a stable peace by a combination of strength and good example. Destiny, believed Wilson, had singled out the American people to preserve Western civilization.

The consequences of these beliefs on policy were far-reaching. To prepare war plans in case the United States became involved against its will he regarded as an unneutral act. Only plans that left the actual conditions of World War I out of account were properly neutral. The gap between reality and the Wilsonian concept of the world was large. The gap between a proper military policy and Wilson's foreign policy (especially his insistence on the maritime rights of neutrals) was equally wide. The great residual power of the United States and the military balance in Europe alone preserved the American people from the consequences of these neglects. It would not always be so.

The task of discussing Wilson's policies toward the belligerents has been ably undertaken by others. There is, however, one aspect of national policy about which much controversy still exists, the general problem of national preparedness for war. The role of the strategists and their relations with Wilson and his Administration can, on the basis of the classified records of the Department of the Navy, be analyzed with some degree of accuracy for the first time. They reveal an appalling lack of coordination between the policies of the Administration and the country's military and naval advisers; they also reveal how the members of the General Board, working in a kind of vacuum, reached conclusions that left the nation unprepared for the actual conflict of 1917.

The President would allow the strategists no share in the

formulation of policy. He clarified his attitude on this point a few weeks after he entered the White House. Relations with Japan were strained at that time, and the California Legislature had passed a bill forbidding Japanese residents to own land. This aroused the bitter resentment of the Japanese government. At the height of the crisis, on May 15, 1913, the Joint Army and Navy Board met to discuss precautionary military steps to be taken if war should come. They recommended that the President move the American cruisers then in the Yangtze to reinforce the defense of Manila. On the following day, the Board sent the President a second letter, urging him to send naval reinforcements to Panama and the Hawaiian islands. But the President furiously resented the Board's "interference" and its attempt, as he touchily put it, to coerce him by sending letters on successive days.[26]

The Cabinet had already settled the question. Warships, it was feared, might provoke the Japanese, and were not to be sent to Manila. Wilson interpreted the Joint Board's second letter as a bid to overrule the President and Cabinet. He instructed the Secretary of the Navy, Josephus Daniels, to inform the officers of the Board that "if this should occur again, there will be no General or Joint Boards. They will be abolished." Daniels thought "it was a glorious thing to see the President's determination that the policy of the Administration should be carried out and no officer in the Army or Navy should be permitted to make war plans . . . when such a policy was contrary to the spirit of the Administration."[27]

On May 17 General Leonard Wood, a member of the Joint Board, hastened to the White House to explain to the President

26. May 15 and Oct. 9, 1913. *Records of the Joint Army and Navy Board.* E. David Cronon, ed., *The Cabinet Diaries of Josephus Daniels, 1913–1921* (Lincoln, University of Nebraska Press, 1963), p. 68. Link, *Wilson and the Progressive Era*, pp. 86–87.

27. Cronon, *Diaries of Daniels*, p. 93.

that he had misinterpreted the Board's intentions. General Wood reported to the Board some months later: "Mr. Wilson stated that he was glad to know this as it looked very much as if such action had been attempted." The Joint Army and Navy Board had never been a very effective body; after 1913 it ceased to play a role in military planning, although it met on a few more occasions. The General Board also lost Dewey's services a few weeks before the outbreak of war in Europe. He suffered from a stroke. Advancing age and infirmity forced him to take a decreasing part in the discussions. The Board's function, moreover, remained purely advisory. Its influence depended on the attitude of the Secretary of the Navy, and Daniels was not disposed to listen to professional advice.

Daniels was an able man in the wrong position. He possessed many commendable qualities; he held staunchly liberal views and genuinely wished to better the welfare of his fellow citizens; he was tough, belying his benign countenance, and obstinate when occasion demanded it. His caution, levelheadedness, and personal loyalty no doubt endeared him to the President. His long experience as a journalist, moreover, could have worked to the advantage of the Navy; a Secretary of the Navy capable of presenting the Navy's case skillfully to Congress and to the American people would be a great asset. His concern for bettering the life of ordinary seamen was deep and sincere. Yet when all has been said the choice of Daniels was extraordinary. Wilson had placed the direction of the nation's principal means of defense in the hands of a pacifist. Daniels evidently supported Wilson's neutrality to the bitter end. At the meeting of March 20, 1917, which Wilson called to hear the views of his Cabinet on whether he should recall Congress and recommend war with Germany, Daniels finally conceded that this was now the only policy left. Secretary of State Lansing recorded the poignant moment in his private diary: "The

President then turned his head toward Daniels who sat opposite Burleson and said: 'Well,' Daniels hesitated a moment as if
weighing his words and then spoke in a voice which was low
and trembled with emotion. His eyes were suffused with tears.
He said that he saw no other course than to enter the war, that
do what we would it seemed bound to come, and that, therefore, he was in favor of summoning Congress as soon as possible
and getting its support for active measures against Germany."
Lansing also recorded his own reaction to Daniel's belated vol-
teface, writing, "his pacifist tendencies and personal devotion to
Mr. Bryan and his ideas were well known. It was, therefore, a
surprise to us all when he announced himself to be in favor of
war. I could not but wonder whether he spoke from conviction
or because he lacked strength of mind to stand out against the
united opinion of his colleagues. I prefer to believe the former
reason, though I am not sure." [28]

Daniels had acted from the first as if he were determined to
alienate the good will of the Navy. He inaugurated a program
of reforms designed to improve its moral tone. He would transform the Navy, he announced in his annual report of December 1914, into the "biggest university in America." Every ship
would be a school. Few naval officers shared this splendid vision; indignation was further aroused by the Secretary's ban
on liquor aboard ship. Rear Admiral Bradley A. Fiske, Aide for
Operations and the Secretary's senior adviser, when he first
heard of the Secretary's intentions, sent Daniels an indignant
letter. This order, he bluntly declared, was insulting to the
honor of the American naval officers. The Admiral's angry
growl has lost none of its force: "The officers of the Navy are

28. Memorandum of the Cabinet meeting, March 20, 1917. Lansing's
Diary, Lansing MSS. First published in full in Grenville, "The United
States Decision for War, 1917. Excerpts from the Manuscript Diary of
Robert Lansing," *Renaissance and Modern Studies*, 4 (Nottingham,
1960).

dignified and high minded gentlemen. Their ideals and standards will compare more than favorably with those of average men in civil life . . . [the contemplated order] was an unmerited indignity, an act of disrespect to a set of men, most of whom are of settled (and good) habits, and many of whom have grown grey in their honored profession." No doubt Fiske was exaggerating when he warned Daniels that the ban on liquor would actually "impair the military efficiency of the Service," [29] but this remark shows how deeply the Admiral's feelings had been stirred. Daniels might have been forgiven his puritanical streak if he had been equally concerned about the fighting capacity of the fleet. Instead he paid little heed to the advice of his most able officers, a grave responsibility for someone who knew nothing of naval strategy.

Although during the first two years of Wilson's Administration the General Board was held in no high regard, its members discussed all aspects of naval policy; what is more the General Board tendered advice to the Secretary of the Navy on a large variety of questions ranging from the disposition of the fleet and the adoption of war plans to the building requirements of the Navy and the proper provision of bases at home and abroad. Daniels would consider the recommendations only when they coincided with his own views or with those of the President.

On the eve of the outbreak of World War I, the General Board met in special session to face the problem of how a continental war might endanger the security of the United States. No one could predict whether the conflict would be confined to the continental powers alone or whether England would also become involved. They warned the Secretary of the Navy that a German victory would in all likelihood be followed by an attack on the Western Hemisphere; Germany, they said, did

29. Fiske to Daniels, May 27, 1914. Daniels *MSS*, Library of Congress.

not accept the Monroe Doctrine and would attempt to secure "the position she covets on this side of the ocean." The United States, so the General Board concluded, must therefore prepare for this eventuality without delay.[30] This memorandum is of significance as it reveals the outlook the General Board maintained until America's entry into the war.

From 1914 until February 1917 the General Board and the General Staff of the Army were preparing not for World War I but for the war which might follow it. The revision of War Plan Black on January 1, 1915, recognized, it is true, that as long as the Central Powers and the Entente were locked in battle there was no threat to the Monroe Doctrine, and that in defense of American citizens maltreated by the Central Powers, America might be forced to fight Germany. But there was no thought of joining in the Allied war effort; in effect the war planning of the United States was limited to meeting any hostile German cruisers in the Atlantic. In the words of the war plan: "No other objective exists for the American fleet, unless an expeditionary force is sent against German South Africa." [31] Admiral Fiske was doubtful whether the assumptions of War Plan Black were valid. The State Department's protest on February 10, 1915, concerning Germany's declaration of war zones led Fiske to remark in his diary: "the note to Germany is nearly an ultimatum, and almost threatens war if a U.S. ship is sunk. The significant fact of this to me is that if war results, the *strategic advantage* will be to Germany, since (in order to interfere with Germany's action) U.S. will have to send ships near Germany. Hitherto, we assumed that war, (if it comes) with Germany will be because of her violation of Monroe Doctrine, in which case she will come to *us*, and we will have the strate-

30. General Board Memorandum, Aug. 1, 1914. Published in the Navy Department's *Annual Report, 1914.*
31. "War Plan Black," p. 60. War Portfolios, Navy Department, National Archives, Washington, D.C.

gic advantages." [32] But neither Fiske's doubts nor the possible repercussions of Wilson's policies had any perceptible influence on war planning. War Plan Black was amended from time to time during 1916 and 1917 to provide for a variety of emergencies against a German fleet operating in the West Indies. The Board recommended the purchase of the Danish West Indies in August 1916 in order to strengthen the defensive American position in the the Caribbean. Wilson had already that same month concluded a treaty with Denmark to that effect. So too the American occupation of Haiti in July and August 1915 and the occupation of Santo Domingo in May 1916 may at least partly have been undertaken for strategic reasons. From the first, the General Board had warned the Secretary of the Navy that one "serious possibility for the United States connected with a great European war lies in the changes of sovereignty in possessions on or adjacent to the American continent that may result from corresponding changes in sovereignty on the continent of Europe." [33] In November 1914 the Board specifically pointed out the danger to the United States arising from the continued "unsettled state of affairs in Mexico, Haiti and Santo Domingo." [34]

But during the first year of the war both the President and Secretary Daniels on other issues rejected the advice of the General Board. The Board recommended in July and September 1914 a substantial increase of naval construction; it asked for four battleships a year until 1923 and also for the neces-

32. Fiske Diary, Feb. 12, 1915, p. 63. Fiske *MSS*, Library of Congress. The authors are indebted to Dr. James E. Hewes, Jr., for drawing their attention to the importance of this manuscript as a source for the study of the naval policy of the Wilson Administration from 1913 to 1915.

33. General Board Study #420–1, General Board to Secretary of the Navy, Aug. 1, 1914. Records of the General Board, Department of the Navy, Washington, D.C.

34. General Board Study #421, General Board to Secretary of the Navy, Nov. 14, 1914. General Board Records.

sary construction of auxiliary vessels, destroyers, supply ships, and oil fuel vessels, without which the fleet could not take to the high seas. The lack of these auxiliary vessels, which the General Board had requested in vain for several years, in its opinion already crippled the movement of the fleet. The Board pointed to the serious shortage of men and officers which it now declared could only be met by passing laws authorizing their enlistment.[35]

While the General Board during the early months of the war urged on the Administration a policy it believed to be necessary for the security of the United States, Theodore Roosevelt and Senator Lodge made themselves the leaders of a public campaign for national preparedness. Critics of the Administration's military policy within the Department of the Navy supplied information. On October 16, 1914, Lodge's son-in-law, Representative Augustus P. Gardner, introduced a resolution in the House stating "The United States is totally unprepared for war, defensive or offensive, against a real power." [36] Assistant Secretary of the Navy Franklin Delano Roosevelt confided to Fiske that he had sat up late the night before and had initiated the idea and even suggested the wording of Gardner's resolution.[37] The New York *Times* and New York *Tribune* gave wide publicity to the campaign for national preparedness. Early in December the *Tribune* carried the headline "Daniels in open disfavor with men under him." Daniels replied to his critics with staggering complacency. On Decem-

35. General Board Study #420–2, General Board to Secretary of the Navy, Nov. 17, 1914. General Board Records.

36. For a disscussion of the preparedness controversy, see esp. Link, *Wilson and the Progressive Era*, pp. 174–96; also Armin Rappaport, *The Navy League of the United States* (Detroit, Wayne State University Press, 1962), pp. 39–62.

37. Fiske Diary, Oct. 16, 1914, p. 10. Fiske MSS, Library of Congress, Washington, D.C.

ber 4, 1914, he released the following statement for publication in the New York *World:*

> If there ever was a time when the American people had cause to be proud of their Navy, it is now. It is not the largest Navy in the world. In fact, in the number of great ships and total tonnage it ranks third. But situated as this country is, we do not need in time of peace to burden the country with the expense of maintaining as large a Navy as either England or Germany, the only navies of greater number and tonnage than ours . . . If the nation wishes to be always on a war footing, the expenses of the Navy must be increased by leaps and bounds. I do not think the American people wish more than the normal increase at this time. Nor do I think this is necessary." [38]

Growing congressional concern about the nation's defenses was not allayed by the Secretary's assurances that all was well. Admiral Fiske arranged to be called before the House Naval Affairs Committee on December 17, 1914, and refuted the Secretary's satisfactory report on the state of the fleet. Behind the scenes he convinced some influential members of Congress that the Department was not organized for war and needed a general staff. The creation of the Office of the Chief of Naval Operations in the spring of 1915 by act of Congress was intended to meet this need. But the Chief of Naval Operations was made directly responsible to a Secretary who was opposed to the whole concept of a general staff. Daniels even berated Rear Admiral Austin M. Knight, the President of the Naval War College and a senior member of the General Board, for advocating publicly the reorganization of naval

38. New York *Times* (Nov. 22, 1914); New York *World* (Dec. 4, 1914); New York *Tribune* (Dec. 7, 1914).

administration: "I told him he was right in saying the Department was not organized for war. . . . he, the War College, the General Board, the Aides and the Secretary were incompetent and should be removed." [39]

He eventually appointed Captain William S. Benson, Commandant of the Philadelphia Navy Yard, as Chief of Naval Operations. Benson lacked both General Board and War College experience, which may well have commended him to the Secretary. Fiske was passed over. He had supported the idea of a general staff and earned the Secretary's displeasure by his testimony before the House Naval Affairs Committee.[40] The Secretary treated Fiske and the officers of the General Board with scant courtesy. He would have liked to do without them altogether but found their advice on the building program of the fleet indispensable. On other aspects of naval policy the Administration ignored the General Board. The war plans remained paper plans since the Secretary and the President did not approve of war plans, and the bureaus in the Department were not instructed to ensure that they could be put into practice. The bureau chiefs were jealous of the contribution the General Board sought to make to the formation of naval policy. In projecting the building needs of the fleet the General Board had taken over responsibilities once vested in the hands of the bureau chiefs. Secretary of the Navy George Meyer's attempt to coordinate the work of the bureaus by creating aides had only added to the confusion when his successor, Daniels, by his own attitude encouraged professional differences. Fiske's recommendations and those

39. Cronon, *Diaries of Daniels*, p. 93. For a discussion of the origins of the Office of Chief of Naval Operations see Henry P. Beers, "The Development of the Office of the Chief of Naval Operations, Part II," *Military Affairs*, 10 (1946), 10–38.

40. Fiske Diary, Dec. 17, 21, and 28, 1914, pp. 38 ff. Fiske predicted on Dec. 28, 1914, "I am confident he [Daniels] will get rid of me if he can." Fiske MSS.

of the General Board were usually opposed in the Department by Victor Blue, Chief of the Bureau of Navigation, and by Albert Gustavus Winterhalter, Aide for Material. For support Fiske could count only on Roosevelt.[41] With Benson's appointment as Chief of Naval Operations, Fiske's last hopes of influencing the policies of the Department vanished and he retired as Aide for Operations in May 1915. From then until the congressional investigation of 1920, professional criticism of naval policy, although not silenced, lacked focus. The divisions in the Navy did not augur well for the great plan endorsed by Wilson in 1916, to build a Navy second to none.

The reasons for President Wilson's reversal in attitude toward national preparedness have been discussed by Arthur S. Link. Germany's submarine warfare against merchantmen and passenger liners had brought the United States to the brink of war. Public pressure on the Administration had greatly increased by the summer of 1915. We probably need look no further for Wilson's motives. The Administration's treatment of the General Board during the war in Europe certainly makes it unlikely that the influence of the strategists was decisive. And so the President, who in October 1914 had laughingly called the preparedness talk a "good mental exercise," asked Secretary Daniels on July 21, 1915, to request the General Board to submit the building program that would best meet the needs of the United States.

Secretary Daniels was left with no alternative but to carry out the President's wishes. His distress may be gathered from

41. Many entries in the Fiske Diary reveal the professional rivalries and struggles within the Navy Department but see esp. Nov. 5, 6, and 10, 1914, pp. 20 ff. Fiske MSS. Fiske's *From Midshipman to Rear Admiral* (London, Werner Laurie, 1920), pp. 526 passim, repays careful study for the early years of the Wilson Administration. Another valuable account is Elting E. Morison's *Admiral Sims and the Modern American Navy* (Boston, Houghton, Mifflin, 1942).

his suggestion to Wilson that the President should publicly announce his intention that once the war was over he would propose worldwide naval disarmament. Wilson wisely replied that if he adopted this suggestion he would find it difficult to explain why the Administration was "apparently going in two directions at once"; instead, to mollify Daniels, Wilson thought he might "speak out plainly again for organized peace." [42]

The General Board was not left an entirely free hand in formulating the plans. Its terms of reference were clearly set out in a letter from the Secretary of the Navy that asked for an opinion "as to what the Navy must be in the future in order to stand upon an equality with the most efficient navy of the world." They were not requested to suggest measures to be taken if the United States were to be drawn into World War I. The Administration in so framing the purpose of the future Navy committed a serious error. A Navy to match any navy in the world would mean the laying down of an enormous battleship program.[43]

The General Board had the disadvantage of planning America's naval needs without being told in what situations the Navy was likely to be employed. The Board sought to fill this vacuum of policy planning by speculating freely about the probable causes of war. In a memorandum of August 6, 1915, the officers of the Board reasoned: "History shows that wars are chiefly caused by economic pressure and competition between nations and races . . . At the close of the present war it is not improbable that the defeated belligerents, with the connivance and perhaps participation of the victors, may seek to recoup their war losses and to expand at the expense of the

42. Daniels to Wilson, Aug. 2, 1916; Wilson to Daniels, Aug. 16, 1916. Daniels MSS.
43. It should be noted, moreover, that after the battle of Jutland on May 31, 1916, a large battleship fleet was of little use to the Allied cause.

new world. On the other hand, perhaps soon, the victor may challenge the United States . . . The naval policy should therefore make the United States secure in the Western Atlantic, the Caribbean and the Pacific Oceans at the earliest possible moment." [44] Even in August 1917 the Board wrote: "A new alignment of powers after the present war must not find our fleet . . . unprepared to meet possible enemies . . . to act singly or jointly with all their naval powers against us." [45] To the strategists, the United States had no friends in the world, only jealous rivals. Their recommendations for a vast building program of battleships and auxiliary vessels over a five-year period was based on these premises. A protracted and bitter struggle in Congress preceded the Naval Act of Appropriation (August 29, 1916). Wilson skillfully persuaded the majority of both houses to compromise and accept a massive program of naval rearmament. The bill as passed endorsed the suggestions of the General Board and even went one better—the new ships were to be laid down over three, not five, years as the General Board had originally proposed.[46]

But the General Board committed a grave error by failing to recognize the submarine menace in time. Early in November 1915 the Board summed up its views: "The deeds of the submarines have been so spectacular that in default of engagements between the main fleets undue weight has been attached to them . . . Yet at the present time, when the allies have learned in great measure to protect their commerce, as they learnt a few months earlier to protect their cruisers from the submarine menace, it is apparent that the submarine is not

44. General Board Study #420-2, memorandum of August 6, 1915, placed with General Board to Secretary of Navy, July 30, 1915. Daniels MSS, Box 257, Navy Correspondence.

45. General Board Study #420-2, General Board to the Secretary of the Navy, Aug. 29, 1917. General Board Records.

46. Sprout, *Rise of American Naval Power,* pp. 334–46.

an instrument fitted to dominate naval warfare." [47] By 1917 it belatedly recognized that the issue of war hung on the success with which the Allies could cope with German submarines. Every destroyer had to be pressed into service to convoy Allied supplies, and the United States had less than fifty destroyers in commission at the outbreak of the war.

And so it was that Wilson's passionate desire for peace, a mediated peace which he held was necessary to save "white civilization," and a grave strategic error in evaluating the submarine led the nation in 1916 to make a great military effort that was peculiarly ill suited to the needs of the day.

Until February 1917 no thought whatever had been given to cooperating with the Allies on land or sea. Not even a rough plan existed to provide for the eventuality of sending an American expeditionary force to Europe; and this despite a remarkable warning that the United States naval and military attachés serving in London and Paris, their assistants, and the two military observers serving with the British Army in France had sent from London on April 4, 1916. In their joint memorandum they suggested that plans should be prepared to mobilize the mercantile marine to carry the United States Army to Europe in the event of war; in forcible language they pointed to the danger of not acting in time: "Any system adopted at the moment and operated without previous study and experience is more than apt to bring discredit on the Navy, and useless danger to the Army and the Nation." [48] Their proposals were not even considered by the Joint Army and Navy Board until November 1916. The Board then ex-

47. General Board Study #420–2, General Board to the Secretary of the Navy, Nov. 9, 1915. General Board Records.

48. Joint memorandum by the American military and naval attachés and their assistants in London and Paris and by the two American observers with the British Army in France, April 4, 1916, referred to in a memorandum of November 14, 1916. *Record of the Joint Army and Navy Board.*

pressed its entire confidence in the competence of the Army
Quartermaster Corps to handle all transport problems and
cited as an illustration of the efficiency of existing arrange-
ments "the recent successful withdrawal of the Vera Cruz
expedition." [49] The war plans held in readiness by the Army
included an American invasion of Canada (1912–13) and also
envisaged such possibilities as an attack on New York by
Great Britain (March 1915) and the defense of the Pacific
coast from a Japanese invasion (February 1915 to March
1917).[50] The first plans for an American expeditionary force to
Europe, not drawn up until late March 1917, were based on
the possibility of invading Bulgaria through Greece and invading France, in alliance with Holland, to the rear of the
German armies.[51] These plans were of little conceivable use.
Consequently the full impact of American intervention was
delayed for many months. Wilson had not provided the leadership to prepare the nation effectively for a war that until the
very last he regarded as disastrous, while the strategists had
failed to consider eventualities their President virtually refused to face.

Regarded as a whole, the years from 1900 to 1917 witnessed
a great change in diplomatic and strategic thought, in which
Dewey played a large part. It is certainly curious that the
most important offensive war plan to be found, Lieutenant
Kimball's, coincided with the period when American power
was only beginning to entitle the United States to be considered as a great power. A striking characteristic of American
war planning from 1903 until 1917 is that it was conceived on

49. Memorandum, November 14, 1916. *Record of the Joint Army and
Navy Board.*
50. Army War Plans, National Archives, card references to folios
Canada, Great Britain, and *Japan.* The actual war plans have not yet
been traced and were possibly destroyed.
51. Army War Plans, National Archives, reference to folio *Germany,*
memorandum, March 29, 1917.

the whole in terms of defense; the possibility of an alliance with Britain or any other power had been given no serious consideration in the shaping of military policy. The strategists continued to regard as axiomatic George Washington's admonition against permanent alliances long after many thoughtful Americans perceived that Washington's advice could no longer preserve the interests of the United States in the twentieth century.

Manuscript Sources

Official Correspondence

UNITED STATES

The Records of the Department of State: National Archives (Washington, D.C.). The Records of the Department of the Navy: National Archives. The Records of the General Board: Department of the Navy (Washington, D.C.). The Records of the Department of the Army: National Archives.

GREAT BRITAIN

The Records of the Foreign Office: Public Record Office. (London). The Records of the Colonial Office: Public Record Office. The Records of the War Office Intelligence Division: Public Record Office.

GERMANY

Microfilm of the Foreign Ministry Archives: Public Record Office. Microfilm of the Records of the Navy: Public Record Office.

Personal Papers

Thomas F. Bayard: Library of Congress. James G. Blaine: Library of Congress. Joseph Chamberlain: Birmingham University Library, Birmingham, England. Grover Cleveland: Library of Congress. William E. Curtis: Library of Congress.

Manuscript Sources

George Dewey: Library of Congress. Donald M. Dickinson: Library of Congress. Bradley A. Fiske: Library of Congress. Walter Q. Gresham: Library of Congress. Charles S. Hamlin: Library of Congress. John Hay: Library of Congress. Henry Cabot Lodge: Massachusetts Historical Society, Boston. John D. Long: Massachusetts Historical Society. Stephen B. Luce: Library of Congress. Alfred T. Mahan: Library of Congress. Daniel Manning: Library of Congress. Manton M. Marble: Library of Congress. William McKinley: Library of Congress. John T. Morgan: Library of Congress. Richard Olney: Library of Congress. Theodore Roosevelt: Library of Congress. Elihu Root: Library of Congress. Third Marquess of Salisbury: Christ Church, Oxford, England. Carl Schurz: Library of Congress. William L. Scruggs: microfilm of journal, Yale University Library. John Sherman: Library of Congress. John L. Spooner: Library of Congress. Henry White: Library of Congress.

Index

Index

Chang, Yen Hoon, 54; signs Immigration Treaty, *1888*, 57; accepts Senate amendments, 58

China, 10, 225; prejudice against, 52–53; Burlinghame Treaty, 53–54; immigration negotiations, 59–63; expected partition, 267–68; market of, 268, 269; rivalry for, 288–89, 304, 312; agreements concerning, 313–16. *See also* Far East

Cienfugos, 301

Cleveland, Grover, 27, 32, 39, 87, 213, 229, 232, 233; inadequacy in foreign affairs, 40–41; personality and rise to power, 41–43; "sound money" candidate for presidency, 43; loyal to financial views of Tilden and Manning, 44; opposes silver lobby, 45–46; seeks to defeat silver movement by diplomacy, 46–51; harmful effects of silver diplomacy, 46; recommends repeal of Bland Allison Act, 50; failure to secure the general support of his party on silver question, 51; recognizes political importance of Chinese immigration, 52, 54; protects Chinese from attack, 54; leaves Bayard to solve problem by negotiation with Chinese government, 54–55; decides to make tariff reduction principal political issue of *1888*, 56–57; urges conclusion of Chinese treaty, 57; seeks to retrieve political fortunes by backing Chinese exclusion bill, 60–62; does not consult Bayard, 61; fails to gain support of four Western states in *1888*, 63; attempts to gain political advantage from failure to settle American-Canadian differences, 63, 66–71; supports Bayard in fisheries question, 66; estimate of his treatment of Chi-

nese and Canadian differences, 72–73; and Hawaiian annexation, 103–15; appoints Gresham Secretary of State, 104; initiates partisan debate on Hawaiian revolution, 112–15; repeal of Sherman Silver Purchase Act, 116; plays more active role in Venezuelan boundary dispute, 140–41; meets Scruggs, 143; discusses Venezuelan question with Dickinson, 150–51; discusses Venezuelan question with Scruggs, 150–51; attitude to Venezuelan boundary question and concern for Orinoco, 152; second interview with Scruggs, 151–53, 160; motives of Venezuelan policy, 158–60; inclines to more active Venezuelan policy, 160–61; supports Olney, 163–65, 181; his special message to Congress, *December 17, 1895*, 155, 165, 167–68; Cuban policy, 180–82, 184, 186, 188–90, 192, 194–95, 196, 199, 236; general estimate of 199–200, 240

Clyde, William P., 94

Cole, Cornelius, 3

Colombia, 81, 127, 128; and Isthmian canal, 82; boundary dispute with Costa Rica, 116–17; relations with United States, 117, 121, 309–11

Columbus *Daily Sun*, 127

Commercial Bureau of American Republics, 92

Conference of American states. *See* International American Conference

Congress of the United States: naval votes in *1870s* and *1880s*, 2; concern over state of Navy, 2–10; opponents of naval expansion in, 10; votes for two battleships, *1890*, 11, 37; passes Marine Schools Act, 15; attitude to Naval War College, 18, 20–

[341]

Index

Index

Goodrich, Caspar F.: advocates establishment of Naval War College, 17

Gorman, Arthur P.: introduces bill on fisheries, 1887, 67; and Hawaiian annexation, 106

Goschen, George, 169

Grant, Ulysses S., 94, 188, 189

Great Britain, 125, 289; relations with United States, 7, 40, 94, 151, 169–70, 207–08, 228, 289, 293; rejection of bimetalism, 48–49, 208; difficulties over fisheries, 65; merchant marine, 79; and Chilean revolution, 97, 99, 100; and Hawaii, 109, 110; and Brazilian revolution, 118; dispute over Mosquito Indians, 118–19; and Venezuelan boundary dispute, 120, 122–24, 136–78; and Nicaragua, 122; reputation for perfidy, 143, 144; dispute with Nicaragua, 148–49; rapprochement with United States, 307. *See also* Canada; Venezuelan boundary dispute; War Plans (British)

Great Lakes, 171, 172

Gresham, Walter Q., 103, 159; personality and early career, 104; Hawaiian policy, 107–15, 162; Latin American policy, 116; intervenes in dispute between Colombia and Costa Rica, 117; and Brazilian revolution, 117–18; and Mosquito Indians, 118–19, 122; and Venezuelan boundary dispute, 120–21, 123–24, 141, 144, 145–46, 150, 161; death, 124, 161

Gridley, Charles B., 171, 172

Guam, 294, 318, 319

Guantánamo, 295, 301, 319

Guiana boundary dispute. *See* Venezuelan boundary dispute

Gutschmid, Baron, 96

Guzmàn, Blanco, 127, 142

Haiti, United States relations with, 84, 94, 100, 303, 327

Hale, Eugene, 8–9, 245

Hampton Roads, 280, 281

"Hancox Case," 129, 131

Hanna, Mark, 245

Harmon, Judson, 194

Harper's Weekly, 86, 87, 105

Harrison, Benjamin, 25; enters White House, 1889, 83; Latin American policy, 83–84, 100–01; attitude to major diplomatic questions, 86, 90; belief in coordinated policies, 87; personality and early career, 87–88; appoints his cabinet, 88–89; relations with Blaine, 89–90; believes in strong Navy, 92, 93; desires base in Santo Domingo, 94; refuses to use force to secure base in Santo Domingo, 95; and relations with Chile, 96–100; and Hawaiian revolution, 105, 109, 113, 114; appoints Scruggs to Venezuela, 128; and Venezuelan boundary dispute, 140

Harvard University, 204, 207, 209

Hawaiian islands, 40, 76, 101, 126, 135, 195, 221, 225, 229, 319; Blaine wants to acquire, 85, 86; revolution in, 102, 104, 221–22; press comments on annexation, 104, 105, 221, 222; Treaty of Annexation, 1893, 106; Cleveland withdraws treaty from Senate, 107; Blount's report, 111; Cleveland and Gresham plan to restore Queen, 111–14; Japanese designs on, 270, 271; annexed by United States, 289, 295. *See also* Cleveland; Gresham; Foster; Pearl Harbor

Hawes, Gilbert R., 132

Havana, 194, 196, 255, 256, 276, 301

Hay-Pauncefote Treaty, 308

Hay, John, 126, 282, 291; adroit

Index

249–50, 256, 260, 261, 262, 282–84; attack on Manila, 268, 269, 270, 272–76, 292; and Cuba, 274, 276–78, 282, 294

Spooner, Henry J., 21

Spooner, John C., 261, 262

Spring Rice, Cecil, 226

State Department, 126, 132, 133, 216, 269; appointment of diplomats, 77–78; neglect by Blaine, 89; and Venezuelan boundary dispute, 121, 123, 128, 135, 146, 147, 148

Stevens, John C., 105, 106, 111, 112, 114, 115, 126, 127, 222

Stillman, Oscar B., 197, 199

Stockton, John P., 3

Storrow, James J., 156, 176

Strong, Josiah, 41

Taft, William H., 311, 317

Taft-Katsura conversation, 314, 315

Taylor, Hannis, 247

Taylor, Henry C.: appointed president of Naval War College, 28–29; appeals to Luce for help, 29–31; and Venezuelan crisis, 171, 172; and plans for war with Spain, 272, 273; advocates General Staff, 299; on Monroe Doctrine, 302–04

Teller, Henry M.: and Chinese exclusion, 61, 201; amendment concerning Cuba, 264, 288

Territorial expansion, 40, 41, 103, 230; Gibson's views, 76; Harrison's views, 85; Blaine's views, 85; Cleveland's views, 103, 106, 107, 108–09; attitudes of Democratic and Republican parties, 115; Hawaiian debate, 223, 224, 225, 229; historians' assumptions about, 240, 241; and the Philippines, 288

Thompson, Richard W., 16

Thurston, Lorrin A., 107, 222

Tilden, Samuel J.: backs Cleveland, 44; supports silver diplomacy, 47, 49, 50

Tracy, Benjamin F., 11, 25, 26; favors Naval War College, 25–26; reappoints Mahan to Naval War College, 26–27; advocates battleship fleet, 1889, 33, 35, 37, 93; asks Mahan's advice on strategy, 93; seeks base in Haiti, 94

Transisthmian canal. See Isthmian canal

Triple Alliance, 125

Trumbull, Lyman, 3

Turkey, 119, 223

United States Army. See Army

United States Naval Institute, 14, 17, 36, 37

United States Navy. See Navy

Valparaiso, 99

Venezuela: relations with United States, 120, 121, 145, 146; civil war in, 120, 121, 128, 129–31, 149, 176–77; Scruggs services to, 134–57; blockaded by Britain and Germany, 1902, 309. See also Crespo; Guzmàn; Rojas

Venezuela Steam Transportation Company, 129

Venezuelan boundary dispute, 104, 117, 120, 122–24, 127, 129, 130–31, 134–79, 307

Vera Cruz, 335

Virgin Islands, 94, 327

Virginius crisis, 1873, 4

Walker, James G.: supports Naval War College, 18, 19, 20

War Board, 1898. See Naval War Board

War College. See Naval War College

War Department, 300

Warner, A. J., 50

War plans (British): against United States, 172–73, 307